THE DECISIVE WRITER

Kathryn Rosser Raign
University of North Texas

THOMSON

WADSWORTH

Australia ■ Canada ■ Mexico ■ Singapore ■ Spain ■ United Kingdom ■ United States

The Decisive Writer

Kathryn Rosser Raign

Publisher: *Michael Rosenberg*
Acquisitions Editor: *Dickson Musslewhite*
Development Editor: *Michell Phifer*
Editorial Assistant: *Cheryl Forman*
Technology Project Manager: *Cara Douglass-Graff*
Marketing Manager: *Carrie Brandon*
Marketing Assistant: *Dawn Giovanniello*
Advertising Project Manager: *Joy Westberg*
Project Manager, Editorial Production: *Lianne Ames*
Print/Media Buyer: *Mary Beth Hennebury*

Permissions Editor: *Norah Piehl*
Production Service: *Jane Hoover, Lifland et. al., Bookmakers*
Text Designer: *Anne Carter*
Photo Manager: *Sheri Blaney*
Photo Researcher: *Sharon Donahue*
Cover Designer: *Anne Carter*
Cover Printer: *Transcontinental Printing*
Compositor: *Publishers' Design & Production Services, Inc.*
Printer: *Transcontinental Printing*
Cover Art: *"Studio Wall" 1973 © Estate of Roy Lichtenstein*

Library of Congress Control Number: 2004116501

Student Edition: ISBN 1-4130-0013-4

Instructor's Edition: ISBN 1-4130-1116-0

Credits appear on pages 525–528, which constitute a continuation of the copyright page.

Thomson Higher Education
25 Thomson Place
Boston, MA 02210-1202
USA

Asia (including India)
Thomson Learning
5 Shenton Way
#01-01 UIC Building
Singapore 068808

Australia/New Zealand
Thomson Learning Australia
102 Dodds Street
Southbank, Victoria 3006
Australia

Canada
Thomson Nelson
1120 Birchmount Road
Toronto, Ontario M1K 5G4
Canada

UK/Europe/Middle East/Africa
Thomson Learning
High Holborn House
50–51 Bedford Road
London WC1R 4LR
United Kingdom

Contents

CHAPTER  **The Design of Writing 85**

Images and Texts

PART TWO

REASONS FOR WRITING   123

CHAPTER

Writing to Persuade   325

The Power of Nature

CHAPTER  **Writing to Respond   373**

Global Icons

PART THREE

CONDUCTING RESEARCH 417

CHAPTER 11

Collecting Information   419
Working in the Library and Online

CHAPTER 13 **Documenting Sources 481**
MLA and APA Styles

Preface

The Decisive Writer is a book about making decisions—the kinds of decisions writers face every time they write. Experienced writers are decisive writers because they have had years of experience in which to learn, by trial and error, how to make effective writing choices. Regardless of the level of talent students bring to a composition class, most of them have very little conscious knowledge of how they can intentionally make effective choices when writing.

While most composition textbooks emphasize the importance of teaching the writing process, they often fail to look at that process as a series of choices. Learning that an essay or other written text is the result of a process empowers students by demystifying the act of writing, but it is even more empowering for students to understand that there is a rationale for every decision they will make as writers and that becoming better writers is a matter of learning to make effective choices during each stage of the writing process. For these reasons, *The Decisive Writer* uses the decision-making process as its controlling paradigm.

Because we live in a world of mixed media, *The Decisive Writer* is visually oriented. Each chapter has a theme to which the graphics, the student essays, the professional essays, and the writing options connect. These themes have been chosen for their relevance to the book's audience and for their ability to prompt effective written responses.

☰ Organization

The Decisive Writer has three parts:

- Part One: How Writing Works
- Part Two: Reasons for Writing
- Part Three: Conducting Research

Part One: How Writing Works

Chapter 1 introduces the rhetorical situation—with its three-part structure of audience, purpose, and occasion—as a tool for making informed writing choices. The text presents questions whose answers lead students to effective decisions in relation to each of these three parts. Students are also shown how to apply the rhetorical situation as an integral part of the writing process. Examples of a student's work at each stage of the writing process are presented, including free writing, a rough draft with peer comments, and a revised draft.

Chapter 2, "Strategies for Writing," explores some of the reasons why people write—to share a personal experience, observation, or information, to solve a problem, to evaluate, persuade, or respond—and includes examples of each type of writing. Linking reasons with methods, this chapter discusses rhetorical strategies for development and organizational methods for shaping a piece of writing. The chapter gives students a working familiarity with strategies and organizational patterns from which they can choose as they write.

Although design used to be considered appropriate course material only in technical communication classes, Chapter 3, "The Design of Writing," presents design as an integral part of effective written communication—whether in a paper or on a Web page. In order to use design to increase the effectiveness of their writing, students have to understand basic design principles.

Part Two: Reasons for Writing

Each of the seven chapters in this part of *The Decisive Writer* discusses how to make choices when writing for a specific reason. Rhetorical strategies appropriate to each reason for writing, as well as organizational methods from which the writer can choose, are considered. Additionally, each chapter has both student and professional writing samples that illustrate the various strategies and methods.

At the end of each chapter is a set of collaborative exercises that may be used for small groups to practice the skills presented in the chapter. Next, a feature called "Writing Picks" presents four writing options from which students can choose. A series of questions based on the application of the rhetorical situation helps guide the student to develop the writing option he or she has chosen. Students are also provided with a series of activities that help them to engage in each phase of the writing process—prewriting, drafting, revising, and editing—in relation to the type of writing the chapter covers.

Part Three: Conducting Research

Chapter 11, "Collecting Information," introduces students to methods of conducting research in both the library and on the Internet. The chapter concludes with three research-based writing options from which the students can choose.

Chapter 12 discusses how to evaluate sources and use them effectively in a research paper. Having chosen one of the writing options introduced in the previous chapter, students are asked to complete a series of exercises that prepare them to write the research paper: an abstract, an outline, and an annotated bibliography.

Chapter 13, "Documenting Sources," provides guidelines and example entries for citing sources in both MLA and APA style. This chapter includes an MLA-style student research paper, complete with outline and Works Cited list.

Features

The Decisive Writer contains a number of features that make it stand out from other rhetoric textbooks.

- *Thematic Content* Every reading relates to the theme of the chapter, and each writing option asks students to respond in some way related to that theme. These themes were chosen to prompt provocative and insightful student responses.

- *Visual Orientation* Each chapter of *The Decisive Writer* includes extensive graphics, as well as at least one visually oriented writing option. Students are also encouraged by the writing exercises to include graphics in their own work.

- *Writer's Breaks* These exercises are intended to help students generate material that will help them in selecting a topic from the writing options found at the end of each chapter and in developing that topic. Students can do these exercises as class assignments or on their own.

■ *Student Essays*   Each of the chapters in Part Two includes two student essays that were written in response to one of the writing options in the chapter. To help readers understand the significance of these essays, each one has been annotated to identify the student's use of specific rhetorical strategies and/or organizational methods. Each essay is also followed by a set of thought-provoking questions titled "Consider This . . .".

■ *Professional Essays*   Each chapter in Parts One and Two contains one to five professional works that relate to the thematic element of the chapter. These readings are intended to give students examples of how an experienced writer addressed the issue being raised by the chapter.

■ *Collaborative Exercises*   These exercises provide students with the opportunity to practice the skills presented in the chapter in preparation for writing their own essays.

■ *Writing Briefs or Picks*   Each chapter concludes with three or four writing options. The options in Part One lead the student to produce a brief piece of writing. In Part Two, each option is intended to result in a complete essay. In Part Three, the options relate to the production of a research paper.

■ *Applying the Rhetorical Situation*   Although students are introduced to the rhetorical situation in Chapter One, *The Decisive Writer* reinforces consistent use of this tool by providing in each chapter a list of questions related to the rhetorical situation and to the chapter's writing options.

■ *Focusing on Process*   In this section of each chapter, students are given specific activities to help them complete the four stages of the writing process.

■ *Grammar Choices*   Each chapter concludes with brief grammar and style lessons, which focus on aspects that often give students trouble and include short activities for applying the material to actual drafts. Chapter One begins by describing four types of sentences, and the next four chapters discuss those types in more detail. Other Grammar Choices sections focus on transitive and intransitive verbs, sentence errors, pronouns, verb tenses, dangling modifiers, faulty predication, pronoun cases, and restrictive and nonrestrictive clauses. Many of them build on skills and concepts previously presented.

■ *Style Choices*   Each chapter includes a brief style lesson that presents a technique students can immediately begin applying to their own writing.

☰ Ancillaries

The following ancillaries provide additional resources as you use this book.

■ *The Instructor's Manual*   This manual includes helpful information for new instructors, including advice on facilitating group work and responding to student writing, a collection of sample syllabi, and specific advice on teaching each chapter. A list of further readings and additional writing options are included in the *Instructor's Manual*. Exercises to accompany the grammar and style lessons that appear in the text are available in the *Instructor's Manual*.

■ *The Decisive Writer Web Site*   The companion Web site contains a wealth of information you will find useful in the classroom. The site features Diction Concept Library, Grammar Concept Library, Mechanics Concept Library, Punctuation Concept Library, Research Concept Library, Student Paper Libraries, Writing Concept Library, and more!

☰ Acknowledgments

Thank you to the many teachers across the country who took the time to review this book, some more than once: Jessie Kapper, Purdue University; Nolde Alexius, Louisiana State University; Mary Ann Bretzlauf, College of Lake County; Stephen Calatrello,

Calhoun Community College; Keri Turner, Nicholls State University; Samantha Morgan-Curtis, Tennessee State University; Michael Neal and Donna Winchell, Clemson University; Kurt Neumann, William Rainey Harper College; Sylvia Stacey, Oakton Community College; Jeffrey Andelora, Mesa Community College; Jerry Ball, Arkansas State University; Debra Black, Arizona State University; Vicki Byard, Northeastern Illinois University; Sujata Chohan, Joel Farson, and Donald Jordan, Heald College; Karen Griggs and Edward Moritz, Indiana University–Purdue University at Ft. Wayne; Martha Kerlin, Tidewater Community College–Chesapeake; Lyle Morgan, Pittsburg State University; Carole Papper, Ball State University; and Beverly Reed, Stephen F. Austin State University. You made this book what it is.

I also thank the following: for their unfailing confidence in my project, Michael Rosenberg, Publisher, and Dickson Musslewhite, Senior Acquisitions Editor; for her endless patience and insightful editing, Michell Phifer, Senior Development Editor; and for all the work they did to produce this book, Lianne Ames, Senior Production Project Manager, and Jane Hoover, copyeditor and Production Manager.

And last, thanks to my family and friends. Dad, you gave me my vision. Mom, you gave me the determination to make it real. Jennifer and Paula, no task was too small or too great. Jer—you stayed when a wiser man might have fled. And all the rest of you—thanks for being there.

Kathryn R. Raign
December 2004

PART ONE

How Writing Works

Roger Ressmeyer/Corbis

AP Photo/Eric Risberg

Ben Martin/Time-Life Pictures/Getty Images

As part of your education, you are learning to make good choices as a writer. Writers such as Alice Walker (left), Maxine Hong Kingston (center), and Gabriel Garcia Marquez (right) have developed this skill to a high degree.

UNLIKELY HEROES

The Rhetorical Situation

In this chapter, you will learn:

- What the rhetorical situation is—the who, why, and when of writing

- How to analyze the three parts of a rhetorical situation—audience, purpose, and occasion

- How to make various decisions to facilitate stages of the writing process

Warner Bros./Zuma Press

Harry Potter is the most unlikely of heroes. Though he appears to be just a schoolboy, he frequently manages to save the day.

Writing is a process of making decisions. When you write, you have many decisions to make. You need to choose:

- A topic
- Writing strategies
- Organizational method
- Stylistic elements
- Tone

Making these choices can be simplified by learning to use the rhetorical situation as a problem-solving tool to help you determine when your writing decisions are good ones. By learning to apply the rhetorical situation to every part of the writing process, you can become a decisive writer.

WHAT IS THE RHETORICAL SITUATION?

The situation in which you write, also called the *rhetorical situation*, has three basic parts:

- Audience
- Purpose
- Occasion

These three components affect—in fact, to a certain degree, they determine—every aspect of what you write. Your familiarity with them will help you make good writing choices and become a decisive writer. If you base all your writing decisions on the three components of the rhetorical situation, you should be able to make them confidently. Moreover, these components apply to any type of writing, not just academic writing, so whether you are writing for a class, for your job, or for personal reasons, the rhetorical situation is the tool you need to make good choices.

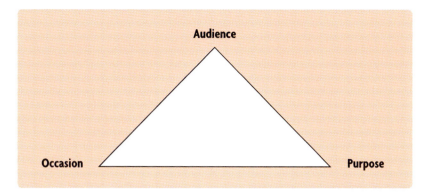

The communication triangle illustrates the flow of information in every rhetorical situation—from the writer to the audience, with a message that serves the writer's purpose.

☰ Audience

Every act of communication involves an audience, even if the audience is only you. The concept of audience is complex; it can mean so many things. Your audience might be a specific person—your composition teacher, your friend, your employer. In these cases, you should have a fairly clear idea of the audience for your writing. However, at other times, the audience might be a group of classmates, people who are trying to install a piece of computer software, anyone who is considering adoption, or employees working in a personnel office. Regardless of how much or how little you know about the particular audience for a piece of writing, in order to determine how best to suit that audience's needs, you need to try to answer several questions:

■   *Who are your readers?* Are your readers young, old, middle-aged? Are they working professionals? Are they college students like you? If you are writing to an audience of people in their fifties and sixties, is it appropriate to use the slang you use when you talk to your friends? Are you making style and content choices that are appropriate for your audience or ones that are comfortable for you? Are your readers people who know how to sift through material to find what they want, or might they benefit from a more structured presentation? Is the diction you are using appropriate? Are you talking over your readers' heads or talking down to them?

- *Are your readers motivated to read what you are writing?* Are they reading because they have to or because they want to? The motivation level of a college student preparing for a test in a required course will likely be different from that of an employee trying to receive a promotion. What can you do to motivate your readers? Is the style of your essay engaging? Is the voice speaking in your essay one to whom your readers will want to listen? Is the information you are providing accurate and believable?

- *What are your readers' expectations for what they are reading?* Are your readers expecting to learn how to do something? To be helped to make a decision? To be persuaded? If readers simply want to complete a task, are you giving them only pertinent information? If readers are interested in studying an issue, are you presenting both sides? If you are claiming to present a fair evaluation of something, are you being objective? If you are sharing an experience, have you included enough detail for readers to feel included?

- *What specialized knowledge do your readers have?* How much you will need to help your readers understand what you are writing depends on what they know. If you are a computer programmer writing to novice users, can you assume that they know what the term *modem* means? If you are writing to a business major, can you assume that she shares your knowledge of modems? Try to determine what your readers know, so you can decide how much you need to tell them.

☰ Purpose

In terms of the rhetorical situation, purpose is twofold: What is your purpose for writing? And what is your audience's purpose for reading?

What is your purpose for writing?

Until you know why you are writing and what you want to accomplish, you can't really move forward on a writing project. Any writing situation includes a purpose of some sort—to fulfill an assignment, to request information, to prove a point, to tell a story. Your understanding of your purpose and your ability to make your writing reflect that purpose will determine how successful you are as a writer. When you are unsure about the purpose for something you are writing, you can consider the following questions:

- *What are you trying to accomplish?* Are you trying to teach your readers something? Do you want them to consider a different viewpoint? Do you want to give them something to think about? Do you want to make them understand your feelings about an issue? Do you want them to consider their own feelings about an issue?

- *What point do you want to make?* If someone finishes reading an essay you wrote and can't answer the question "What was the point?" the essay has a problem. Your goal as a writer should be for your readers to take something away from everything you write. For example, an essay you write might help someone reconsider her feelings about homosexuality by offering her a viewpoint and experience different from her own. Another essay might allow someone to have a more sympathetic view of younger siblings, to laugh about a sensitive topic, or to feel better about a personal disappointment.

- *What reaction do you want readers to have?* Do you want to make your readers angry? Do you want to make them feel concerned? Do you want them to question something? Do you want to make them laugh? As a writer, you have the power to make your readers react simply through the choices you make. You can use language to shock, to create suspense, to cast doubt, to clarify, or to question.

Writer's Break

Choose one of the three Writing Briefs at the end of this chapter. Write the topic you chose at the top of a piece of paper.

- Assume that you are writing an editorial for a local newspaper. Who is your audience? Make a list of everything you know about those readers.

- Make a list of reasons for writing about the topic. What could your purpose be? To inform? To persuade? To alarm?

- Why are you writing about this topic now? List at least three reasons other than that it's an assignment.

What is your audience's purpose for reading?

Readers usually read for a reason—they want to learn something; they want to be entertained; they want information; they're curious. Readers have many reasons for reading. Consider why your readers might be reading, and you'll be more successful at meeting their expectations.

If you can successfully match your reason for writing with your reader's reason for reading, you will both be satisfied with the result. For example, when your history professor asks you to write an essay on the economic effects of the Civil War, he or she does not want a handwritten poem or song expressing your personal feelings about the war. He or she expects an academic essay typed in the usual format and including a list of reputable sources. On the other hand, it would be inappropriate to use a formal convention such as the third person when writing to a close friend.

Language is a powerful tool, but to use it effectively, you have to use it intentionally. Decide what your goal is before you begin writing, and then make your word choices accordingly.

In the following essay, the writer describes her personal response to the terrorist attacks of September 11, 2001. Does she use her understanding of the rhetorical situation to make good decisions? Her writing strategies are identified for you. These strategies will be discussed in Chapter Two.

Reason for writing: personal

Organizational method: chronological with an alternation between past and present and between her mother's story and her own

September 11, 2002: Impersonating a Survivor

Amy Barth

A year ago today, my day was really not that bad. My house was a comforting place to go when I got off work early. The sky was a brilliant blue, the sunshine was warm and golden, and as it turned out, my classes were cancelled too. A year ago, while I sat on my couch in the cool air-conditioning doing nothing but watching TV, my mother was running for her life.

My mother, Nancy, has worked for the Department of Defense as a civilian employee since 1981. She loves her job as a Supply Systems Analyst, and last year at this time, she worked for the Defense Logistics Agency. Her office was in the Pentagon.

A long-distance view of the towers

Last year at this time, I was working at Boeing, in Corinth, Texas as a part-time secretary. I was oblivious to the news that morning until I got to work. People were standing motionless around a radio listening to a news report in solemn silence. A plane had crashed in New York City. We dispersed one by one to act like we were working until we heard a second plane had crashed. Most of us decided to go and watch the reports on television at the security room downstairs.

I remember I was eating lemon yogurt while I watched the horrible crashes replayed in real-time, then in slow motion, repeating over and over. It was very easy to be detached from the scenes on TV because it seemed so much like a movie set with special effects somehow gone horribly wrong. I stood outside the glassed-in security room, looking through my reflection at the images on the screen. Then I heard the words, "We have just received a report that the Pentagon has been hit by a third plane."

My day was still easy, even then. Even as I watched my reflection on the security glass melt into panicky tears and felt myself heave into a fit of hyperventilating, I was fine. Even though they sent me home from work with compassionate pats on the back, pressing tissues into my hands, I was really doing quite well. At the same time I had been numbly watching the day's events reveal themselves, two thousand miles away, my mother was seeing it all in person.

Narration—her mother's past story again

That morning her office had celebrated a coworker's birthday, and they were just settling into work when they heard about the World Trade Center. In the midst of their own shock and fear about what was happening in New York, they suddenly felt the entire building shaking. In seconds, the halls were filling up with white smoke, and someone yelled that the walls and

ceiling were falling in. Alarms were blaring, lights were flashing.

My mom and her officemates grabbed what they could of

their personal belongings and ran. In their suits and ties, skirts

and heels, they ran down the maze of corridors to the center of

the Pentagon. They thought it had been a bomb or missile and

figured the center of the building would be safest. When they

understood it had been a plane that crashed, like in New York,

mom said, "We knew we had to get out in case it exploded, or

heaven forbid, another plane hit us."

They ran once more through the building and out again,

following orders to get to the outer edges of the parking lot as

© Reuters/Corbis

A view of the damaged Pentagon

fast as they could. Looking back at the fire and smoke in disbe-lief, my mother realized the plane had crashed into the building where her office had been just three weeks prior. The surreality of the situation soon became full blown when Air Force fighter jets appeared in a swarm overhead.

Narration—her own past story

I didn't know any of these details until much later. All I saw on TV were short blurbs about the fire at the Pentagon--nothing about evacuees was ever mentioned. I hoped my mother's office was in some far away corner close to an exit. I prayed she was far from the turmoil. My fears, though, kept asking, "What if she was in there? What if I never see her again?"

Narration—her mother's past story

Mom's office group committed to staying together and ultimately decided to climb the steep interstate embankments to cross the highway to a nearby shopping mall. Mom later told me she wished, among other things, that she had thought to grab her tennis shoes before she left because the going wasn't easy in her fitted skirt and pumps. From the mall, my mom called my father, who was working at another Army installation about twenty miles away. He didn't answer the phone at his desk, so she left a voice mail and countless calls to his pager to let him know she was okay. He got the first message, but never talked to her in person that morning because all the phone lines and satellites were jammed with the sudden influx of calls to the area.

It soon became apparent that she and her team of coworkers would have to find their own way out of Washington. Neither the commuter buses nor the conventional trains were running and the highways were blocked off for miles. Despite their fear of more insidious attacks (Could they be gassed? Maybe there could be a bomb?) they decided to risk the only available escape: The Metro--the subway system in the area. After buying tickets and determining which train each of them should ride, the team of coworkers parted, unsure of when they would see each other again. After reaching the southernmost stop in Virginia, mom had to take a taxi to get the rest of the 30 miles home. It was about 3:00 PM when she walked in the door. I didn't hear her voice until later in the day when the phone lines were finally free.

Far away in Texas, I had been sitting on the couch, intermittently crying and pacing, glued to the television all day. I looked for glimpses of my mother in the few bits of evacuation footage they showed at the Pentagon, but I never saw her. I could only sit and wait, fitfully clean my house, and call local people I knew from the East Coast. No one knew anything about Washing-

Narration—her own past story

ton DC, though. I was so frustrated that there wasn't more information available to me specifically about the Pentagon. All the news reports were focused on New York, understandably, but what about the other crash? What about my mom?

I expected the sky to cloud over and thunder to crash, but it didn't. The weather was lovely, almost cool for mid-September in Texas. And I had a free day to enjoy it, but of course I didn't. I would rather have had the bad weather. It would have been a reflection of my mood--of everyone's. It would have made me feel like I was somehow more connected to the awful events going on that day if I had something, anything, physical to bear. Even something as mundane as thunderstorms would have helped.

Narration—her own present story

That all happened about a year ago. No matter how many times I tell this story, I cannot help but mention my anguish and frustration at the jammed phone lines and the uninformative media. I play up my pain like it really matters to someone besides me. I recognize my mother's story is the true thing of interest and import, but I want to have my experience remembered too. Why? It was nothing really. It was an easy day for me. But it wasn't. If I could have traded places with my mother, I would have done it in a second. If I could have charged into those buildings in New York, I would have. If I could have wiped the ashes off their faces, I would have done it until the last one was clean. But I couldn't do anything. I was two thousand miles away.

My not so subtle assertion of suffering is pitiful, I know, but it is the only connection I have to the events of that day. From this far away I have been able to do very little to make Mom's experiences any easier to bear or understand. She does not seem to have many problems with what happened to her. The feelings of helplessness and survivor's guilt were fairly mild for her, although she did have to question God's logic in the beginning. Prayer and meditation have increased her faith and assuaged her questions.

I still want to assume that if I had been there to act as a leaning post for her, she would have been better off. When I was still at home, Mom often relied on me for support. If she had a fight with dad, I was there to be her shoulder to cry on. When she was depressed about my brother's problems at school, I was there to be her cheerleader and back-up tutor for my brother. When she had cancer, I was there to take care of her and the house as well as I could. The difference

Writer's Break

Try an idea map. Look at the example on page 25 before you start.

- Write the topic of the Writing Brief you chose earlier in the center of a piece of paper.

- Using this topic as a starting point, write as many ideas as you can around it.

- After you have written all your ideas, use different colored markers to draw links between similar ideas.

this time was obviously the fact that I wasn't there. I wish I could have done more--more than just sitting at home watching TV, more than having too short and too few phone conversations long after the fact. If I could have just hugged her when she came home that day, it might have given me the simple satisfaction of "doing" something for myself. Of course, she doesn't blame me for not being there, but that is what I'm doing to myself.

I understand that the entire experience is mine only by proxy. While I have been waiting to find my way out of the fear and guilt that day inspired, mom has healed. She saw the damage up close, and she saw the damage repaired. She changed jobs and offices but keeps in touch with her team of officemates from that day. Plus, she has joined a gym to have a physical outlet for stress relief. "Don't forget, but move on," seems to be her motto.

After seeing her progress, I realize that I've been playing victim by proxy and now it is time to become a survivor by proxy. I know what I need to do is take strength from her in the same way I took the experience from her. She connects me to that day, to that history, and she is the only one who shows me how to survive it: by living life to its fullest, by forgiving but not

Narration—her mother's present story

Narration—her own present story

forgetting, by rebuilding and strengthening, but understanding that life is not under our control and being okay with that. A year ago today my mom became a survivor of a terrorist attack. Today, I begin to understand how to become a survivor myself.

Consider this . . .

- What was this writer's reason for writing?
- Did she choose an effective organizational method?
- Did her essay have a point to which you could relate?

≡ Occasion

Writing doesn't occur in a vacuum. Something prompts us to write. This something is the occasion, the third part of the rhetorical situation. For example, you may be writing because a teacher gave you an assignment. Such an occasion for writing might be described like this:

> My history instructor asked me to record a current event to document it for historical purposes. I am supposed to pretend that my essay will be part of a high school history book that will be used in the year 2020.

In this case, your occasion for writing is to fulfill an assignment and receive a grade. Part of the assignment is to write in a certain style—as though your essay will appear in a history book. Consequently, you have to base your writing decisions on this occasion

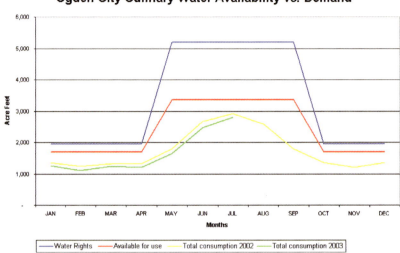

This is an example of a graph from a professional document.

and attempt to meet your instructor's expectations by making choices consistent with the writing done by historians.

The occasion for writing is often closely related to the type of writing you are doing. Most of your writing can be classified as one of these types:

- *Academic writing* is writing you do for school. Academic writing includes essay exams, research papers, and persuasive essays.

- *Professional writing* is writing you do for work. Professional writing includes resumes, business letters, reports, and proposals.

- *Personal writing* is writing you do for yourself. Personal writing includes journal entries, personal letters, poems, lists, and notes.

Clearly, not all occasions for writing are academic. Your occasion might be to ask a friend for advice, or you might be writing a resume because you are attempting to find a job. You might feel motivated to write a letter to the editor of a favorite magazine in response to something that was published there. All of these are occasions for writing, and because they are different, they all require a different type of response. Think about your occasion for writing and use it as your guide for making writing choices.

In the next essay, Margaret Atwood asks us to imagine the choices that might be forced on us by famine. Why did she write this essay? What point is she trying to make? Who is her unlikely hero?

BREAD

Margaret Atwood

Imagine a piece of bread. You don't have to imagine it, it's right here in the kitchen, on the bread board, in its plastic bag, lying beside the bread knife. The bread knife   1

is an old one you picked up at an auction; it has the word BREAD carved into the wooden handle. You open the bag, pull back the wrapper, cut yourself a slice. You put butter on it, then peanut butter, then honey, and you fold it over. Some of the honey runs out onto your fingers and you lick it off. It takes you about a minute to eat the bread. This bread happens to be brown, but there is also white bread, in the refrigerator, and a heel of rye you got last week, round as a full stomach then, now going moldy. Occasionally you make bread. You think of it as something relaxing to do with your hands.

Photodisc/Getty RF

Imagine a famine. Now imagine a piece of bread. Both of these things are real but   2
you happen to be in the same room with only one of them. Put yourself into a different room, that's what the mind is for. You are now lying on a thin mattress in a hot room. The walls are made of dried earth and your sister, who is younger than you are, is in the room with you. She is starving, her belly is bloated, flies land on her eyes; you brush them off with your hand. You have cloth too, filthy but damp,

and you press it to her lips and forehead. The piece of bread is the bread you've been saving, for days it seems. You are as hungry as she is, but not yet as weak. How long does this take? When will someone come with more bread? You think of going out to see if you might find something that could be eaten, but outside the streets are infested with scavengers and the stink of corpses is everywhere.

3   Should you share the bread or give the whole piece to your sister? Should you eat the piece of bread yourself? After all, you have a better chance of living, you're stronger. How long does it take to decide?

4   Imagine a prison. There is something you know that you have not yet told. Those in control of the prison know that you know. So do those not in control. If you tell, thirty or forty or a hundred of your friends, your comrades, will be caught and will die. If you refuse to tell, tonight will be like last night. They always choose the night. You don't think about the night, however, but about the piece of bread they offered you. How long does it take? The piece of bread was brown and fresh and reminded you of sunlight falling across a wooden floor. It reminded you of a bowl, a yellow bowl that was once in your home. It held apples and pears; it stood on a table you can also remember. It's not the hunger or the pain that is killing you but the absence of the yellow bowl. If you could only hold the bowl in your hands, right here, you could

withstand anything, you tell yourself. The bread they offered you is subversive, it's treacherous, it does not mean life.

There were once two sisters. One was rich and had no children, the other had five   5
children and was a widow, so poor that she no longer had any food left. She went to her sister and asked for a mouthful of bread. "My children are dying," she said. The rich sister said, "I do not have enough for myself," and drove her away from the door. Then the husband of the rich sister came home and wanted to cut himself a piece of bread; but when he made the first cut, out flowed red blood.

    Everyone knew what that meant.   6

    This is a traditional German fairytale.   7

The loaf of bread I have conjured for you floats about a foot above your kitchen   8
table. The table is normal, there are no trap doors in it. A blue tea towel floats beneath the bread, and there are no strings attaching the cloth to the bread or the bread to the ceiling or the table to the cloth, you've proved it by passing your hand above and below. You didn't touch the bread though. What stopped you? You don't want to know whether the bread is real or whether it's just a hallucination I've somehow duped you into seeing. There's no doubt that you can see the bread, you can even smell it, it smells like yeast, and it looks solid enough, solid as your own arm. But can you trust it? Can you eat it? You don't want to know, imagine that.

Writer's Break

In Margaret Atwood's essay, she takes bread, a common object that we take for granted, and makes it strange to us by imagining the significance it would develop if we found ourselves in one of several imagined scenarios. Choose a common object like bread (for example, shoes, water, or aspirin). Then, in your writer's notebook:

- Describe what it means to you now.
- Describe what it could mean to you if it was taken away from you by a war or natural disaster.
- Why are such reminders useful?

Consider this . . .

- ■ Why did Margaret Atwood choose bread as the focus of her essay? Was it a good choice?

- ■ Did you think her "let's pretend" approach was effective? Why or why not?

- ■ Did this essay make you feel sad, angry, guilty? What did you feel, and why? What do you think the writer wanted you to feel?

THE WRITING PROCESS

You are probably familiar with the major stages of the writing process:

- ■ Prewriting

- ■ Drafting

- ■ Revising

- ■ Editing

Each of these parts of the writing process requires you to make choices. That is, at every step of writing a paper, from jotting down a few notes to revising the last sentence, you need to make decisions. Thus, becoming more decisive is key to improving as a writer.

≡ Prewriting

Prewriting, sometimes called *invention* because you are inventing material, is everything that happens before you start to draft. The types of invention are limited only by your imagination, but some helpful techniques you can choose to use include these:

- ■ Free writing

- ■ Listing

- ■ Idea mapping

- Talking to others
- Exploring common aspects

Free writing

Free writing is like running warm-up sprints. You put your pencil to the paper or your fingers on the keyboard, and you don't stop writing until the end of a designated time period. Free writing warms up your writing mechanism. There is no one way to free write, but you might try either of the following methods.

Method One: Take a piece of paper, and write a topic—a phrase or a word—at the top of the page. Give yourself three minutes, and start writing. At the end of the three minutes, read what you've written and circle any sentence, phrase, or word that surprises or interests you. Spend another three minutes writing in response to what you've circled.

Method Two: Without prompting yourself in any way (no word or phrase as a starting topic), simply start writing. Don't stop for three minutes. Again, look for a sentence, phrase, or word that interests you, and use that as a prompt for further free writing.

Unlikely Heroes
- *Unknown heroes*
- *People who did the right thing when you didn't expect them to*
- *People who have never been heroic before*
- *People who do things you never thought they could do—someone in a wheelchair walks*

A brief example of free writing based on the first method described in the text

Listing

Listing works best if you have some sort of controlling idea or theme on which to base your list. If you don't have anything that close to a topic, you can use listing as a way of developing ideas. Try either of the following methods.

Method One: Write your controlling idea or theme at the top of a piece of paper; then list every related idea you can come up with, no matter how remote the association with the main idea. When you have listed everything you can, start connecting similar ideas to reveal patterns. To do this, you can draw lines or highlight in different colors.

Method Two: Start with one of these prompts: "Things I would like to write about" or "Things I wouldn't like to write about." You can also try making a list of reasons for writing or reasons for not writing. After you produce the list (taking care to include anything that pops into your head, no matter how ludicrous it might seem), choose one of the listed items as a starting point for free writing.

Idea mapping

Many people learn best visually, and idea mapping is one visual approach to free writing. The basic method for idea mapping is to write a question, statement, phrase, or word in the middle of a piece of paper, circle it, and then begin drawing connecting branches that lead to possible subtopics. Each branch should represent one train of thought, though any branch may split into two or more. Start a new branch for every new idea. You may want to use different colors to highlight branches or even drawings to express your ideas. You can also include images or words cut from magazines or newspapers.

Talking to others

You don't have to develop all of your ideas alone; find a couple of classmates who want to work with you and start a writing dialogue: Use e-mail to write them your opinion on a topic, ask for help choosing a topic, or simply pose an interesting question. Let the dialogue develop from there.

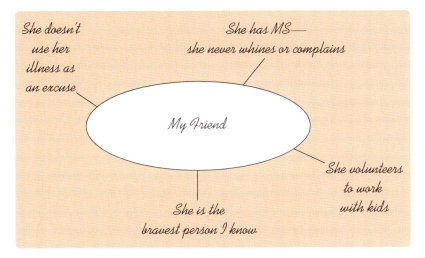

An example of an idea map

Exploring common aspects

Exploring common aspects is a method that involves asking questions to help you discover more about a topic. Here is a list of
questions you might use to explore aspects of a topic:

- What is it?

- To what is it similar? How is it similar?
  What is it different from? How is it
  different?

- What is its cause? What effect does it have?
  What is its opposite?

- What was it like in the past? Has it
  changed? Have people's ideas about it
  changed?

These questions help you generate information
by asking you to look at a topic in different ways.
We all tend to favor our own viewpoints, but applying a set of standard questions can help you
consider other ways of looking at issues.

Writer's Break

Before you begin writing an essay, develop a
writing process:

- Choose a time and a place.

- Choose a free-writing technique, and use
  it.

- Write a rough draft based on the results
  of your free writing.

After you write the rough draft, evaluate your
process. What will you change next time?

☰ Drafting

You have choices when you begin drafting as well. When, where, and how you draft can affect the outcome of the writing process. Consider the following recommendations, and decide whether they might help you.

- *Try to write at the same time every day.* Over time, you will find yourself starting to get in the writing mode as that hour approaches, and you will waste less time trying to get into the right frame of mind. Commit yourself to an hour or two every day, and you will soon be getting your papers done early—and enjoying the process of writing them.

- *Create a writing environment for yourself that is conducive to work.* If distractions bother you, close the blinds and turn off the TV or the stereo; don't log onto your email account. You may want to fix yourself a snack before you sit down. If you do this ahead of time, you won't have an excuse to go down the hall to the soda machine, or into the kitchen where you are sure to find more compelling things with which to occupy yourself.

- *If you don't already compose on the computer, learn to.* By establishing a connection between your hands and the keyboard, you don't have to waste time retyping your paper after you've written it.

☰ Revising

When you revise your writing, you aren't looking for misspelled words and missing commas—that is what you do when you edit, and editing is the last stage of the writing process. Revising is what you do when you are still looking at big issues—including organization, completeness, and effectiveness. When revising, you answer questions like these:

- Do I have a clear and relevant thesis?

- Is my topic significant, or will readers think "So what?"

- Do I use the best strategies to get my point across? For example, do I use description to give readers a clear picture of a place? Do I use comparison to show how my view of this place was different before I moved away?

- Do I present the material in a logical order?

- Have I said everything that needs to be said? Do I answer the questions readers are likely to have? Do I consider both sides of the issue? Do I include all the pertinent details?

- Is the tone I use appropriate? Have I said anything that will alienate my audience? Have I made unfair accusations when pointing out what I consider wrong in a given situation? Is humor a good choice for this topic?

- Is the diction I'm using appropriate to my purpose? To my audience?

- Will readers recognize a personality behind the words? Am I in there somewhere, or is my paper voiceless? What can I do to give it a distinctive voice?

To help you revise your writing more effectively, you can choose any of the following techniques:

- *Get a second opinion.* Form a group with some of your friends from class, and read one another's papers. Take your paper to someone who has more writing experience than you. Always get a second opinion.

- *Work with your teacher.* Your teacher keeps office hours. Go to them! Ask your teacher questions. Show your teacher your rough draft. Get some feedback.

- *Read what other people write.* The best writers are usually the best readers. Reading will help you to write more fluently. After reading writers you admire, you will find yourself hearing their voices echo in your mind as you write. This will positively

Writer's Break

After you finish the Writing Brief at the end of this chapter, revise that piece of writing in terms of its structure and style. When you're done, ask yourself these questions:

- Is the piece better or worse than I thought?

- Did I make any significant changes?

- What was the most difficult part of revising?

Share your answers with the class.

influence your writing by increasing your repertoire of writing techniques.

≡ Editing

Editing means working at the local level—the word and sentence level—and asking questions like these:

- Have I used punctuation correctly?

- Are all my sentences complete?

- Have I varied my sentence structure?

- Have I used correct grammar? Are there any dangling modifiers or subjects and verbs that don't agree?

Editing is a skill that requires practice. When it's new to you, there are techniques you can choose to help you:

- *Give yourself some distance.* Always give yourself at least 24 hours from the time you finish a paper to the time you begin editing. You have to distance yourself from your own work in order to be objective.

- *Find another reader.* Have someone who represents the audience you are writing for read your paper. For example, maybe you're writing a paper for a school organization. Ask someone from the organization to read your paper and let you know whether you targeted the pertinent issues.

- *Read backwards.* When you read from left to right, top to bottom, you read what you expect to see almost as often as what is actually on the page—especially if you are the writer. Look at this sentence:

    I went to to the grocery store to by milk.

How many errors in the sentence did you catch? Errors like the repetition of *to* and the spelling *by* instead of *buy* are hard to spot. Our eyes don't expect to see *to* twice, so we don't. We know that *by* is a word, so we don't realize it should be *buy* in this context. If you read sentences backwards, you can no longer "guess" at what comes next because you have removed the context. The individual words have no meaning in relation to each other, which allows you to focus on finding errors.

- *Read out loud.* Since your eyes can't be depended on to catch all the errors, read your paper aloud. Your ears will hear things that your eyes won't see.

- *Be resilient.* The purpose of editing is to improve your writing. If you approach your paper as though each draft is evolving, getting closer to the final version, it will be easier to make necessary changes.

Look at the student paper that follows. The student's prewriting exercises and drafts are included, so that you can see the choices he made as he wrote. The rough draft includes peer comments.

Free Write

Heroes. Heroes. Superheros. Superman. Mighty Mouse. The Power Rangers. I'm not any of those things. I'm not a hero. How am I a hero? Heroes do great things. I was in the navy and never left home. Some hero. I did join the Navy — that took guts. What a horrible experience. Maybe heroes are people who don't give up?

Free Write

Hero

Ordinary hero

Ordinary person who does brave things.

My mom is a hero.

My dad is a hero.

I am a hero.

I didn't quit school and move home.

I made a choice and stuck with it.

Making tough choices is part of being a hero.

Aren't we all heroes?

No. Some people take the easy way out.

Real heroes don't.

List Exercise

I joined the navy.

I wanted to do something with my life.

It wasn't what I expected.

I still did my best.

I got kicked out because of my bad knee.

Idea Map

Batman
|
Superman — Superheroes — Spiderman

Unlikely? ——— (Hero) ——— Real heroes don't do it for attention
|
Unrecognized

Undeserved   Unexpected

Me? ——— Real heroes
|
No way

My mom   My dad

Cancer survivor   Took care of us

More heroic to do right thing

My New Home (Peer-Reviewed Draft)

Trevor Hartman

When I was 19, I did what any 19-year-old male would do in my position . . . I joined the military. My father drove me to the federal building in downtown Dallas and drove off.

I spent the first half of the day proving that I could bend my knees, snap my fingers, and urinate into a cup (not all at the same time). I was found clean of marijuana and alcohol. I received a plane ticket and a government check for $50. I

What position were you in?

He didn't say anything?

began my five hour journey by taking a shuttle bus from the federal building to the airport.

Around 10 pm, we arrived at O'Hare airport in Chicago. The map that I had been given to navigate this virtual maze and find the USO was weak. After nearly half an hour of searching, questioning security guards and stopping for no less than three bathroom breaks, my companions and I arrived at the USO office.

Almost three-dozen other men were sitting in a large carpeted area and talking, watching TV, or sitting quietly. I could feel the tension in the room. Each person had joined for reasons of his own, and each person was now unsure of what would happen next.

After nearly an hour of waiting, one of the petty officers who had been ignoring us the entire time stood up and began yelling.

I hurried to obey fearing she might direct her powerful voice at me if I moved too slowly. I found the beginnings of a line on the left wall, and placed myself six or seventh from the front. Not more than a minute after I had taken my place in line, the Petty Officer began screaming again.

She chose a particularly indecisive male, and personalized her attack just for him, she was really hard on him, and he just

Why were you in charge of the other people?

Can you show the tension, rather than talking about it?

Show—what did she look like? What did she say?

What was she screaming about? Did you do the wrong thing or did someone else?

stammered. Without waiting to see if he complied, she walked up to the front of the two lines.

Working quickly, she had all of us head onto a small commercial bus parked right outside of the front doors. Two seconds after the last person had taken his seat another Petty Officer stepped on the bus. He was a large white male, with a hard face and bulging biceps and triceps. He really scared us!

After an hour bus ride that I spent watching the video and staring at the blackened window, which offered no view of the outside, the bus pulled to a stop. All of us piled out of the bus and made a dash for the nearest building, the Recruit Orientation Center. It was almost midnight by now, and the sky was pitch black. I took a deep breath of the cold air and immediately began coughing up phlegm (I didn't stop for nine weeks). Reaching the inside of the building, I entered a place which I would visit many more times.

When all of us had lined up (for the second time that night), a grizzly looking Chief Petty Officer told us to wait for our names to be called and respond by yelling out our social security numbers and then report for temporary uniform issue at the end of the hall. The third person had a zero in his social security

Show don't tell. What did he stammer? What did she say?

What did he do to scare you?

How cold was it?

What did it look like?

number, but he pronounced it as the letter 0. He was awarded with an extremely summarized version of his family lineage with several references made to dogs then sent on his way. No one else made the same mistake.

> Good example—
> you should do
> more of this.

I received tennis shoes, sweats, ski mask, gloves, skivvies, undershirts, socks, a blanket, some sheets and a pillow case, a scarf and a trench coat, which didn't fit. All of the toiletries I was given were placed in my newly issued sea bag. My new clothes in tow, I, along with 70 other men whom I would be spending the next 8 weeks of my life with, began my journey down the 3-mile road (yes, literally), which would bring us to our ship (barracks).

> When and where
> did this all
> happen?

> Was it an easy
> trip?

After what seemed like hours and was actually only an hour and a half we arrived at our final destination. A blinding flash of yellow light penetrated the fog covering my glasses, and I could immediately feel the blood in my ears begin to flow again. As the fog cleared, I found myself heading up a long set of black metal stairs which turned to the right after about fifteen steps before continuing up another flight. The interior of my ship looked old. Reaching the second floor (there were three in all), I followed the fifteen or so people in front of me into a darkened room.

> What do you mean
> it looked old? Can
> you describe it?

There were no lights on in the room, but I could sense the room was fairly large. Rack upon rack of bunks crossed the length of the walls.

How big? How many bunks?

"Welcome to your new home," a cold voice said in the darkness. "I'm going to make sure your stay here is a pleasant

Great dialogue— creepy.

one."

Your essay just sort of ends. How did you feel about your choice at this point? What's the point of this essay? Can you make that clear?

My New Home (Final Draft)

Trevor Hartman

At the end of my first semester of college, I had only two things to show for it: Three hours of credit from an Intro to Computer Science class I tested out of with an A and a shiny trophy I won at a speech tournament. Apparently, refraining from turning in your work is not conducive to receiving a decent grade. Facing the very real prospect of flunking out of college as well as the wrath of my parents, I did what any 19-year-old male would do in my position . . . I joined the military. My father drove me to the federal building in downtown Dallas, and after a few quick words of advice, "Keep your mouth shut, do what you're told, and don't volunteer for ANYTHING," my father gave me a quick hug and drove off. Thus I began a journey that lasted eight weeks and earned me a little over $2,000.

I spent the first half of the day proving that I could bend my knees, snap my fingers, and urinate into a cup (not all at the same time), and I was found clean of marijuana and alcohol, and I received a plane ticket and a government check for $50. I began my five hour journey by taking a shuttle bus from the federal building to the airport.

Around 10 pm, we arrived at O'Hare airport in Chicago. I had been placed in charge of a group of three others since I was the one going into the Navy as an E3 (Seaman) as opposed to an E1 (Seaman Recruit). At the recruiter's office, I offhandedly remarked that I had taken three years of high school Junior Reserve Officer Training Corps. This ended up gaining me two extra rank grades. O'Hare airport was huge. Thousands of people of all different shapes, sizes, and races bustled through the same area trying to reach their next flight. The map that I had been given to navigate this virtual maze and find the USO was wholly inadequate. After nearly half an hour of searching, questioning security guards and stopping for no less than three bathroom breaks, my companions and I arrived at the USO office.

Almost three dozen other men were sitting in a large carpeted area and talking, watching TV, or sitting quietly. I could almost smell the stink of fear upon each person. I could feel myself drowning in that emotion, riding along the wave of uncertainty we created. Each person had joined for reasons of his own, and each person was now unsure of what would happen next.

After nearly an hour of waiting, one of the petty officers who had been ignoring us the entire time stood up and began yelling. She was a short, round black woman who looked about 40, and she had a surprisingly deep voice. "All of you form up outside into lines on either side of the wall," she bellowed.

I hurried to obey fearing she might direct her powerful voice at me if I moved too slowly, but several men became so nervous they couldn't choose a wall. I found the beginnings of a line on the left wall, and placed myself six or seventh from the front. Apparently, I had made the correct choice. Not more than a minute after I had taken my place in line, the Petty Officer began screaming again, "Can't any of you do a single f***ing thing right?"

She chose a particularly indecisive male, and personalized her attack just for him, "Why the f*** are you still standing there? Didn't I tell you to get in line?" She paused for a moment, waiting for his response.

He nervously stammered, "S-s-s-sorry Ma'am." "Do I look like a Ma'am, to you? I'm a petty officer. Now let's try that again!" she screamed, her voice rising to an impossible pitch.

"Sorry Petty Officer," he said again, sounding surer of himself this time. He was wrong again.

"Are you calling me a sorry Petty Officer?" she asked (a question I would hear repeated dozens of times in the upcoming weeks), venom dripping from her voice. "No Ma'am . . . I mean, Petty Officer," he managed to finish.

"You're d*** right you're sorry. Sorry doesn't even begin to describe you. Now get in line and shut the f*** up." Without waiting to see if he complied, she walked up to the front of the two lines.

Working quickly, she had all of us head onto a small commercial bus parked right outside of the front doors. Two seconds after the last person had taken his seat another Petty Officer stepped on the bus. He was a large white male, with a hard face and bulging biceps and triceps. "Everyone shut the f*** up," he said unnecessarily since I along with everyone else in the bus was too afraid to speak at this point.

After an hour bus ride that I spent watching the video and staring at the blackened window, which offered no view of the outside, the bus pulled to a stop. All of us piled out of the bus and made a dash for the nearest building, the Recruit Orientation Center. It was almost midnight by now, and the sky was pitch black. I've heard that in the Great Lakes there are two temperatures, hot and very, very cold. Since it was December 20th, the temperature was the latter as opposed to the former. I took a deep breath of the cold air and immediately began coughing up phlegm (I didn't stop for nine weeks). Reaching the inside of the building, I entered a place which I would visit many more times. Green doors with small rectangular windows lined both sides of the marshmallow white walls. Looking upward, I could see a silver banister crossing the length of the open walkway above me.

When all of us had lined up (for the second time that night), a grizzly looking Chief Petty Officer told us to wait for our names to be called and respond by yelling out our social security

numbers and then report for temporary uniform issue at the end
of the hall. The third person had a zero in his social security
number, but he pronounced it as the letter O. He was awarded
with an extremely summarized version of his family lineage with
several references made to dogs then sent on his way. No one
else made the same mistake.

What followed over the next hour was a series of trips from
one room to another where I received tennis shoes, sweats, ski
mask, gloves, skivvies, undershirts, socks, a blanket, some sheets
and a pillow case, a scarf and a trench coat, which didn't fit. All
of the toiletries I was given were placed in my newly issued sea
bag. My new clothes in tow, I, along with 70 other men whom I
would be spending the next 8 weeks of my life with, began my
journey down the 3-mile road (yes, literally), which would bring
us to our ship (barracks). I couldn't stop coughing from the cold,
and my glasses had fogged over from my own breath. I tried to
keep myself positioned behind the man in front of me, and for
the most part, I succeeded. Pushing back thoughts of complain-
ing, I forced myself to continue in silence.

After what seemed like hours and was actually only an
hour and a half, we arrived at our final destination. A blinding

flash of yellow light penetrated the fog covering my glasses, and I could immediately feel the blood in my ears begin to flow again. As the fog cleared, I found myself heading up a long set of black metal stairs which turned to the right after about fifteen steps before continuing up another flight. The interior of my ship looked like it had seen many years of service. Dingy yellow walls, a black banister with peeling paint and a slight musk of mold all added to the impression of age. Reaching the second floor (there were three in all), I followed the fifteen or so people in front of me into a darkened room. There were no lights on in the room, but I could sense the room was fairly large. A couple of minutes later my eyes finally adjusted to the light, and I could see that the room was roughly the length of two basketball courts and the width of half a basketball court. Rack upon rack of bunks crossed the length of the walls.

"Welcome to your new home," a cold voice said in the darkness. "I'm going to make sure your stay here is a pleasant one."

Placing my sea bag upon a bunk, I realized that THIS was the beginning of my journey, and for some reason the Petty Officer's words didn't make me feel any better about my choice.

Consider this . . .

- You may not normally consider profanity a good choice when you are writing an essay, but this writer used it several times. Was this a good choice? Why or why not?

- The writer used both formal and informal tones in this essay. Do you think this is appropriate? Why?

- What point is the writer trying to make with this story?

WRITING IS A PROCESS of making choices. However, if you understand the rhetorical situation, you do not have to make random choices. You can use your knowledge of your audience, your purpose, and your occasion for writing to guide your choices. As you become more skilled and decisive, the process of writing an essay will become easier for you.   ▪

WRITING BRIEFS

Each of the options that follow asks you to write a brief paper—no more than one page. Use these writing exercises as preparation for the longer assignments in Part Two of this book.

Option One

What makes a hero?

Heroism is a very popular theme in films, books, songs, and TV shows. Why is it such a popular theme? Do movies and TV series realistically depict heroes? For example, would you consider any of the characters in the long-running series *Friends*, *The Simpsons*, or *Everybody Loves Raymond* an accurate depiction of a hero? What about characters in movies like *G.I. Jane*? Write a one-page paper in which you either defend or refute a depiction of a hero that is well known in American culture.

Corbis/Sygma

The film G.I. Jane *addresses the controversial issue of women in combat.*

Option Two

The force of circumstances

The essay by Margaret Atwood is a powerful reminder of how circumstances sometimes force people to make difficult choices and thus become unlikely heroes.

Write a one-page paper in which you describe an unlikely hero you have known.

Mother Theresa devoted her life to helping the poor and homeless in Calcutta, India.

Because of Rosa Parks's heroism, African Americans established equal rights to seating on public buses— a move that helped to end segregation.

Option Three

Uncle Sam wants you

The U.S. Army home page contains a great deal of information intended to persuade you to enlist. Visit the Web site; then, write a one-page paper discussing specific ways in which this site tries to encourage you to sign up by emphasizing the concept of heroism.

Grammar Choices

TYPES OF SENTENCES

There are four types of declarative sentences:

- Simple sentences
- Compound sentences
- Complex sentences
- Compound complex sentences

In order to identify these types of sentences, you need to understand the following terms:

A **subject** is a word or group of words that is the topic of the sentence and so acts or is acted on or described.

A **predicate** consists of all the words after the subject, which give information about what the subject is, what it is doing, or what is being done to it.

An **independent clause** is a clause that can stand alone and function as a simple sentence; it contains a subject and a predicate.

A **dependent clause** is a clause that cannot stand alone without an independent clause to complete its meaning; it contains a subject and a predicate.

A **coordinating conjunction** is a linking word such as *and*, *but*, *for*, *nor*, *or*, *so*, or *yet*, which joins independent clauses.

A **subordinating conjunction** is a linking word such as *because*, *since*, *although*, *until*, or *while*, which often begins a dependent clause.

Simple Sentences

A **simple sentence** consists of one independent clause. An independent clause must have a **subject** and a **predicate**.

Apparently, **refraining from turning in your work** is not conducive to receiving a decent grade.

At the moment though, **I was more concerned with the temperature**.

Rack upon rack of bunks crossed the length of the walls.

Compound Sentences

A compound sentence is made up of two independent clauses linked by a **coordinating conjunction** or a conjunctive adverb:

He popped a video into the VCR stationed at the front of the bus, **and we were directed** to watch several former recruits talk about their experiences and what Recruit Training Command was going to be like.

There **were** no **lights** on in the room, **but I could sense** the room was fairly large.

Complex Sentences

A **complex sentence** has one independent clause and one dependent clause, joined by a **subordinating conjunction**:

I had been placed in charge of a group of three others **since I was** the one going into the Navy as an E3 (Seaman) as opposed to an E1 (Seaman Recruit).

Since it was December 20th, the **temperature was** the latter as opposed to the former.

Compound Complex Sentences

A **compound complex sentence** contains two independent clauses and at least one dependent clause:

Doubts clouded my mind for a moment, **as I watched** his blue Chevy Blazer recede into the distance, **but I** quickly **pushed** them back **as I realized** that my choice had already been made, **and thus I began** a journey that lasted eight weeks and earned me a little over $2,000.

It was almost midnight by now, **and the sky was** pitch black **as I tried** to keep up with the man running frantically in front of me, **as if his life depended** on reaching the building.

Learning to recognize these four types of sentences is the key to understanding how to punctuate them. This has been an overview of the types. Each type will be looked at in greater detail in the Grammar Choices section in one of the next four chapters.

Making It Work

- Identify the type of each sentence in your draft. Is it simple, compound, complex, or compound complex?

- Count how many of each type of sentence you have. Do you have at least two of each type of sentence?

- Revise selected sentences to make sure that you have at least two examples of each type of sentence in your paper.

- Does your draft have more sentence variety now?

Style Choices

SENTENCE VARIETY

Everyone likes variety. That's why ice cream comes in flavors besides vanilla and not all cars are black. The same is true of writing. Writing that lacks variety is boring. Look at this example.

Mom's office group committed to staying together and ultimately decided to climb the steep interstate embankments to cross the highway to a nearby shopping mall. **[simple]** Mom later told me she wished, among other things, that she had thought to grab her tennis shoes before she left because the going wasn't easy in her fitted skirt and pumps. **[complex]** From the mall, my mom called my father, who was working at another Army installation about twenty miles away. **[complex]** He didn't answer the phone at his desk, so she left a voice mail and countless calls to his pager to let him know she was okay. **[compound]** He got the first message, but he never talked to her in person that morning because all the phone lines and satellites were jammed with the sudden influx of callers to the area. **[compound complex]**

This paragraph is good for two reasons, both related to the writer's use of sentence variety:

- Because the words have a varying rhythm, the writing is not repetitious or stagnant.

- The meaning of the information in the sentences is clear because one idea is subordinated to another. This allows us to understand how the writer relates one idea to another.

Making It Work

- Choose a paragraph from the paper you are currently writing.
- Identify the type of each sentence in the paragraph.
- How much sentence variety does the paragraph have?
- How could you add more?

MANY VOICES, MANY IDEAS

Strategies for Writing

In this chapter, you will learn:

- How writing can teach you many things

- Reasons for writing—to share a personal experience, an observation, or information, to solve a problem, to evaluate, to persuade, or to respond

- Writing strategies— narration, description, example, definition, interview, comparison/contrast, division/classification, process, cause/effect, and argumentation

- Organizational methods— chronological, spatial, conceptual, topical, alternating, emphatic, and logical

Roger Ressmeyer/Corbis

AP Photo/Eric Risberg

Ben Martin/Time-Life Pictures/Getty Images

Successful writers—such as Alice Walker (top), Maxine Hong Kingston (middle), and Gabriel Garcia Marquez (bottom)—use a variety of writing strategies.

It's natural to be unsure of your writing abilities. Most of you have been writing in school for at least twelve years, and in that time, you've probably had your fair share of criticism. Constructive criticism is a good thing—it helps us to improve our skills; however, a steady diet of criticism can make anyone insecure. The purpose of this chapter is to build your confidence by helping you identify reasons for writing.

Just as you may never have thought about whether you have a writing process, you may never have thought about when to write other than for a class assignment. However, compelling reasons to write arise daily. Part of being a decisive writer is learning to recognize and exploit these occasions.

LEARNING BY WRITING

If you consider every essay you write as an opportunity to learn and try to find a compelling reason to write, you will learn something from what you write:

- You may learn about yourself.

- You may learn about a research topic you've chosen.

- You may learn a new writing technique.

- You may learn a new way of looking at the world or some part of it.

For example, you will probably do a fair amount of writing in college. Your professors do not ask you to write just to keep you busy. They know that writing is a way to learn. You can read about capital punishment and gather facts, but you can only say you have really learned about capital punishment when you have synthesized and analyzed what you've read and then developed your own opinion concerning the topic. A written paper is the most effective medium to share an opinion you've developed. Once you've done this, you've moved beyond the phase of just repeating what other writers say and begun expressing what you've learned in your own words. At this point, others can learn from you.

Writing can always teach you something if you approach it seriously and think about what you write rather than just putting words on the page to fulfill an assignment. Read the following two essays, and decide which writer learned more about writing.

Writer's Break

- Identify six compelling reasons to write.
- For each of the six reasons you identified, briefly describe the motivation to write and how you would respond.
- After you finish writing, post your list so that your classmates can access it, or if you are not using a computer, make copies to share with at least four other people in your class.

Essay One

Writing is a very valuable resource in today's society; furthermore, writing can come across as a powerful message if expressed clearly with a structured format. It is important to acquire well-developed writing skills for everyday use, class essays, and job opportunities.

Writing is an everyday skill which is extremely useful. Countless times during the day writing is used. Whether in class or in a letter to your mother, it is important to use some kind of structure in writing. Structure in writing organizes thought and helps the reader understand the reading. Strong writing skills are an asset which helps a writer become more organized and clarified in his thoughts.

Another reason it is important to learn how to write well is for class essays and reports. As stated before, writing can become a powerful message if expressed correctly. When turning in a class assignment, professors tend to look for structure and format, and if they find a lack of it they may conclude that the excerpt was unorganized. With good writing skills, a writer can persuade the audience and seem quite intelligent about the topic even if he knows little about what he has written on.

Finally and most importantly, an individual must learn to write strongly to earn job opportunities or promotions. In order to get a job, a person must turn in a resume, which requires writing of some sort. Moreover, some companies ask workers to write self-evaluations for promotions and pay increases. Often success is determined on what these people write and how they present material. Another reason learning to write well is a must is because many individuals judge intelligence on how a person writes. In conclusion, writing is not only a valuable asset in everyday matters; it can also determine the success of an individual.

Essay Two

I like to write because it is a way for me to express myself more vividly. Writing allows me to express myself better by thinking more critically as I am putting words onto paper, rather than just blurting out the words without too much thought beforehand. Writing also allows me to become more involved in myself; consequently, I learn more about myself when I write.

I am an individual who likes to talk and involve myself in conversation. Many times during conversation my thoughts get caught up, and they do not flow as well as I would like them to. My thoughts are better expressed on paper. I have time to think about and elaborate on how I am feeling. The words do not have to flow out so quickly because I have time to examine my thoughts. Many times during conversation you know what you want to say, but it can be difficult putting it into words. Many times you have to sit back and get your thoughts together. While you're doing that, the listener has lost interest in what you have to say. When you write, you have time to sit back and think of what you want to say. When your words are in writing, the words are flowing and the reader does not lose interest. For that individual not to lose interest in what you are saying, you need to express yourself vividly.

When I am expressing myself on paper, I become one with myself. I become more involved in feelings, beliefs, and expectations of myself. Writing allows an individual to explore his or her own mind. When you're collecting your thoughts you may find out things about yourself that you thought were not there. In several of my English classes we had to write persuasive papers. When I began to write I may have felt a certain way about the topic; during the middle, my views may have changed.

About eighty percent of the time my thoughts are better written than said. Writing is simply a way for me to involve myself in my own little world. My world is nothing but thought and feeling; feelings that allow me to become more involved with myself mentally.

Considering that both of these essays were written in class and that the students had limited time, they are fairly well-written. However, the ways in which these writers respond to the prompt "Why is writing important?" are very different. The first writer takes no risks. It is difficult to get a sense of either him or his opinions regarding writing:

Writing is a very valuable resource in today's society.

This sentence doesn't say anything beyond the obvious. Do you, as the reader, get any sense of this writer's true opinions concerning the value of writing?

The writer of the second essay makes a much more successful attempt at communicating clearly. Consider the opening line of that essay:

I like to write because it is a way for me to express myself more vividly.

This writer doesn't make vague references to "society." She throws herself and her opinions right out in front of the reader—she communicates an idea that she believes. This attitude is expressed throughout the essay. Consequently, even though the essay is not better in the sense of being more correct, it is better in the sense that the writer took the assignment she was given and chose to turn it into more than another class exercise. By investing some of herself in what she wrote, she created an occasion for writing, and she learned something valuable in the process:

About eighty percent of the time my thoughts are better written than said. Writing is simply a way for me to involve myself in my own little world. My world of nothing but thought and feeling, feelings that allow me to become more involved with myself mentally.

There will be times when you feel compelled to write and times when you have to write. However, there should be no time when you don't learn from writing.

REASONS TO WRITE

There are many reasons to write. You can write for academic reasons, business reasons, or personal reasons, but most often, essays are written for one of these reasons:

- To share a personal experience
- To make an observation

- To impart information

- To solve problems

- To evaluate

- To persuade

- To respond

Although we are going to discuss each of these reasons individually, it is important to remember that they can overlap. For example, in the process of writing about a personal experience, you might solve a problem. Or you might share a piece of information in order to persuade someone to accept your opinion about what you have shared. Most essays have a primary focus—one of the reasons to write listed above. You shouldn't feel constrained by this list, though. If the point you want to make requires blending several of these reasons, that's fine.

Writer's Break

For each of the seven reasons to write:

- Identify a possible writing topic.

- For each topic, write one or two sentences justifying your choice.

Be prepared to share your material with the class.

≡ To Share a Personal Experience

There are many genres of personal writing, including memoir, autobiography, and diary or journal. The personal writing you do for this course will be in the form of short essays. Some of these essays will give you the opportunity to share and explore experiences you have had.

Interestingly, personal writing often becomes public writing at some point. For example, personal writing often provides the only insight into ancient cultures. Look at this example from an ancient journal:

> A man who teaches a woman to write should recognize that he is providing poison to an asp.

This passage, which was copied out by male school children in Greece in the fourth century BCE, is attributed to the comic poet Menander. It tells us a great deal concerning the attitudes of the time.

Owali-Kulla/Corbis

Even before the invention of any system of writing, early humans used pictures to record information and to share their experiences.

Personal writings of historical figures also allow us to understand past events in a more accurate context. Journals written by victims of the Holocaust, such as *The Diary of a Young Girl*, by Anne Frank, help us get a glimmer of understanding about an inconceivable event.

Start writing now. Keep a journal. Jot yourself notes. Write a line or two on the back of photos. Some day those little scraps of personal writing might help you write something bigger and better. In fact, next time you're stuck for a topic, spend some time going through your junk drawer looking at old notes and photographs. Your history is worth writing about. Writing is something that lasts. It gives you a way of recording memories and events. When should you write for personal reasons? Every time you get the chance.

☰ To Make an Observation

When you write to share an observation, you make an experience or event the focus of your writing. Genres of observation-based writing include travelogues, news reports, and photo essays. Observational writing allows you to share the significance of something you observed.

The following passage, written by Samuel Pepys in 1666, describes the Great Fire of London, which destroyed four-fifths of the central city. We now know that this tragedy had the felicitous effect of helping to wipe out the plague by killing the rats that infested the city. Pepys records only the visible horror of the moment:

FROM THE DIARY OF SAMUEL PEPYS

So I rode down to the waterside . . . and there saw a lamentable fire. . . . Everybody endeavouring to remove their goods, and flinging into the river or bringing them into lighters that lay off; poor people staying in their houses as long as till the very

The Great Fire of London, 1799 by J. C. Stadler. Guildhall Library, Corporation of London, UK/Bridgeman Art Library.

The great fire of London devastated the city and killed thousands of people.

fire touched them, and then running into boats, or clambering from one pair of stairs by the waterside to another. And among other things, the poor pigeons, I perceive were loth to leave their houses, but hovered about the windows and balconies, till they some of them burned their wings and fell down.

Observational writing like this allows the writer to make sense of what he or she saw while providing the reader with the opportunity to share an experience vicariously.

≡ To Impart Information

When you write to share information, you make details about a specific topic the focus of your writing. Genres of information-based writing include feasibility studies, instructions, consumer reports, and records of experiments. In the following brief informative essay, scientists speculate about the origin of clothing.

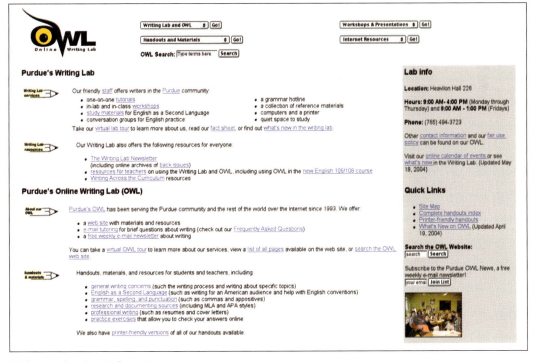

Web sites also share information.

HUMANITY'S BIG COVERUP

Nell Boyce

1   When a school sends home a note about lice, most parents simply shudder and give their kids the once-over. But Mark Stoneking, on seeing the note, got intrigued. Cooties, realized the Max Planck Institute for Evolutionary Anthropology scientist, might reveal the naked truth about clothing and identify the first early humans to put it on.

2   Furs and fabrics tend to rot, leaving no trace in the fossil record. But lice can serve as a living fossil. Head lice make their home on hair while body lice reside in clothes. If Stoneking could figure out when body lice branched off from their hair-living brethren—presumably because they found a new home in a prehistoric wardrobe—that could be the date of clothing's origin.

3   **The lice clock.** Stoneking's group studied the genetic differences among 40 head and body lice, as well as their distant ancestor, the chimpanzee louse, to see how louse genes change over time. They calculated that body lice appeared sometime between 114,000 and 30,000 years ago. The more recent date corresponds to the age of ancient sewing needles, as well as to a sudden outburst of creativity and migration that occurred in early modern humans. "I think it fits very well with the idea that clothing may have been associated with the first migrations out of Africa into colder climates," says Stoneking, whose work appears in ***Current Biology***.

4   But some evidence suggests that humanoids may have needed covering even earlier. They seem to have lost their dense body hair over a million years ago, and archaic Neanderthals were living in cold regions of Europe 150,000 years ago. Richard Klein of Stanford University thinks that they, too, must have worn some covering, though perhaps only rough wraps instead of tailored clothes with seams where lice like to hide. "The question is, what is clothing?" observes Klein philosophically. "Whether we would call that clothing doesn't matter. It's what the lice think of it."

In this essay, the writer shares information about a new area of anthropological study that can shed more light on the life of early humans—a topic to which we can all relate.

≡ To Solve a Problem

When you make some issue or difficulty and its possible solution the focus of a piece of writing, you are writing to solve a problem. Genres of problem-solving writing include proposals, essays, and case studies. In the following excerpt from a proposal, the writer identifies a specific problem and proposes a solution.

The irregularities recently encountered in physical wet and dry bulb measurements on the Cargocaire air dryers have caused process moisture control to become a major problem. One solution is to purchase a hygrometer to standardize the moisture reading. A hygrometer will allow us to make control decisions much more quickly and with greater confidence.

The hygrometer best suited for our system is the Shaw Model SH4, 4 point manual meter with alarm delay. I recommend purchase of the Shaw Hygrometer for the following reasons:

- Sensors would be located in each of the three 16-inch diameter process air risers from the Cargocaire to determine individual machine performance.
- One sensor would be located in the 20-inch diameter main header to determine overall moisture content.
- Our maximum moisture content of 10 grains/lb. corresponds to a dew point of –11.11°C, and would require the medium range (–60 to 0°C) "Yellow Spot" sensors.
- Accuracy should be 2 grains, and minimum sensor service should be 3 to 5 years.

Although this proposal identifies a specific problem and suggests a possible solution, some problem-based writing simply explores a problem that may or may not have a solution.

≡ To Evaluate

When you write to evaluate, you make your opinion of something—a person, a situation, a piece of literature, an action—the focus of your writing. Genres of writing to evaluate include reviews and critiques.

In the following excerpt, the writer evaluates *Buffy the Vampire Slayer*.

FROM WHY *BUFFY* KICKED ***
Virginia Postrell

Buffy was right all along.

For those who somehow missed its cult success, *Buffy* tells the story of an unlikely hero—a pert, blonde teenager whom fate has destined to be the Slayer, the "one girl in all the world" endowed with the supernatural strength to protect humanity against the demon hordes. Buffy would rather be a cheerleader and prom queen, but a normal life is not to be. "No chess club and football games for me," she says. "I spend my free time in graveyards and dark alleys." . . .

The mere existence of *Buffy* proves the declinists wrong about one thing: Hollywood commercialism can produce great art. Complex and evolving characters. Playful language. Joy and sorrow, pathos and elation. Episodes that dare to be different—to tell stories in silence or in song. Big themes and terrible choices. . . .

Buffy assumes and enacts the consensus moral understanding of contemporary American culture, the moral understanding that the wise men ignored or forgot. This understanding depends on no particular religious tradition. It's informed not by revelation but by experience. It is inclusive and humane, without denying distinctions or the tough facts of life. There are lots of jokes in *Buffy*—humor itself is a moral imperative—but no psychobabble and no excuses. . . .

In this essay, the writer tries to show why a popular television show earned its popularity and to suggest that it has lasting value. Most evaluative writing functions in the same way.

☰ To Persuade

When you write to persuade, you make an attempt to change your readers' opinions or sway their decisions the focus of your writing. Persuasive writing genres include proposals and editorials.

The events of September 11, 2001, rocked the world, and the citizens of the United States are still recovering from those horrifying events. The following passage offers one writer's opinion of the event:

FROM LETTERS AT 3AM
Michael Ventura

Is this the first event of World War Three, a war unlike any before, to be fought in ways unlike any before? It may be. As I write I feel like I'm whispering, because in such a time all words that are not shouted feel like whispers—small breaths of sound spoken in the dark, their meanings tentative and incomplete. It is very late, it may be too late, but still I propose a toast and raise my glass:

To the compassionate and brave.

In this piece of writing, the author offers two opinions—September 11 may be the beginning of World War Three, but we should not crouch down and hide. We should salute our heroes. Persuasive writing always addresses a point that can be argued. That is what makes the act of persuasion necessary.

☰ To Respond

When you write to respond, you write about something produced by someone else—a piece of writing, an idea, a work of art. The focus of your writing is your response to what the other person created. Response genres include reviews, literary analyses, and prefaces to larger works. In the example that follows, the writer responds to a novel.

FROM TEACHER TO TEACHER
Gary Salvner

Though it didn't overwhelm me at first reading, Gary Paulsen's *Hatchet* (Bradbury Press, 1987) has since become my favorite young adult novel. After numerous readings I've begun to understand why it has sold over three million copies and continues to rivet both young adult and adult readers. With *Hatchet*, the delight is in the details. As Brian Robeson, wholly unschooled in outdoor survival, begins to understand the Canadian wilderness he crash lands into, we learn about it as well. Brian discovers through trial and error which berries are edible, how to construct hunting tools, and how to use all his senses to alert himself to weather changes and animal behavior. It is the vivid descriptive details, the sense that Paulsen authentically knows what he's writing about, that makes this survival adventure convincing.

In this review, the writer tells us why he considers the novel *Hatchet* an excellent example of the genre of young adult literature. He does this by referring specifically to the text itself and to the literary techniques used by the writer. This is how you respond to a published work.

CHOOSING WRITING STRATEGIES

Writing strategies, which are sometimes called *modes*, are the tools you use to write your essays. The writing strategies we will consider are as follows:

- Narration
- Description
- Example
- Definition
- Interview
- Comparison/contrast
- Division/classification
- Process
- Cause/effect
- Argumentation

Writer's Break

- Choose five of the writing strategies listed here, and find an example in a piece of writing of the use of each strategy.
- Put your examples in your writer's notebook, and label them.
- Be prepared to share your information with the class.

Although we will discuss these strategies individually, it is important to remember that you will typically blend them in your essays. After all, you are not likely to complete a complex task using only one tool. Writing an essay is a very complex task, so it stands to reason that you will need to use more than a single tool in order to achieve your purpose. Based on your reason for writing, you may use one strategy more than another, but you will almost always use more than one. For example, if you are writing a proposal, you will clearly use argumentation, but you might also use narration to provide background information or comparison/contrast to weigh possible solutions. In the following essay, the writer's primary reason for writing is to discuss a problem and a solution, so she uses cause/effect as her primary strategy. However, she also uses two other strategies. Each of these is labeled for you.

REBUILDING EDEN

Jocelyn Selim

During the 1990s, Saddam Hussein instituted a series of draining projects that have reduced an 8,000-square-mile refuge of freshwater wetlands—regarded by some as the historical Garden of Eden—to a small, salt-encrusted remnant. A United Nations report described the loss of this ecologically abundant area as "one of the world's greatest environmental disasters." Now that Hussein is gone, an international team of wetlands experts has formed a consortium, called the Eden Again Project, to restore the oasis before it vanishes into the desert.

1 Reason for writing: to solve a problem

Cause—Hussein's draining projects

Effect—destruction of wetlands

Solution—Eden Again Project

Located along the southwestern Iran-Iraq border at the confluence of the Tigris and Euphrates Rivers, the wetlands provided a key rest stop for migratory birds and a nursery for the shrimp and fish of the Persian Gulf. The region also supported more than 300,000 Marsh Arabs, whose opposition to Hussein's regime allegedly provoked the draining project. Since the wetlands began drying up, dozens of endemic species, including smooth-coated otters and Euphrates soft-shell turtles, have vanished, and Gulf fish populations have fallen by half.

2

Description—effects of the problem

Geologist Suzanne Alwash of El Camino College in Torrance, California, director of the Eden Again Project, recognizes that restoring Iraq's unique marsh

3 Argument—complications of solution

Corbis

ecology will involve navigating thorny issues of postwar reconstruction and water distribution in a parched region.

4   "A project of this scale is going to require enormous funding, and that's provided we can overcome political issues between Iraq and its neighbors that could prevent getting enough freshwater into the country. But it looks like the U.N. and the United States and Iraqi governments are ready to give the support we need," Alwash says. Then come the scientific challenges: "You can't just flood the area. It's a delicate process that involves simultaneously controlling the amounts, the salinity, the quality and all sorts of possible contaminations," says wetlands ecologist Mary Kentula of the Environmental Protection Agency, and adviser to the Eden Again Project.

Effect—reintroduction
of species

5   *If* the project proceeds as intended, some areas could return to their wetland state in five years. Then Alwash and her colleagues plan to reintroduce displaced species and monitor how they coexist with returning Marsh Arabs. In this case, researchers do not see humans as obstacles to success: "They have been essential to this ecosystem for over 10,000 years," Alwash says.

≡ Narration

A narrative tells a story. Narrative writing normally follows a chronological order, but the writer can reverse the order of events for emphasis or to build suspense. Consider the following excerpt, which places past events before a present one.

FROM MY MOTHER NEVER WORKED
Bonnie Smith-Yackel

From her wheelchair she canned pickles, baked bread, ironed clothes, wrote dozens of letters weekly to her friends and her "half dozen or more kids," and made three patchwork housecoats and one quilt. She made balls and balls of carpet scraps—enough for five rugs. And kept all her love letters.

"I think I've found your mother's records—Martha Ruth Smith; married to Ben F. Smith?"

"Yes, that's right."

"Well, I see that she was getting a widow's pension. . . ."

"Yes, that's right."

"Well, your mother wasn't entitled to our $255 death benefit."

"Not entitled! But why?"

The voice on the telephone explains patiently:

"Well, you see—your mother never worked."

≡ Description

Descriptive writing creates a verbal picture of how something or someplace looks, sounds, smells, tastes, and/or feels. The following excerpt is an example.

FROM THE WAY TO RAINY MOUNTAIN
N. Scott Momaday

Descending eastward, the highland meadows are a stairway to the plain. In July the inland slope of the Rockies is luxuriant with flax and buckwheat, stonecrop and larkspur. The earth unfolds and the limit of the land recedes. Clusters of trees and animals grazing far in the distance cause the vision to reach away and wonder to build upon the mind. The sun follows a longer course in the day, and the sky is immense beyond all comparison. The great billowing clouds that sail upon it are shadows that move upon the grain like water, dividing light. Farther down, in the land of the Crows and Blackfeet, the plain is yellow. Sweet clover takes hold of the hills and bends upon itself to cover and seal the soil. . . .

☰ Example

Exemplification is the process of using specific examples to support a general statement. The following excerpt uses exemplification to support the writer's position that illiteracy carries a high cost.

FROM THE HUMAN COST OF AN ILLITERATE SOCIETY
Jonathan Kozol

Illiterates cannot read the menu in a restaurant.

They cannot read the cost of items on the menu in the *window* of the restaurant before they enter.

Illiterates cannot read the letters that their children bring home from their teachers. They cannot study school department circulars that tell them of the courses that their children must be taking if they hope to pass the SAT exams. They cannot help with homework. They cannot write a letter to the teacher. They are afraid to visit in the classroom. They do not want to humiliate their child or themselves.

☰ Definition

A definition tell us what something is by listing its parts, explaining how it works, telling us what it does, or comparing it to similar things. In the next excerpt, the writer defines *wife* by listing many activities traditionally seen as part of that role.

FROM I WANT A WIFE
Judy Brady

Why do I want a wife? . . . I want a wife who will take care of my physical needs. I want a wife who will keep my house clean. A wife who will pick up after my children, a wife who will pick up after me. I want a wife who will keep my clothes clean, ironed, mended, replaced when need be, and who will see to it that my personal things are kept in their proper place so that I can find what I need the minute I need it. I want a wife who cooks the meals, a wife who is a good cook. I want a wife who will plan the menus, do the necessary grocery shopping, prepare the meals, serve them pleasantly, and then do the cleaning up while I do my studying. I want a wife who will care for me when I am sick and sympathize with my pain and loss of time from school. I want a wife to go along when our family takes a vacation so that someone can continue to care for me and my children when I need a rest and a change of scene.

☰ Interview

You use interview as a writing strategy when you base your essay on information you get directly from someone else. The interview is a very popular genre of writing, and you will find examples of it in magazines like *Rolling Stone*.

THE RIGBY MYSTERY

Jenny Eliscu

More than 200 Beatles songs are credited "Lennon/McCartney," but the degree of collaboration varied, and who gets credit for songs has occasionally been a source of tension. 1

Paul McCartney has said that he wrote lyrics and music for "Eleanor Rigby" almost entirely on his own: "I wrote it at the piano. John helped me on a few words, but it came down eighty-twenty to me." 2

But in a 1980 *Playboy* interview with David Sheff, John Lennon painted a different picture: "The first was his, and the rest are basically mine. . . . I finally went off to a room with Paul and we finished the song. Who said what to whom as we were writing, I don't know. I do know George Harrison was there when we came up with 'Ah, look at all the lonely people.'" 3

By changing the credit on *Back in the U.S.*, McCartney "is kidnapping 'Eleanor Rigby,'" says Elliot Mintz, a spokesman for Ono and a friend of Lennon's. "It lays the groundwork for Paul to adopt however many songs he chooses." 4

☰ Comparison/Contrast

You compare and contrast when you make it clear how two or more things are similar or different. In the next excerpt, the writer compares Ray Kroc, founder of McDonald's, with Walt Disney by stressing their similarities:

FROM WALT AND RAY: YOUR TRUSTED FRIENDS
Eric Schlosser

Despite all their success as businessmen and entrepreneurs, as cultural figures and advocates for a particular brand of Americanism, perhaps the most significant achievement of these two men lay elsewhere. Walt Disney and Ray Kroc were masterful salesmen. They perfected the art of selling things to children. And their success led many others to aim marketing efforts at kids, turning America's youngest consumers into a demographic group that is now avidly studied, analyzed, and targeted by the world's largest corporations.

☰ Division/Classification

When you use division, you take a single topic and divide it into parts. For example, if you were writing about the government of the United States, you would probably divide the topic according to the three main branches and their parts. When you classify, you take separate topics and group them into categories according to a shared element. For example, you might take several cartoonists and place them in the category of political satirists based on their shared traits. The writer of the next excerpt divides college students and people in general into economic classes.

FROM THE MEN WE CARRY IN OUR MINDS
Scott Russell Sanders

A scholarship enabled me not only to attend college, a rare enough feat in my circle, but even to study in a university meant for the children of the rich. Here I met for the first time men who had assumed from birth that they would lead lives of comfort and power. And for the first time I met women who told me that men were guilty of having kept all the joys and privileges of the earth for themselves. I was baffled. What privileges? What joys? I thought about the maimed, dismal lives of most of the men back home. What had they stolen from their wives and daughters? The right to go five days a week, twelve months a year, for thirty or forty years to a steel mill or a coal mine? The right to drop bombs, die in war? The right to feel every leak in the roof, every gap in the fence, every cough in the engine, as a wound they must mend? The right to feel, when the layoff comes or the plant shuts down, not only afraid but ashamed?

☰ Process

When you write about a process, you tell how something happens or how something is done, by listing the steps in chronological order, as the writer does in this excerpt.

FROM HOUSE
Tracy Kidder

The building site slopes gently. Locke calculates by how much it does so. He turns the scope of the transit until he sees the cross hairs rest upon a numeral inscribed on a long, numbered staff. Judith's father has volunteered to carry the staff. Locke directs him to and fro. For a benchmark, Locke has chosen an electrical box planted in the ground nearby. He sends his staff-bearer to that spot first. The numbers Locke reads through his scope tell him how far below his transit's scope the benchmark rests. He sends the staff-bearer to a stake that represents the southeastern corner of the house to come, and through the scope he determines how far below the benchmark that corner lies. Locke checks these numbers against ones inscribed on a blueprint opened on the ground beside him. Soon he knows the relative elevations of the land at each corner of the house. He will be able to tell through his spyglass when the cellar hole has been dug to the proper depth. The ceremony can begin, as soon as the bulldozer arrives.

☰ Cause/Effect

Cause-and-effect writing explores why something happens and the result of its happening. The next excerpt explains how television has caused damage to family life.

FROM TELEVISION: THE PLUG-IN DRUG
Marie Winn

Home and family have changed in important ways since the advent of television. The peer group has become television-oriented, and much of the time children spend together is occupied by television viewing. Culture generally has been transformed by television. Participation in church and community activities has diminished, with television a primary cause of this change. Therefore it is improper to assign to television the subsidiary role its many apologists insist it plays. Television is not merely one of a number of important influences upon today's child. Through the changes it has made in family life, television emerges as *the* important influence in children's lives today.

☰ Argumentation

When you write argumentatively, your focus is a controversial topic, on which you have a specific opinion to share. Your goal is to persuade your readers to accept or even adopt your opinion. In the following excerpt, Martin Luther King, Jr. eloquently argues against segregation.

FROM LETTER FROM BIRMINGHAM JAIL
Martin Luther King, Jr.

We have waited for more than 340 years for our constitutional and God-given rights. The nations of Asia and Africa are moving with jetlike speed toward gaining political independence, but we still creep at horse-and-buggy pace toward gaining a cup of coffee at a lunch counter. Perhaps it is easy for those who have never felt the stinging darts of segregation to say, "Wait." But when you have seen vicious mobs lynch your mothers and fathers at will and drown your sisters and brothers at whim; when you have seen hate-filled policemen curse, kick, and even kill your black brothers and sisters; when you see the vast majority of your twenty million Negro brothers smothering in an airtight cage of poverty in the midst of an affluent society; when you suddenly find your tongue twisted and your speech stammering as you seek to explain to your six-year-old daughter why she can't go to the public amusement park that has just been advertised on television, and see tears welling up in her eyes when she is told that Funtown is closed to colored children, and see ominous clouds of inferiority beginning to form in her little mental sky, and see her beginning to distort her personality by developing an unconscious bitterness toward white people; when you have to concoct an answer for a five-year-old son who is asking, "Daddy, why do white people treat colored people so mean?" . . .

CHOOSING AN ORGANIZATIONAL METHOD

In addition to finding a reason to write and choosing writing strategies that suit your purpose, you also have to choose an organizational method. These are the most commonly used methods:

- Chronological order
- Spatial order
- Conceptual order
- Topical order
- Alternating order
- Emphatic order
- Logical order

Again, it is important to remember that while most essays will use one organizational method predominantly, you can use a combination of two or more methods within an essay. The rhetorical situation should guide your organizational choices.

Writer's Break

- Look at the five pieces of writing you chose for the Writer's Break on page 66.
- Determine which organizational method each writer used.
- Did any writer use more than one method? Which one is predominant?
- Share your information with the class.

☰ Chronological Order

When you use chronological order, you arrange description or information according to the order in which it happened. Among the excerpts presented earlier in this chapter, these use chronological order: "My Mother Never Worked" and *House*.

☰ Spatial Order

When you use spatial order, your writing is organized to reflect the movement of the eyes. For example, the focus moves left to right, up to down, or near to far. Spatial organization is especially useful for descriptive writing. The following excerpt uses spatial organization: *The Way to Rainy Mountain*.

☰ Conceptual Order

When you use conceptual order, you introduce points related to your topic and then develop and link them. This organizational method is used in the excerpts from "The Men We Carry in Our Minds" and "Television: The Plug-In Drug."

☰ Topical Order

When you use topical order, you present several related topics and then develop them. For example, if you were writing about the destruction of Mt. Everest, you might cover several related topics in order to make your point: the history of the mountain, famous climbs, the current state of the mountain, and the lack of regulation that is causing the problems. The excerpt from *The Human Cost of an Illiterate Society* is organized topically.

☰ Alternating Order

You use an alternating organizational method when you identify a problem and then propose a solution. "Rebuilding Eden" uses this pattern.

You also use an alternating order when you compare two things to show how they are similar or contrast them to show how they are different. You can alternate by discussing first one thing and then the other or by using a point-by-point pattern. The excerpt from "Walt and Ray: Your Trusted Friends" is a comparison organized in alternating order.

☰ Emphatic Order

When you use emphatic order as your organizational method, you arrange your information in order of importance—usually from least important to most important, though this order can be reversed. This method is often used in persuasive writing. The following excerpt uses emphatic order: "Letter from Birmingham Jail."

☰ Logical Order

When you use logical order as an organizational method, you have two options: You can begin with a general statement and then present specific details to elaborate on the statement, or you can begin with specific details and follow with a general statement of their significance. The following excerpt uses logical order: "I Want a Wife."

SO WHAT DOES ALL this have to do with learning how to write essays? Everything. Writing is like anything else—the more you do it, the better you will be at it. If you look for opportunities to write rather than looking for reasons not to write, you will not only be surprised by how often you will find good occasions for writing, but by how quickly you become a more confident writer. Rather than always picking up the phone, write a letter to a friend. When a situation seems unmanageable, write about it. If the mechanic who fixed your car overcharged you, write a letter demanding a refund. The next thing you know, you'll find yourself dreading writing less, and what you learn in your composition class and from this book will start making sense. So when should you write? Whenever you can. ▪

COLLABORATIVE EXERCISES

Group Exercise One

- Talk about times when you had to use writing to represent yourselves. Try to identify an example of each of the types of writing discussed in this chapter.

- Did you feel like you represented yourselves as well as you would like?

- Write a brief impression based on what you discovered.

- Share your work with the class.

Group Exercise Two

- As a class, make a list of the qualities papers written in response to Options One and Two in Writing Briefs should have.

- As a class, develop a list of criteria you could use to evaluate those papers.

- Individually, write three questions for your peer evaluators. Each question should address a concern you have about your paper.

WRITING BRIEFS

Option One

And the winner is . . .

We are frequently asked to demonstrate who we are by writing about ourselves. For example, if you answer a personals ad, you respond in writing, and someone decides whether or not to meet you based on your choice of words. When you apply for a job, you are asked to submit a letter and a resume. A prospective employer will decide whether to interview you based on your choice of words. Choose a job ad or a personals ad that requires you to write a letter (or use one of the examples shown below), and write the letter that is required.

Attractive woman in love with romance seeks a suitor who can woo her with words. Send me a poem, send me a letter, send me a song. Don't send me a picture. Let your words of romance sweep me away.

Acctg. Software Sales Rep
Tulsa based firm is expanding Blackbaud non-profit accounting practice to Dallas Area. Looking for a salesperson w/accounting systems background. Exp. in the non-profit industry a plus. Please fax, email or mail resume to:

HQ Technology Group
6717 S. Yale Avenue Ste 104
Tulsa OK 12345

Option Two

Why did I do that?

Words and images are often powerful enough to influence us: We buy things because of advertisements; we join organizations because of what they tell us; we change ourselves because of images we see. Choose a piece of writing or an image that you consider powerful or persuasive, and write a one-page analysis of the reasons for the piece's success. Consider the creator's reason for communicating and the strategies he or she used.

Mark Wilson/Getty Images

When we believe that a celebrity supports a cause, we are more likely to support it.

Recruitment posters like this one played a vital role during World War II.

The Advertising Archive/The Picture Desk, Inc.

Many weight loss ads depend on before and after photos to sell a product.

Option Three

Worth a thousand words

In this photo, Walker Evans, who photographed victims of the 1930s Dust Bowl in the American Midwest, shares a great deal of information. What do you think were his reasons for taking this photo? What do you think he wanted to share with his audience? Using the reasons for writing, the writing strategies, and the organizational methods discussed in this chapter, analyze this photograph to determine why you think Evans took it and what his message is.

"Wash Stand" by Walker Evans/Corbis

Grammar Choices

SIMPLE SENTENCES

A **simple sentence**, also called an **independent clause**, must have a **subject** and a **predicate**. Look at these examples:

Culture **generally has been transformed by television**.

I **thought about the maimed, dismal lives of most of the men back home**.

They **cannot write a letter to the teacher**.

They **are afraid to visit the classroom**.

Each of these simple sentences contains a subject and a predicate. Each predicate contains a verb and also contains modifying words and phrases.

Culture generally **has been transformed** by television.

In this sentence, the adverb *generally* and the phrase *by television* modify the verb.

I **thought** about the maimed, dismal lives of most of the men back home.

In this sentence, *about the maimed, dismal lives* is a prepositional phrase that modifies the verb *thought*, and *of most of the men back home* is a prepositional phrase that modifies *lives*.

They **cannot write** a letter to the teacher.

They **are afraid** to visit the classroom.

In these sentences, the verb is followed by a phrase that completes the meaning of the verb.

Making It Work

How do you identify a simple sentence?

▪ Find the subject.

▪ Find the verb.

Style Choices

USING SIMPLE LANGUAGE

When we write, we have a tendency to want everything to sound bigger and better. In terms of word choices, this often results in the use of inflated language. Inflated language characterizes our writing when we choose a word like *utilize* instead of *use*. Look at these other examples:

facilitate	help
inquire	ask
endeavor	try
require	need
terminate	end
affirmative	yes

Don't be a writer who sounds like he or she swallowed a thesaurus. Use simple language; in most cases, it communicates more clearly.

Making It Work

- Read your paper out loud.
- Underline every word you wouldn't normally use in everyday speech.
- Do they belong in your paper, or have you used inflated language?

IMAGES AND TEXTS

The Design of Writing

In this chapter, you will learn:

- What visual rhetoric is and how visual texts work to convey meaning

- The basic elements of design—headings, fonts, white space, lists, and graphics

- How to use the basic design elements to increase the accessibility and impact of your essays

- How to use design to create effective Web pages

Both the design and the content of a document are important in conveying your meaning.

WHAT IS VISUAL RHETORIC?

Rhetoric, loosely defined, means persuasive speaking or writing, and most of the writing skills you will learn in this book will help you make your writing more persuasive (user-friendly, clear, concise, compelling, organized, and so forth). However, in addition to verbal rhetoric, we also have to consider visual rhetoric—how visual texts convey meaning. You are bombarded each day by visual texts: television, Web pages, political cartoons, advertising. How do these visual and verbal combinations persuade, and how can you harness such power in your own writing?

Though it's a cliché, a picture *can* be worth a thousand words, and words and pictures together have incredible persuasive power. In the story that follows, the writer Antoine de Saint-Exupéry explores the role of visual metaphor—how a picture of one thing can represent another—specifically focusing on how an image can be as easily misunderstood as words.

> ### Writer's Break
>
> Make a list of images you see so often that you don't really see them anymore—for example, stop signs and "no smoking" symbols.

FROM THE LITTLE PRINCE

Antoine de Saint-Exupéry

1 So I lived my life alone, without anyone that I could really talk to, until I had an accident with my plane in the Desert of Sahara, six years ago. Something was broken in my engine. And as I had with me neither a mechanic nor any passengers, I set myself to attempt the difficult repairs all alone. It was a question of life or death for me: I had scarcely enough drinking water to last a week.

2 The first night, then, I went to sleep on the sand, a thousand miles from any human habitation. I was more isolated than a shipwrecked sailor on a raft in the middle of the ocean. Thus you can imagine my amazement, at sunrise, when I was awakened by an odd little voice. It said:

3 "If you please—draw me a sheep!"

4 "What!"

5 "Draw me a sheep!"

I jumped to my feet, completely thunderstruck. I blinked my eyes hard. I looked   6
carefully all around me. And I saw a most extraordinary small person, who stood
there examining me with great seriousness. Here you may see the best portrait that,
later, I was able to make of him. But my drawing is certainly very much less charm-
ing than its model.

That, however, is not my fault. The grown-ups discouraged me in my painter's   7
career when I was six years old, and I never learned to draw anything, except boas
from the outside and boas from the inside.

Now I stared at this sudden apparition with my eyes fairly starting out of my   8
head in astonishment. Remember, I had crashed in the desert a thousand miles
from any inhabited region. And yet my little man seemed neither to be straying un-
certainly among the sands, nor to be fainting from fatigue or hunger or thirst or
fear. Nothing about him gave any suggestion of a child lost in the middle of the
desert, a thousand miles from any human habitation. When at last I was able to
speak, I said to him:

"But—what are you doing here?"   9

10   And in answer he repeated, very slowly, as if he were speaking of a matter of great consequence:

11   "If you please—draw me a sheep . . ."

12   When a mystery is too overpowering, one dare not disobey. Absurd as it might seem to me, a thousand miles from any human habitation and in danger of death, I took out of my pocket a sheet of paper and my fountain-pen. But then I remembered how my studies had been concentrated on geography, history, arithmetic and grammar, and I told the little chap (a little crossly, too) that I did not know how to draw. He answered me:

13   "That doesn't matter. Draw me a sheep . . ."

14   But I had never drawn a sheep. So I drew for him one of the two pictures I had drawn so often. It was that of the boa constrictor from the outside. And I was astounded to hear the little fellow greet it with,

15   "No, no, no! I do not want an elephant inside a boa constrictor. A boa constrictor is a very dangerous creature, and an elephant is very cumbersome. Where I live, everything is very small. What I need is a sheep. Draw me a sheep."

16   So then I made a drawing. He looked at it carefully, then he said:

17   "No. This sheep is already very sickly. Make me another."

18   So I made another drawing.

19   My friend smiled gently and indulgently.

20   "You see yourself," he said, "that this is not a sheep. This is a ram. It has horns."

21   So then I did my drawing over once more. But it was rejected too, just like the others.

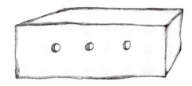

22   "This one is too old. I want a sheep that will live a long time."

23   By this time my patience was exhausted, because I was in a hurry to start taking my engine apart. So I tossed off this drawing.

24   And I threw out an explanation with it.

25   "This is only his box. The sheep you asked for is inside."

26   I was very surprised to see a light break over the face of my young judge:

27   "That is exactly the way I wanted it! Do you think this sheep will have to have a great deal of grass?"

"Why?"   28

"Because where I live everything is very small . . ."   29

"There will surely be enough grass for him," I said. "It is a very small sheep that   30
I have given you."

He bent his head over the drawing: 31

"Not so small that—Look! He has gone to sleep . . ."   32

And that is how I made the acquaintance of the little prince.   33

Consider this . . .

- How do the illustrations amplify the power of this story? Would the narrative have the same impact without the drawings?

- Why is the little prince's ability to see beyond the surface reality of the pictures to a deeper meaning significant in this story?

- How do text and graphics work together in this story?

In this story, the writer explores how illustrations communicate in ways that words cannot. He never says that drawings should replace words, but simply shows that the presence of one strengthens the meaning of the other. His own book is a clear example of this close relationship between text and graphics.

You do not have to be an artist to include visual elements in your writing. You simply have to be aware of how the visual elements can be used to affect someone else. Can you think of anything you've written that would have been strengthened by the inclusion of a graphic of some sort?

Writer's Break

Collect at least five graphics that you consider interesting.

- What do you think these images are trying to say?

- Did the creator of each image successfully convey a message?

HEART RATE MONITOR

Courtesy Timex Corporation

Advertisements are a classic example of the combining of text and graphics to convey meaning. Look at the Timex advertisement. How do the text and the graphics work together? What does a large meal of cholesterol-laden food have to do with a heart rate monitor? Why is the picture of the heart rate monitor much smaller than the picture of the food, even though the monitor is the product being sold? What do the words "Life is ticking" mean?

Clearly, the advertiser is hoping to encourage readers to purchase the heart monitor, a fitness device, by confronting them with the harsh reality of a common American breakfast. If the fear inspired by the food is not enough motivation, the text adds further impetus with its message of doom: "Life is ticking." Are you running out of time? Is it too late? Can this heart rate monitor save you? In this ad, both text and graphics are equally important. The photo catches the eye and causes the reader to question the meaning of the objects it shows, and the text serves to answer the reader's question. Life is ticking along; a heart monitor can help you keep your heart ticking along with it.

Advertisements are an excellent source of examples of visual rhetoric. Flip through some magazines, and see what you can discover. What makes the ads persuasive? How do the different communication media work together?

Consider the following essay, which appeared in *The New Yorker* in 2002. In this case, the writer relies on graphics to convey a great deal of the piece's meaning visually because the artists' renderings of imagined memorials are an integral part of the whole work.

AFTER THE TOWERS

Calvin Tomkins

The agonizing work of cleanup and recovery at Ground Zero, which ended officially a month ago, was carried out by men and women whose shared purpose made them a united force. Now comes the far more controversial job of rebuilding. The Lower Manhattan Development Corporation is about to release up to six detailed proposals for the site, with public hearings to follow. A separate design process will eventually lead to the selection of a memorial to the victims, but community organizations, victims' families, business interests, the city, Governor Pataki, and other interested parties are anything but united about the nature, the size, and the location of this key element. With that in mind, we asked several artists to think about the void downtown—not so much to design a memorial but, rather, to conjure up visions, with no constraints regarding the cost, scale, or feasibility. The results, a selection of which are reproduced here, were gratifyingly unfettered, diverse, and a long way from what a committee would think up or reality permit.

Artists seem to have a direct line between mind and eye. Who else would plant a dairy farm down there, with twin red silos and contented cows grazing right up against the rebuilt Cortlandt Street subway entrance? In this case, it's two artists, Vitaly Komar and Alex Melamid, born in Moscow and transplanted to studios in lower Manhattan, where they work on joint projects marked by an incisive, ironic wit. "This is a very intense area," Melamid, whose apartment is one block from Ground Zero, says. "We need something pastoral here, real cows, smell of manure, and, of course, everything organically fed and grown and so forth. In the middle of hell, you know. The subway is real hell. Every city needs a milk farm."

J. Otto Seibold, a multimedia artist and children's-book illustrator, came up with an interesting concept that links the ancient culture of Afghanistan with the vertical geometry of New York. Jenny Holzer would use her signature xenon-light projections to bathe two of the surviving World Financial Center buildings in a constant, nighttime stream of poetry and other texts, each one relevant in some way to the tragedy and its aftershocks. Nancy Rubins, a California-based sculptor of found-object constructions, who admits that she doesn't like to go above the second floor of a building, had the notion of going down instead of up—a hundred and ten stories down into the lower-Manhattan bedrock, where the remembered shape of the Twin Towers would be forever safe from aerial attack, and where their phenomenal presence, unseen but not unfelt, might serve to counterbalance the hectic ephemerality of life aboveground.

4   That sense of uncertainty, of the isolated and compartmentalized quality of urban life, hovers over the strange labyrinth in Alice Aycock's drawing. "When I try to take in the entire event," Aycock, whose work is often designed for public places, says, "I think first of the moment when someone is on the phone, doing business, doing some stock trading, maybe, or calling the family, and suddenly there you are, stopped in time. I saw it as a section of all those different labyrinths, unable to communicate with each other." Can there be, conversely, too much communication? Tony Oursler's proposal, the darkest and most ambiguous of those received, is for twin scaffoldings with video screens on which all the film and video coverage of the disaster would be projected, in a continuous loop from the moment the first jet exploded into the north tower until both structures collapsed. Oursler, one of the most original video artists at work today, conceded that his piece can be seen as a comment on our obsession with the media's endless replaying and reprocessing of reality. "A lot of young people I know don't want to see any more of that footage," he said. "They're fed up with it." His saturation screening could run for a limited time, and then "maybe it should all be buried," he suggested. "It should consume itself."

5   There is no trace of ambivalence or irony in Elyn Zimmerman's quiet elegiac design for two reflecting pools on the site of the vanished towers. One mirrors the site as it is, or will be; the other gives back what was, in images projected onto the surface that show the Twin Towers at different times of the day and night. Zimmerman is another artist who frequently does commissioned works for public places. Her sculptural memorial to the victims of the first World Trade Center bombing, installed on the plaza between the towers, was destroyed on September 11, but a small fragment was recovered and is being preserved by the Port Authority.

6   Like most of the artists who participated in the project, Art Spiegelman lives close to the site. The idea of replacing the twin hundred-and-ten-story towers with a forest of a hundred and ten one-story towers suggests those cheesy replicas of the

Empire State Building found in tourist traps along Forty-second Street, but Spiegelman's range of allusion doesn't stop there. He really misses the old towers, even though he wasn't too crazy about them before. "It's not like I love the way my nose looks," he said. "I just don't want somebody ramming a plane into it. Anyway, the idea of being able to bring them back in a more manageable way was in there someplace. One could learn to live with them and look them in the eye."

"Free Trade" by J. Otto Seibold. Originally published in The New Yorker.

The Buddhas destroyed by the Taliban are envisioned in New York, and the towers house refugees in Bamiyan, Afghanistan.

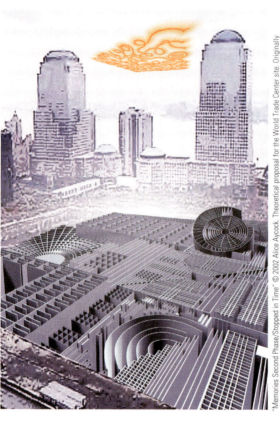

"Memories Second Phase/Stopped in Time" © 2002 Alice Aycock. Theoretical proposal for the World Trade Center site. Originally published in The New Yorker.

The moment of the disaster, "Stopped in time," for Aycock, recalled "different labyrinths, unable to communicate with each other."

"Mirror of Memory/WTC" © 2002 Elyn Zimmerman. Originally published in The New Yorker.

Zimmerman says of her twin pools, "One reflects the world as it is. In the other, projected images create a mirror of memory."

"Hudson Ferry," by James Schuyler, and "Could Have," by Wislawa Szymborska, are projected on surviving buildings.

IT COULD HAVE HAPPENED.
IT HAD TO HAPPEN.
IT HAPPENED EARLIER. LATER.
NEARER. FARTHER OFF.
IT HAPPENED, BUT NOT TO YOU.
YOU WERE SAVED BECAUSE
YOU WERE THE FIRST.
YOU WERE SAVED BECAUSE
YOU WERE THE LAST.
ALONE. WITH OTHERS.
ON THE RIGHT. THE LEFT.
BECAUSE IT WAS RAINING
BECAUSE OF THE SHADE.
BECAUSE THE DAY WAS SUNNY.
YOU WERE IN LUCK—
THERE WAS A FOREST.
YOU WERE IN LUCK—
THERE WERE NO TREES.
YOU WERE IN LUCK—
A RAKE, A HOOK, A BEAM, A BRAKE,
A JAMB, A TURN, A QUARTER INCH,
AN INSTANT.
YOU WERE IN LUCK—
JUST THEN A STRAW
WENT FLOATING BY.
AS A RESULT, BECAUSE,
ALTHOUGH, DESPITE.
WHAT WOULD HAVE HAPPENED
IF A HAND, A FOOT,
WITHIN AN INCH,
A HAIRSBREADTH FROM
AN UNFORTUNATE COINCIDENCE,
SO YOU'RE STILL HERE?
STILL DIZZY FROM ANOTHER DODGE
CLOSE SHAVE, REPRIEVE?
ONE HOLE IN THE NET
AND YOU SLIPPED THROUGH?
I COULDN'T BE
MORE SHOCKED OR SPEECHLESS.
LISTEN,
HOW YOUR HEART POUNDS INSIDE ME

and there's
Miss Strong Arm,
toting her torch

it's another city
going back
the moon one night
past its full
writes signs
vanishing hypnotically
downtown
the towers block massively
at the rail
a man who rests his hands

looks heroic:
he works at night:
going from or to?

I don't know
I hardly know
why I'm on the river
late at night.

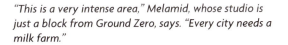

"This is a very intense area," Melamid, whose studio is just a block from Ground Zero, says. "Every city needs a milk farm."

> ### Consider this . . .
>
> - Did the graphics in the article communicate as effectively as the text?
> - Are the graphics essential to this essay?
> - Could incorporating graphics into your writing process help you express yourself more effectively?

BASIC DESIGN GUIDELINES

Once you have written the text of your paper, you need to consider the design. How you arrange the parts of the text affects the audience's response.

☰ Headings

Headings identify major portions of your paper. The more specific the heading, the more useful it is. For example, a heading such as "Paragraph Three" doesn't tell readers anything about what they will be reading. A heading such as "The Early History of the Volkswagen" tells a great deal more. Using headings allows you to create a visual outline of your paper that guides your readers from one portion of the text to the next. Such a visible skeleton facilitates the reading process for the reader—and the writing process for you. Using headings will help you stay on track while you write.

☰ Fonts

Fonts, different type styles, allow you to draw attention to the different portions of your paper in order to create a visual hierarchy of the information in the text. For example, if you want to draw attention to levels of information with your headings, you use different fonts and/or font sizes, as in this example, which uses a sixteen-point font for the title, a fourteen-point font for major headings, and a twelve-point font for subheadings:

The Threat of Global Warming

Global Warming

Warming of atmosphere due to human activities

Greenhouse effect

Effects on Our Planet?

El Niño effect

Melting ice caps

Increasing sea level

The Evidence

The earth's changing composition

Greenhouse gases

Uncertainties

Levels of greenhouse gas

Effect on humans

Preventing Global Warming?

Emissions

Penalties for corporate pollution

Alternative energy sources

A quick glance at this outline of headings and subheadings allows readers to distinguish the two levels because they are different fonts and sizes. This use of different fonts and sizes allows you to visually indicate to the reader the levels of information within your paper. Just from this outline, readers know what major divisions the writer has created to organize the paper, and what supporting evidence he or she will use in each section

≡ White Space

Readers can be put off by large blocks of unbroken text. White space allows you to break your text into manageable pieces that a reader can understand and remember. You should use white space to accentuate headings and to separate one block of text from the next. In general, follow these guidelines:

- Double-space the text.

- Justify the left margin, but use a ragged right margin.

- Space between headings and text.

- Space between the end of one block of text and the heading that follows.

Lists

If you have three or four specific points to make or examples to present, a list can be an effective way to emphasize them. A list visually emphasizes important information and breaks up the text to increase the memorability of what is important. For instance, the writer of the paper on global warming might list the three types of greenhouse gases he or she will discuss in a bulleted list. In this case, the writer doesn't want to use a numbered list because numbers imply that the items of information have a hierarchy of importance. Bullets are neutral:

- Carbon dioxide

- Methane

- Sulfate aerosols

Graphics

You may assume that graphics are pictures: drawings or photographs. Actually, a graphic is anything that is not simply text: a graph, a table, a chart, a diagram, and so on. Even a box containing text, such as the example on the next page, is a graphic that can break up blocks of text.

Graphics are useful for two reasons: They allow you to present information in a nonverbal format, and they make the page visually interesting. Different readers learn in different ways, and using graphics increases your chances of helping your readers understand what you are trying to say. For example, the writer of "The Threat of Global Warming" might use graphics from the articles he or she read to research the topic. Emphasizing a point with a graphic adds validity to an argument, especially for those readers not familiar

Title (16 pt)

Always use text to introduce every heading.

Major Heading (14 pt)

Introduce subheadings as well as major headings. Your paper should not look like an outline.

Subheading (12 pt)

You should not have more than two levels of headings in most papers. You may, however, have bulleted lists within paragraphs under either major headings or subheadings:

- Lists can be bulleted or numbered.

- Lists should have extra space between items.

- A list should contain at least three items, but not more than six.

---

with the topic. If you are discussing art, it makes sense to include examples of the works you are discussing. If you are comparing information, why not include a graph, table, or chart?

Always remember to include the source for any graphic you use. Chapter Thirteen will provide more information about using sources.

What you should avoid is gratuitous graphics. Nothing is more distracting to a reader than cute pictures that have no relevance to the paper's topic. Should you include a funny cartoon in a paper about a serious issue? Should you include pictures just because you can? The answer to these questions is no. Graphics are great, but use them sparingly and be sure that they add rather than distract.

USING DESIGN IN AN ESSAY

Very few writers of nontechnical documents consider it important to pay attention to design when they are writing, but readers of essays are just as interested in having an easy reading experience as anyone else. Consequently, you need to remember to use the basic principles of design for every paper you write.

The first thing readers see when they look at your paper is not the words themselves—it's the shape of the written words on the page. The initial visual impact of your paper creates a first impression that will affect how positively a reader responds, regardless of the actual content. Look at the following two writing samples:

Sample One

Because my father was in the army, I didn't grow up in one place. I grew up all over the world. I would have to say growing up like I did is both a blessing & a curse.

Sample Two

My self-image was shaped by what many people might deem a unique experience growing up. My hometown of Roby, Texas, population 600, is in a dusty, tumble-weed filled place called West Texas. The cows probably outnumber the people. The first time I rode a horse by myself, I was six-years-old. I flipped my Dad's pick-up truck when I was fourteen. If you took a stroll in my backyard, you'd see a cotton field, an orchard, and a cow pasture. My dad works tirelessly as a cotton farmer, and my mom works as a "homemaker," but she works in both the home and on the farm. Occasionally she even drives a tractor. My parents pressured me to do well in school because they thought an education was my way out of Roby — a way to change our family image.

Which sample did you like better? Which one did you want to read first? Regardless of the skill of either writer, the second sample is more appealing and easier to read because it is typed. No one wants to struggle with someone else's poor handwriting. We tend to assume that the first writing sample is not as good because the writer didn't care enough to make it look professional.

In order to make your writing more persuasive, you need to create a document that is visually pleasing. This doesn't mean making your document "pretty." A document printed in an italic or script font on blue paper might be "pretty," but it would also be very hard to read. A document is visually pleasing for the following more pragmatic reasons:

- The reader can easily identify a hierarchy of information.

- The reader is not overwhelmed by the bulk of the text to be read.

- The information is accessible.

- The document looks professional.

☰ Establishing a Hierarchy of Information

A well-designed document makes it possible for a reader to identify the most important information. It is helpful for a reader to know where to concentrate his or her attention, and the ordering of information in a clear hierarchy facilitates the reader's retention. It also helps the writer guarantee that he or she has emphasized his or her major points. Look at the example that follows. These instructions came with a child's sewing kit.

Step 1: Cut out the rectangle surrounding the lines in Diagram 1. Line these marks up at the 3 3/8 inch mark on the fabric and pin it down with the thicker needle in the kit. Use this as a guide for the 11 lengths of beaded fringe to be sewn on bag.

Step 2: Using the long beading needle, the needle threader and the thread, follow instructions in Diagram 2 to string a 36-inch long thread. Tie a double knot at the end before you start sewing.

Step 3: Use the ruler on this instruction sheet to make sure that the dots are 3 3/8 inches from the top of the fabric before beginning to sew on the fringe.

Step 4: See Diagram 4 to begin the first row of beaded fringe. Follow the pattern on the reverse side of this page to finish all 11 rows of beads. Important Note: You may need to "tie off" several times to complete all of the fringe. When you near the end of a length of thread, wait until you have the needle back on the "inside" of the bag, make sure that all thread has been pulled through, and tie a strong double knot. Cut off extra thread. Now re-thread the needle, tie a double knot, and begin the next line of fringe.

Step 5: Follow the instructions on page 2 to finish all of the fringe.

Because the writer did not create a visual hierarchy of information, it is very difficult for the reader to make any sense out of the instructions without reading them word for word. Even the "Important Note" is buried within the other text. Now consider the following revised version:

MAKING THE BEADED FRINGE

Step 1: Marking the Line for the Fringe
- Cut out the rectangle surrounding the lines in Diagram 1.
- Line these marks up at the $3\frac{3}{8}$ inch mark on the fabric and pin it down with the thicker needle in the kit.
- Use this as a guide for the 11 lengths of beaded fringe to be sewn on the bag.

Step 2: Threading the Needle
- Cut a 36-inch length of thread.
- Thread the beading needle using the needle threader.
- Tie a double knot at the end of the thread before you start sewing.

Step 3: Marking the Sewing Dots

- Use the ruler on this instruction sheet to measure $3\frac{3}{8}$ inches from the top of the fabric.
- Mark dots $\frac{1}{2}$ inch apart across the line.

Step 4: Stringing the Beads

- See Diagram 4 to begin the first row of beaded fringe.
- Follow the pattern on the reverse side of this page to finish all 11 rows of beads.

Important Note:
You may need to "tie off" several times to complete all of the fringe. When you near the end of a length of thread, wait until you have the needle back on the "inside" of the bag, make sure that all thread has been pulled through, and tie a strong double knot. Cut off extra thread. Now re-thread the needle, tie a double knot, and begin the next line of fringe.

The revised version is much easier to read because it has a visual hierarchy. By using white space and bulleted list items, the writer makes it easy for the reader to identify the four main steps and their substeps and to notice the "Important Note." Even without reading, a reader could identify the most important information on the page just by the placement of the headings.

Within essays, there is always a hierarchy of information. The title is the first level of information, and the topic of each paragraph is the second level of information. You may have a third level of information within paragraphs. You can make these levels of information visible by using headings and lists in your essays.

Breaking the Text into Manageable Chunks

When we read, many of us begin by skimming the document to get a sense of its length. For example, when you begin a chapter from this book, do you flip through the pages to see how long it is before you start reading? The more unbroken text a reader sees, the more bulk he or she will perceive. In other words, pages and pages of nothing but words, words, and more words can be intimidating. A considerate writer breaks text into manageable chunks, so that the reader isn't overwhelmed before even starting.

☰ Making the Information Accessible

Readers don't like to work any harder than necessary. If you make the information easy for them to get, they will be more inclined to read your paper. As the preceding examples show, information that isn't obscured by bad handwriting, hard-to-read fonts, or blocks of uninterrupted text is more appealing to readers. Accessibility also makes readers more likely to get your point. Consider the next example.

April 8, 2003
Full Time Faculty and Staff
Parking Permit Renewals

To avoid long lines at the Parking Office, faculty/staff permits for 2003–2004 will be available for renewal through campus mail starting May 14, 2003. To obtain your permit through campus mail, please fill out the attached registration card. Return it with appropriate fees to the Parking Office. The deadline for renewing through campus mail is August 14. Requests after the deadline will be returned.

Permits will be mailed to the departments in July. If you prefer to have the permit mailed to your residence, please enclose a self-addressed stamped envelope with your payment. Faculty/staff who do not participate in renewal by mail can purchase their permits any time after July 20 at the parking office located in the Sullivant Visitor Center at 902 Avenue E. Again this year, if you make less than $1,250 gross pay per month, you may choose to purchase a permit in two payments. The first payment should be sent before August 14, to renew by campus mail. The second payment will be due January 4, 2004. To exercise this option, please complete the attached card and return with your check for $23.50.

We encourage you to become familiar with the regulations of the university, which are updated each academic year. If we can be of further assistance, please contact the parking office at extension 3020.

The reader, who is a busy professor or staff member, must read this entire confusing document in order to know what it contains. If the information were more accessible, this would not be necessary. A revised version follows.

RENEWING PARKING PERMITS THROUGH CAMPUS MAIL

Beginning May 14, 2003, faculty/staff can renew their parking permits through campus mail.

1. Fill out the attached registration card.
2. Attach the appropriate fee:
   - One-payment option: Enclose $47.00.
   - Two-payment option: If you make less than $1,250 gross pay per month, you may choose to purchase a permit with two payments of $23.50. The first payment is due by August 14. The second payment is due January 4, 2004.
3. Return the card with appropriate fees to the Parking Office by August 14.
4. Enclose a self-addressed stamped envelope if you want the permit mailed to your home. Otherwise, we will mail permits to the departments.

STANDARD PURCHASE

After July 20, purchase your permit at the parking office located in the Sullivant Visitor Center at 902 Avenue E.

If we can be of further assistance, please contact the parking office at extension 3020.

The revised document is much more user-friendly because the writer made the information accessible by using headings and white space to emphasize information. The reader can find the information he or she needs more quickly.

☰ Giving the Document a Professional Look

Your writing represents you, and when it's full of errors or looks sloppy, it reflects badly on you. Why should anyone take the time to read a paper you didn't even bother to proofread or type? If you want your work to look professional, be sure to:

- Always run a spell check. (However, remember that a spell check program will not find every error. For example, it will not recognize when *their* should be *there*.)

- Use a good-quality printer.

- Proofread.

USING DESIGN IN A WEB PAGE

More and more of the information we rely on is published on the Web. You might think that designing a Web page is just like designing a text document, but even though there are similarities, there are also differences. In order to design an effective and usable Web page, you need to remember these basic principles:

- Consistency

- Simplicity

- Appropriate use of fonts

☰ Consistency

Like books or articles published on paper, Web sites often have multiple pages. However, you can't flip through the pages of a Web site, and you can't look at more than one at a time. The order in which the pages are viewed is determined completely by the user's choices, and because every user is different, the order will be different every time.

Because a Web site doesn't have a linear order, you have to create a design that will help readers find what they want and keep track of where they are. Look at the two Web pages from the Dallas Off-Road Bicycle Association (DORBA). Even though you reach the membership page by clicking on the red link in the center of the home page that says "Click here to join or renew online," the second page looks so different from the first page that you might wonder if you are still in the same site.

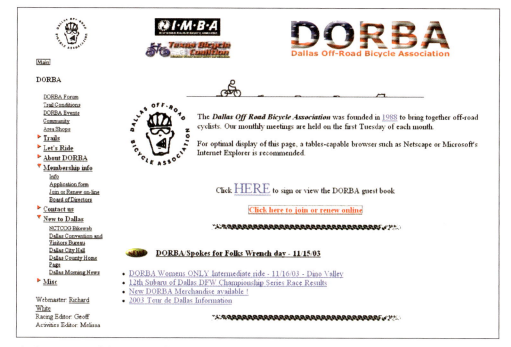

The home page of the Dallas Off-Road Bicycle Association (DORBA)

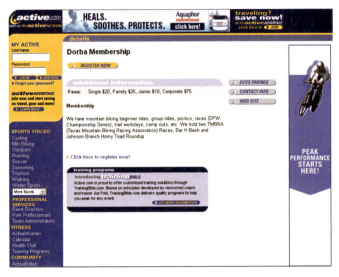

The membership page from the DORBA Web site

Now look at the two pages from the All Music Guide. By clicking on the "explore by" link on the home page, you can get to the
page dedicated to classical music or some other genre. You can easily tell that you are still in the same Web site because the design of
the genre page is consistent with the design of the first page.

The home page of All Music Guide

A genre page of the All Music Guide site

This sort of consistency is essential when designing a Web site. Once you choose a visual theme, you use that same theme for each page. For example, if you choose aqua as the background color of your home page, that should be the background color of the other pages. If you make links orange, they should always be orange. If you have a logo, it should appear in the same place on each page.

Simplicity

Because computers make it so easy to add so many details to a design, it is easy to get carried away and make Web pages so busy that they have no focus. Look at the page for the World Karate Federation (WKF).

This page is so busy that readers may have trouble finding information. The page has no focal point and no clear hierarchy of information. The blue links are difficult to distinguish from headings that also appear in blue. The use of different fonts increases the reader's confusion in response to this too cluttered page.

Web page for the World Karate Federation (WKF)

Web page for a Save the Whales event

In contrast, because of its simplicity, the page for a meetup day for Save the Whales activists is much easier to navigate. The focal point is in the upper left-hand corner and is the brightest spot on the page. Directly below the focal point, in a shaded box, are the primary links. The majority of the page contains registration information easily distinguishable because of its white background.

The WKF page is more flashy than the one for Save the Whales, but it is also much less useful. Remember, the primary function of a Web site is to communicate. If your readers are too distracted by the busyness of your page, they will not find or understand the information it contains.

☰ Appropriate Fonts

Choosing effective fonts is important when designing any document, but it is especially so for Web pages. Computer screens are more difficult to read than printed pages because of the glare, and the almost unlimited font options can make it even more difficult to make good decisions. Just remember these basic guidelines:

- *Do not use ALL CAPITAL LETTERS*. Capital letters are more difficult to read than lowercase letters because there is less visual difference between the letters. Consequently, when you string together a series of capital letters, you unnecessarily slow down the reading process.

- *Do not use all italics*. Like capital letters, italicized letters are more difficult to recognize and read, especially on a computer screen, where the glare and the use of colors can cause one letter to bleed into another.

- *Do not place text over graphics*. Avoid the inclination to place text over a patterned background or a photo. It is very difficult to read text that runs across an image because our eyes don't know where to focus. Keep your backgrounds simple.

- *Do not use animated text*. The Web is full of sites that have flashing, spinning, bouncing, disappearing, and otherwise moving text. No one wants the words they are trying to read to be a moving target—avoid animation.

ILLUSTRATIONS DON'T BELONG just in children's books, and how you design the text of an essay is just as important as how you design an advertising brochure. Although text is important, it is not more important than images. You shouldn't throw unrelated graphics into the papers you write. However, you can benefit from remembering these things:

- We live in a visually oriented world. When you are writing, don't feel obligated to limit yourself to words if a graphic can communicate what you want to say more effectively or if it can supplement your words in an effective way.

- When you are looking for inspiration, be sure to take advantage of visual prompts. An image might be the catalyst for your next great idea.

- Don't randomly litter your writing with unrelated graphics. Such hit-or-miss graphics can detract from your words rather than adding to them.

COLLABORATIVE EXERCISES

Group Exercise One

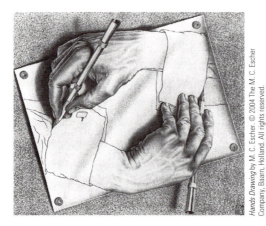

Choose one of the graphics shown here, and, as a group, write a paragraph that explains what you think the image means. To do this:

- Develop several possible meanings for the image.

- Choose the one or two you consider most plausible.

- Write your analysis, including specific details about the image to support your theory.

Share your analysis with the class.

Group Exercise Two

Read the following essay and answer these questions:

- What visual text does the writer analyze?

- How does she explain its deeper meaning?

- What techniques does she use that you think are especially effective?

Share your answers with the class.

Yin Yang and Its Application to the Martial Arts

Erin Lee

I know that Yin Yang is important. We all know this. In class we hear, "More Yin Yang. Yin Yang is power." During tests Grand Master Han tells us, "Pretty good, but you need more Yin Yang. You understand?" And we all nod our heads and say "Yes sir!" I don't know about you, but I am a liar because I know Yin Yang is important, but I don't understand it. I don't know what it means. I don't know how to get it, and I'm sure I don't have it. How do I get more of what I don't have, don't understand, and probably wouldn't recognize if it gave me a roundhouse to the head?

I know Yin Yang is important; you know Yin Yang is important. Now let's see if we can begin to understand what it means to us as martial artists.

 We see the Yin Yang symbol everywhere: on t-shirts, tattooed on people's bodies, on luggage, on bumper stickers, on billboards--even on birthday cakes and rocks. Like most symbols that are exploited by people who really don't understand them, the Yin Yang symbol's primary force has been diluted, and if familiarity truly breeds contempt, the Yin Yang symbol is in deep trouble.

According to Buddhist philosophy, reality is whole and unified, and it is the human mind that separates reality into its opposite parts: light and dark, hard and soft, good and evil, strong and weak. Yin (light) is the more passive, gentle factor, while Yang (dark) is more active and loud. Yin Yang is also defined as balance. You can imagine the central core of your body as the source of your Yin Yang. When you develop internal balance--a balance between what you want versus what you need, what you like versus what is good for you, play versus work--then external forces can affect you temporarily, but your internal balance will always return. When you create an energy system in which energy flows from you, then it is returned to you in an uninterrupted flow.

As martial artists we try to avoid seeing the world in its parts; instead, we try instead to see it as a whole. When we see the world as a series of opposites, it becomes too easy to focus on the negative and forget the positive. For example, when you spar, it is very easy to consider a kick or a punch directed at your body a threatening and therefore negative action that you should avoid. This is because you are separating good from bad and focusing just on the bad rather than seeing the good in the situation. If a punch represents the force of Yang, the martial artist responds by becoming Yin; for example, a punch that appears threatening to you is also an opening that you can use to your advantage. As the other person throws his or her punch, he or she becomes momentarily vulnerable--the Yin within the Yang.

ROB & SAS/Corbis

As martial artists we have the opportunity to not only strengthen our bodies, but to strengthen our spirits as we work to develop internal balance--Yin Yang. Rather than seeing life as a series of potentially bad things that might happen to us at any moment, we can choose to see life in its wholeness. We can choose to see the Yin within the Yang, and we can begin to understand that every experience has both good and bad aspects within it. We can learn to find the positive within a negative situation, the weakness within a strong fighter. By developing Yin Yang within ourselves, we can begin to truly understand the meaning of Pak Juk Pul Gul: "You may strike me down 100 times, but you will never break me, for I am resilient and will never give up."

WRITING BRIEFS

Option One

The power of the image

We are surrounded by visual texts that have the power to affect us. What is it about Walker Evans's photo of the Dust Bowl family that allows you to feel their pain and desperation? Why is the Web page for the American Humane Association persuasive?

For this assignment, choose a visual text (it can be one of those shown here) and write a one-page paper explaining how it affected you and why you think it had the power to do so.

Dust Bowl family by Walker Evans. Corbis

In this photo, Walker Evans compassionately depicts a family stricken by poverty during the Dust Bowl.

The American Humane Association's Web site clearly presents the organization's mission to protect the well-being of children and animals.

Option Two

With eyes open

Can you identify some common type of visual text that you normally accept as part of the landscape and explain its deeper meaning? For example, what about the t-shirts and bumper stickers that show almost anything with a circle around it and a slash running across it? Why do cereal boxes contain so much information? What about restaurant menus? They do much more than show pictures of food followed by names and prices. How about comic strips? How do the pictures communicate as clearly as the words? Select a form of visual text that you see regularly, and write a one-page analysis of its meaning. What is its significance? Why does it keep reappearing?

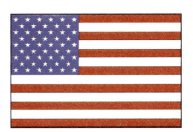

Option Three

Responding to design

In a one-page paper, analyze the design of the Queuent Web site, explaining why you do or don't think it is well-designed. Give specific examples from the site to support your argument. Be sure to explain how the design does or does not make the site more accessible.

Grammar Choices

COMPOUND SENTENCES

In order to be able to identify and punctuate compound sentences, you need to add the following words to your vocabulary:

A **coordinating conjunction** is a word such as *and, but, for, nor, or, so,* or *yet,* which links two independent clauses.

A **conjunctive adverb** is a word such as *however, consequently, therefore, thus, hence, furthermore, moreover, afterward, indeed,* or *otherwise,* which links two independent clauses.

A **correlative conjunction** a pair of linking words such as *either/or, neither/nor, both/and,* or *not only/but also.*

A compound sentence is two or three independent clauses (simple sentences) joined in one of four ways:

▪ By a comma followed by a **coordinating conjunction**

We can choose to see the Yin within the Yang, **and** we can begin to understand that every experience has both good and bad aspects within it.

My dad works tirelessly as a cotton farmer, **and** my mom works as a "homemaker," **but** she works in both the home and on the farm.

▪ By a semicolon followed by a **conjunctive adverb** and a comma

As martial artists we try to avoid seeing the world in its parts; **instead**, we try instead to see it as a whole.

If a punch represents the force of Yang, the martial artist responds by becoming Yin; **for example**, a punch that appears threatening to you is also an opening that you can use to your advantage.

▪ By a semicolon alone

My world is nothing but thought and feeling; these feelings allow me to become more involved with myself mentally.

I know Yin Yang is important; you know Yin Yang is important.

- By a **correlative conjunction**.

  When you create an energy system in which energy flows from you, **not only** is it returned to you in an uninterrupted flow, **but** it is **also** regenerated.

  Either wait for me here, **or** meet me at home.

Making It Work

- Identify every compound sentence in your draft.

- Determine whether you used a coordinating conjuction, a conjunctive adverb, a correlative conjunction, or a semicolon to combine the clauses.

- Make sure you used the correct punctuation in each sentence. Correct any errors that you find.

- Can you combine any other independent clauses to increase the coherence of your essay?

Style Choices

KEEPING ACTOR AND ACTION TOGETHER

Every action has to be done by someone or something. Consequently, it is best to keep the subject of a clause or sentence near the verb. If you separate the **actor** (subject) from the **action** (verb), the reader can lose the meaning of the sentence:

> **Katie**, who wore the red shirt, **kicked** the ball, and **she broke** the window.

> **The jockey**, who had a history of winning races, **won** the Triple Crown.

From these sentences, the reader might think that the color of Katie's shirt or the record of the jockey is more important than what she did or he did, but it's not.

Look at the following sentence:

> Now, it's not as if the 40-year-old **Bo Jackson**, 6 feet 1½ inches tall and a biscuit or two over his Los Angeles Raiders and American League playing weight of 230, **is going to join** the PGA Tour anytime soon.

What is important in this sentence? What Bo Jackson is not going to do. However, because the writer separated the actor and the action, this information is lost at the end of the sentence. Consider this revision:

> Now, it's not as if **Bo Jackson is going to join** the PGA Tour anytime soon. The 40-year-old **Jackson is** 6 feet 1½ inches tall and a biscuit or two over his Los Angeles Raiders and American League playing weight of 230.

The information is divided between two sentences and both keep the actor and the action together.

In the next sentence, the writer does a good job of keeping the actor and the action together:

Against lefthanders **Pujols hits** with a 33-ounce bat, an ounce heavier than the one he swings against righties, to keep him from always trying to pull the bat.

When you are revising your own papers, keep this guideline in mind. Look at your sentences carefully, and revise when necessary to bring actor and action together.

Making It Work

- Look for the subject (actor) and the verb (action) in each sentence of your draft.

- Are actor and action kept together?

- Revise any sentence in which actor and action are separated.

PART TWO

Reasons for Writing

Stelios Varias/Reuters/Landov

Artists, whether using words or some other medium for conveying their message, take into consideration the context for their work—that is, they pay attention to the occasion, the audience, and the purpose.

GROWING UP DIFFERENT

Writing about Personal Experiences

In this chapter, you will learn:

- How to decide whether an event or experience is worth writing about and, if so, how to focus on its significance

- Strategies you can use to write about an experience—narration, description, and comparison/contrast

- How to organize an essay that narrates or describes an experience

Roy Morsch/Corbis

We all have unique experiences as we grow up.

We are storytellers by nature. We tell our friends stories about our past and current experiences. Our parents and other older relatives tell us stories about events we don't remember. We immerse ourselves in the stories told in movies and on television. How often do your conversations with someone else involve telling a story?

What purpose do stories serve? Of course, stories are entertaining, but what else are they?

Writer's Break

For each of the prompts below, list at least three possible stories you could tell:

■ An event that shaped your life

■ A rite of passage that you experienced

■ Someone you know who grew up differently than you did

■ *We learn about ourselves from stories.* When we listen to other people tell stories about us, we learn how the the rest of the world sees us, and we add a new dimension to our understanding of who we are. Sometimes the person a family member describes in a story may not even feel like someone you know, but to the storyteller, that identity is you. How does your family describe you? Are you comfortable with that description? Does it fit you? What does it tell you about who your family thinks you are?

■ *We learn about others from stories.* Stories give us the opportunity to learn about people we may never meet or about another side of a person we thought we knew. We can also come to know historical figures better by reading their stories in biographies and autobiographies. When you listen to stories about the youthful adventures of a parent or grandparent, does it seem impossible that the person in the story and the person you know are the same? Is that twenty-year-old who wrecked his father's '57 Chevy still somewhere inside the skin of the sixty-year-old you know? How can stories about someone change your opinion of that person?

■ *We create identities for ourselves in stories.* We all like to think we know ourselves fairly well, but even if we do, we constantly recreate ourselves. Stories give us an opportunity to create versions of ourselves that we want to share with other people. When we tell stories about ourselves, we craft our responses to situations and interpret our actions in ways that make sense to us—even if we didn't understand our motives originally. In stories, we can be the people we wish we were all the time. Instead of being the person who panicked when someone choked in a restaurant, yet managed to save the day, you can be the person who was calm and collected while everyone else lost their heads. What identities do you give yourselves in stories? Do you have any alter egos?

■ *We make sense out of past events.* When we tell stories about an event in our lives, we have the chance to reconsider the event, the occurrences leading up to it, our response to it, the response of others involved, and so on. This is especially true if we are writing about an event that occurred when we were much younger. We can also read stories of historical events—the Holocaust, the sixties, the civil rights movement—in order to understand them more clearly. We are never quite the same person we were when an event happened, even if it happened yesterday; telling the story allows us to make sense out of the event in a way that wasn't possible when it was happening. What events would you like to reconsider? Why do you feel that they have something to teach you?

MAKING CHOICES WHEN YOU WRITE FOR PERSONAL REASONS

One of the most difficult aspects of writing about a personal experience is choosing which event to write about. We have all lived lives full of events, but when we are asked to write about an event, we tend to think EVENT, as though something is not worth writing about unless it is momentous in some obvious way. But, remember, it's not the scope of the occurrence that determines its significance.

≡ What Is an Event?

An event does not have to be big in the standard sense. In other words, for an event to be worth writing about, it doesn't have to be an obvious mile marker: a birth, a death, a graduation, a wedding. Some experiences are a mélange of many smaller experiences. Many of the experiences that affect us most profoundly are those we don't fully understand until much later or those that happen so quickly we can't respond until later. Consider these examples:

- *An interaction with a stranger.* Some homeless person called me a rich snob when I wouldn't give her any money. But I'm not that kind of person.

- *An unexpected conflict with an authority figure.* I was asked to leave a movie theater for talking. What did I do?

- *Seeing someone after several years have passed.* I can't believe my friend dropped out of high school and has two kids. I keep remembering her as she was—full of plans for a future career as a designer.

- *Finding an old photo, note, or letter.* I know those young people in the funny clothes are my relatives, but who were they really? They're laughing and having fun. What was it like to be eighteen years old in the 1940s? What were they laughing about?

- *Learning something unexpected about yourself, your family, or a friend.* My grandfather worked for the mob? That doesn't seem possible. My grandmother had another husband before she married my grandfather. I didn't know that.

An event worth writing about can be anything that meets any of the following criteria:

- It had a lasting effect on you.

- It has pertinence for others.

- It made you think.

Did you have a best friend when you were a child? Do you have one now? How do you define "best friend," and how can such a thing change you?

It has a lasting effect

Stories are made up of events worth telling, and events are worth telling when they have a lasting effect on us. When you have an argument with a friend over who scratched a CD, you probably are not affected in some lasting way. All friends fight and make up and then go on. But when you and a friend have a fight over a more sensitive issue—sex, drug use, racial bigotry, religion—it might have affected you in a more lasting way. Anyone can have a bad date, but a date that involves violence is deeply significant. Some event from childhood that had little significance to you at the time might become very significant later. For example, you might not have believed your mother when she told your five-year-old self not to worry about the bully who picked on you because what goes around comes around. You might remember these words and reconsider them years later when you hear the bully has been arrested for spouse abuse.

Events have the power to change us. Most of us take our safety for granted until something happens to compromise it. After you've been in a car accident, you may find yourself jumping every time you hear a horn honk, or brakes squeal. If you've ever been bitten by a dog, even if it was your own, you will never feel quite the same way about dogs. When someone you trust lies to you, it can seriously damage your ability to trust again. Even small events can change us. A ten-second exchange with a homeless person might permanently change how you feel about the issue of homelessness.

We look at the world through a lens created of our own experiences, and we can't help but be affected by changes these experiences cause in us.

Relationships that we form with others can have lasting effects on our lives—both positive and negative.

It has pertinence for others

Just because you found an experience life-changing, you can't assume that other people will see it the same way. It is your job as a writer to show readers that your experience has pertinence for them. For example, if someone wants to write about her recovery from anorexia, that's fine; the topic has potential. If the writer fails to give the topic pertinence for her readers, however, her paper will fail.

> When I was growing up, I was always pudgy, and the other kids made fun of me. By the time I was fourteen, I had enough, and I went on a diet. I began by cutting out one meal a day. When that worked, and I lost weight, I started cutting out two meals a day so I could lose faster. Soon I was down to one meal every other day. I had a problem, and I needed help.

There is nothing really wrong with this paragraph, but it is difficult for a reader to invest in it because it is all about the writer. She doesn't give readers any way to understand how her experience can teach them something. Here is her revised version:

> When I was eight, the boy next door used to call me Alliesaurus because he said I was as big as a dinosaur. The girls in my ballet class all laughed when my feet thumped loudly when my bulk landed. "It's the dancing hippo," the skinny girl in the pink tights used to giggle. By the time I was fourteen, I had had enough, and I started dieting. I was going to look like those girls in the magazines if it killed me. I began by cutting out one meal a day. When that worked, and I lost weight, I started cutting out two meals a day so I could lose faster. Soon I was down to one meal every other day. I had a problem, and I needed help. But the real problem wasn't my dieting. The real problem was that I didn't know I needed help because the negative comments had stopped coming. Now I heard, "She is so thin. How does she do that?" The fat girl now had bonier hips than anyone, and I was never going to be the Alliesaurus again. I was going to fit in, and it was killing me.

In this revised paragraph, the writer does more than talk about her problem with anorexia. She also explores the cause of her problem—peer pressure based on the need to conform to stereotypical ideals of beauty. Furthermore, she takes responsibility for her own role in the situation by acknowledging her failure to recognize that she had a problem. This is writing to which readers can respond because they can recognize themselves in this scenario in one of the roles: the victim, the tormentor, or the sufferer. Because she presents us with a multidimensional problem, rather than a self-centered one, this writer provides many openings that readers can use to access this essay in ways that will make it pertinent for them as individuals.

It is thought-provoking

A good piece of writing leaves you intrigued. It leaves you with questions that linger in your mind because they don't have easy or obvious answers. If you finish an essay, put it aside, and think "So what?" the essay has failed. Your job as a writer is not to provide all the answers. In fact, you might not provide any answers, but you should provide your readers with food for thought. Look at these two paragraphs:

> Growing up is very hard. Most of us have felt the bumps and bruises of childhood traumas. Many of us had problems at home, and we found ways to cope with those problems. Finding coping mechanisms is very important for children.

> When I was seven-years-old, I used to hide in my closet with a flashlight and look at books. When I was in that dark, warm, cage, I knew no one would look for me. I probably didn't even need to hide. No one ever looked for me anyway. I was the quiet child, the last child, the child it was easy to ignore. Maybe I should have screamed like my teenage brother, or hit like my adolescent sister; instead, I just hid in my closet. How many other children spend their childhood hiding from something, or nothing?

The first paragraph tells us nothing new. It does not leave us with anything to think about. Your reaction might have been, "Yeah, kids need coping mechanisms. So what?"

The second paragraph, on the other hand, asks many questions that are worth thinking about. Why do some children feel like they have to hide? What are they hiding from? Did you ever hide? Is hiding a good coping mechanism? This paragraph leaves us wanting more because it gives us food for thought.

≡ Making an Event the Focus of a Paper

Every paper needs a focus—a topic or a point of view. However, as we discussed before, every essay must have a point, a reason for taking up space on a page. Thus, your choice of an event to write about can't be random. You have to choose an event because it has a special significance that will let you make a specific point. What event is the focus of the photo below? What point was the photographer trying to make with this photo?

"Lunch Atop a Skyscraper" (1932) by Charles C. Ebbets. Corbis.

Writer's Break

In the Writer's Break on page 126, you identified stories you could tell about three events.

■ Write two or three sentences in which you explain how you could make one of the events the focus of an essay.

■ What point could you make by focusing on this event?

■ What could your reader take away from your essay?

When you choose an event to write about, you are making a pertinent statement about some experience you've had. This may sound difficult, but you actually do it all the time. When you are sitting around with friends telling stories, don't you contribute when you feel like your story is somehow pertinent to what another person said? For example, if one of your friends is telling a story about how some salesperson at an expensive shop made him feel worthless because he wasn't dressed right, you might follow with a story about the time you didn't buy a car from a specific dealership because the salespeople kept ignoring you as though they didn't think you were serious about buying. Your story is pertinent because it reinforces your friend's point about how people misjudge other people based on appearance. What would have happened if you had followed his story with one about a time you got really sick from eating too much fried food? Everyone would look at you oddly because your story didn't fit. It didn't reinforce the point of the original story—it introduced a totally unrelated topic.

Why do you think the writer of the next essay chose the event he did as the focus of his paper? What point was he trying to make?

Perry Mason

Edrick Smith

Reason for writing—to share a personal experience

For five long years, I dreaded watching TV after 10:00 at night. Okay, I was only seven, and I shouldn't have been awake at all, but what my parents didn't know was okay, right? So there

Organizational method—chronological blended with topical

I was in front of my TV each night, scared witless, watching Perry Mason.

CBS-TV/The Kobal Collection/The Picture Desk

He doesn't look very scary, does he?

Perry Mason you might ask? What is scary about Perry Mason? He's the good guy. I knew that. I understood that he was out to get the bad guys, but that didn't prevent me from putting my head under the pillow while it was on. I'm still not sure why I didn't just turn it off, but in retrospect, I'm glad I didn't. Perry didn't just take care of the bad guys--he helped me turn my life around.

When I was in elementary school, material things meant a great deal to me. I wasn't happy just to have clean clothes and shoes that fit. I wanted Polo shirts and Nike shoes. Even though they worked hard, my parents couldn't afford these things, so I started hanging around with a tough crowd making bad choices. I suspect it was my guilt over my sins that made me fear Perry so much. While I watched Perry prosecute the bad guys and put them away, I was reliving the petty crimes I had committed that day. Before I knew it, I was imagining Perry putting me away. I

First point of essay

Narrative

began to question my actions when I stole bubble gum or ice cream from the candy store. My parents both worked during the day, so I had a lot of unsupervised time on my hands.

I can't blame my parents. They taught me right from wrong, and they did the best they could. I chose to steal knowing full well that they would have been shocked and disappointed if they had known. I kept my crimes from my parents, but I couldn't keep my crimes from Perry. Each night at 10:00, I felt like he looked into my soul and judged me a criminal.

Second point of essay

As time passed, I began to seriously consider the direction my life was taking. I didn't want to continue to be one of those kids my mother warned me about. I wanted to change my life before Perry sent me away. I began to practice doing what was right. I resisted the urge to steal what I wanted, and I learned to make do with what I had. I worked hard to develop the integrity to resist the taunts of my former friends. My conscience became clean, and I no longer hid my head under the pillow when Perry Mason was on.

I remember the first night I sat up in bed and watched the entire show without a single fear. Before that night I had always imagined myself in the role of the criminal. That night I began to imagine that I was Perry. I still watch Perry Mason whenever I get a chance, and I still stick to the straight and narrow path. I hope to be a lawyer some day, and I hope I can scare other kids into going straight. Thanks Perry. You're a great guy.

Final point of essay

Consider this . . .

- Why do you think the writer chose the event he focuses on?
- Did he choose appropriate writing strategies?
- Did the essay have pertinence for you?

CHOOSING STRATEGIES FOR WRITING ABOUT AN EVENT

You can choose any of the writing strategies discussed in Chapter Two to write about an event. However, you are most likely to use narration, description, and comparison/contrast.

≡ Narration–Telling a Story

When you use narration, you tell a story or part of a story. When you tell a story, you need to give attention to the following details:

- Characters
- Setting

- Action

- Dialogue

- Sensory detail

Writer's Break

- Make a list of at least five rites of passage that you have gone through.

- For each one, describe three ways in which it shaped who you are now.

- For each one, identify at least one way in which a reader could relate to your experience.

Characters

Every story has characters—the people who do the action of the story. When you are telling a story, you have to let your readers know who the people are that you want them to care about. No story will hold a reader's interest if it does not evoke concern for the characters. In order to make a reader care about someone in your story, you have to make that person seem real. You have to give him or her a name, a personality, an appearance—you have to make the person three-dimensional. We don't care about flat, boring generalities. We care about developed, interesting, flawed, and realistic people.

Setting

The people in your story have to act and interact somewhere; that somewhere is the setting. The setting can be one place or many places, the past, the present, or the future. How important the setting is to your story will vary. For example, if you are telling about your experience revisiting your first home, the setting is obviously of key importance. On the other hand, if you are writing about a relationship, the place where the action occurred might be secondary to the action. Either way, you have to give your readers some sense of where events are occurring. This will help them visualize the action and will give it a sense of immediacy.

Action

Once you have your characters in place, your readers expect them to do something—the action. What they do will be determined by the story, but they should be doing something—walking, talking, touching, yelling, deciding. Consequently, it is very important to use active verbs when writing a narrative. Active voice helps you show what is happening, rather than telling about it. (Active voice is discussed in Style Choices at the end of this chapter.)

Dialogue

If there is more than one person in your story, you will need to use dialogue. What is the difference between these two passages?

> She said I was worthless, and her harsh words really hurt me.

> As I was walking away from her desk, she said, "I wouldn't have wasted so much time on you, if I'd known you have no talent and no desire to improve!" I started to turn around and respond, but my eyes were full of tears, and I didn't want to give her the satisfaction of seeing how much she had hurt me.

In the first sentence, the writer tells us about something someone said to her, but rather than letting the person speak for herself, she paraphrases her words. Clearly, "She said I was worthless" does not tell us as much as ". . . you have no talent and no desire to improve." In the second passage, the writer lets the speaker speak for herself,

Without dialogue bubbles, a comic strip like this would be just a series of pictures with no clear meaning. The dialogue lets us hear what the characters are saying, while the pictures let us know what they are feeling.

and we can judge the content of her words for ourselves. We can appreciate the depth of the writer's pain when we "see" the tears in her eyes. It is difficult to feel anything for the writer of the first sentence because we know so little about what really happened. Always let people speak for themselves. The words people use tell a great deal about them and give your papers a sense of reality.

Sensory detail

We read to experience another person's reality. We can only have this experience if the writer provides us with enough detail to allow us to form complete images of the setting and characters. Read the following passage:

> The pizza restaurant smelled really good. It made me want to eat there.

This description is flat and boring. Now read this passage:

> When I walked into the pizza restaurant, I was assaulted by a wave of warm air carrying the blended aromas of baking bread, fresh garlic, and spicy tomato sauce. The hint of burned cheese just served to cut the sweetness of the other scents. By the time I reached the counter, my mouth was watering.

This description could make you run to the nearest pizzeria and order a large with everything. The difference between the two passages lies in the use of sensory description. Here the sensory words in the second passage are underlined:

> When I walked into the pizza restaurant, I was assaulted by a wave of <u>warm</u> air carrying the blended <u>aromas</u> of <u>baking bread</u>, <u>fresh garlic</u>, and <u>spicy tomato sauce</u>. The hint of <u>burned cheese</u> just served to cut the <u>sweetness</u> of the other <u>scents</u>. By the time I reached the counter, my mouth was <u>watering</u>.

Writer's Break

Choose one of your favorite stories, songs, movies, or advertisements.

- What makes it memorable: the characters, the setting, the action, the dialogue? Why is this element so memorable?

- What sensory details does the work include? How do they help you create a visual image of the scene?

- How can you apply these same techniques to one of your story ideas?

Each of these words invokes one of our senses: smell, sight, sound, taste, touch. We don't know what "smelled really good" actually means because we weren't there. We can imagine the smell of baking bread because we all know how good it smells. These words let us feel as though we were in that restaurant with the writer—he lets us share his experience viscerally.

The Cheat by Georges de lat Tour. Erich Lessing/Art Resource, NY.

In this painting, who are the characters? What are they doing? Where are they? What details allow you to imagine you are there? What do you think the people are saying to one another? If the painter of this work could show so much detail, how much detail do you think you could include in an entire paper?

☰ Description—Showing Not Telling

When we show rather than tell, we allow our readers to step into our shoes and share an experience from our point of view. We give our readers the details they need to visualize the event we are narrating. Look at this passage:

> Through the door of the classroom I could hear the students talking. As soon as I walked in, they stopped talking. I was very nervous, and I wished they would keep making noise. I thought they must realize I was a fraud, not a teacher.

Writer's Break

Rewrite each of the following sentences, so that it shows rather than tells. You may invent details as needed.

- She told me that I wasn't a nice person.
- I felt very bad when I lost the karate tournament.
- She seemed to be very frightened.
- The room was beautiful and inviting.
- I had never seen such a horrible place.

Do these words paint a vivid image in your mind? Can you hear and see the students? Imagine how the teacher feels? Not really, because this writer told us about her experience, she didn't show it to us.

Now consider this revised version:

> As I approached the door of the classroom, I heard the low hum of talk, snatches of conversations that didn't include me: "Who's the teacher for this course? I hate English classes. Required courses are lame. Can I borrow your cell phone?" My hands were sweating, and I wiped them on my carefully chosen black skirt before I took a deep breath and pulled open the door. As I walked into the classroom, the hum subsided, and even though I carefully avoided making eye contact with anyone, I could feel twenty-seven pairs of hostile eyes boring into me. Flop sweat slowly trickled down my sides, and I sent up a silent prayer, "Please don't let them realize I'm a complete fraud!" Drawing a shaky breath, I turned into the blur of faces and squeaked, "My name is Ms. Rosser." "Oh no," I thought. "They must think they have Minnie Mouse for a teacher."

This passage truly allows us to step inside the writer's skin and experience that first day of teaching. Even if you never plan to teach, you can still sympathize with this new teacher. This writing shows. It does not tell. We can hear the students talking, and we can see and feel what the writer experienced. This is what good writing provides: a vicarious experience.

☰ Comparison/Contrast

In the two essays that follow, the writers share experiences related to growing up, though they do it very differently. Both writers use comparisons and contrasts to develop their ideas.

Will the Real Adult Please Stand Up?

Kari Harris

It was a clear sunny day although I couldn't see the sun from the windowless room in which I sat. I was sitting at one end of a long oval table facing six unsmiling professionals. A long battle had led me to this room, this moment. I knew I was just as much an adult as any of the other people in the room, but I felt more like an unruly student facing the principal. As I sat there listening to the principal drone on, images of the years leading up to this meeting flashed through my mind.

My first child, a daughter, had been born eleven years earlier. My husband and I did the best we could to act like we believed parents were meant to act, but I secretly felt more like a little girl playing house. A year later my son was born and though I was a very competent mother by that time, I still continued to feel like a child masquerading as an adult. Luckily, the

> Reason for writing—to share a personal experience

> Organizational method: chronological blended with comparison/contrast

> Narration—cause of primary event

years rolled smoothly along and no bumps in the road caused me
to question my role.

Then my son entered kindergarten. A day never passed
that he wasn't disciplined at least once. He and the principal
were on a first name basis. I wasn't surprised. He was a good kid,
with a big heart, but he was also very active. To make matters
worse, he was also in danger of repeating kindergarten because
his teacher claimed he wasn't learning the alphabet and couldn't
count. Shy of criticizing the teacher--a real adult--I began teaching him at home, and he soon caught up.

When my son was placed into a remedial reading program
at the beginning of the first grade, I actually became concerned
enough to visit the school principal, a woman I admired. She put
my mind at ease and also asked me to begin working as a substitute teacher. It was as a substitute teacher that I began to learn
something about my rights and responsibilities as a parent;
unfortunately, we moved the following year.

After two good years with exemplary teachers, my son
entered the third grade. This is when the battle royal began. I
suspected that my son had ADD, and I knew from his experience

with his previous teachers that he needed extra time for assignments, but his teacher consistently insisted that he just needed
to work harder. Unfortunately, his school did not have a diagnostician on staff, so after numerous conferences with his teacher,
and much begging, I finally decided to play hard ball. I requested
that the school pay a contract diagnostician from another dis-
trict, which they did--unwillingly.

Perhaps I was more sympathetic toward my son than I
should have been, but I remembered how I had felt growing up.
Staying still and paying attention was always hard for me, and
my grades reflected this. Rather than trying to discover the
source of my problem, my parents simply criticized me. My parents never met with a teacher, and never considered the possibility that anyone other than me might have been at fault. They
never took my side. It was this realization more than anything
else that made me grow up.

The day I went to the school to learn the results of my
son's test and demand that his needs be met, I wore a helmet of
hairspray, lots of make-up, a nice dress, and high-heeled shoes. I
felt like I needed to be fully armored in my "grown-up clothes"

Narration—writer's childhood

Narration—present event

Description

from top to bottom before I could face the enemy. I was petri-fied of those people I considered the real adults. I don't know why they seemed so much more grown-up. Maybe it was their titles, or the fact that they had desks to sit behind. I don't know, but I was intimidated. But there was one thing I did know, and it was the shield I carried into battle. I was the authority where my son was concerned.

"Mrs. Harris, your son barely qualified for the special edu-cation program," a tall graying woman told me. "His test results indicate he should be in regular classes." I nodded and smiled. I had expected it to be close.

"What would you like to happen now?" asked the principal. "Do you want him in special education classes full-time? It really doesn't seem fair considering the number of other children who need those classes more. Perhaps he just needs to work harder." I could tell from his tone of voice that he was prepared to be adversarial.

"That won't be necessary," I replied. "All he needs is extra time to finish his assignments and access to the Content Mastery Lab."

Use of dialogue to show event and characters

"That's all you wanted?" said the astonished principal.

"Yes," I replied, "and if you, or my son's teacher, or anyone had listened to me the first ten times I came in, this meeting would not have been necessary because I wouldn't have requested the testing."

When I walked out of the school that day, I no longer felt like a student caught smoking in the bathroom. I was an adult, and I was a parent, and I had what it took to protect my children.

Point of essay

It is not always easy to be a grown-up, and many of us may feel like children playing dress-up. However, when you make the choice to have children, you sacrifice your right to be a child. After all, the only way your children can be free to be children is if you have the strength to be an adult.

Consider this . . .

- Did the writer of this essay make appropriate choices when she chose her writing strategies?
- Do the strategies she used help her make her point?
- Does her story have pertinence even for those readers who have no children?

Writer's Break

■ Make a list of three people you know who grew up differently than you did.

■ List three significant ways in which their experience was different from yours.

■ List at least three questions you would like to ask that person about his or her childhood.

GIRL

Jamaica Kincaid

Wash the white clothes on Monday and put them on the stone heap; wash the color clothes on Tuesday and put them on the clothesline to dry; don't walk barehead in the hot sun; cook pumpkin fritters in very hot sweet oil; soak your little clothes right after you take them off; when buying cotton to make yourself a nice blouse, be sure that it doesn't have gum on it, because that way it won't hold up well after a wash; soak salt fish overnight before you cook it; is it true that you sing benna [calypso songs] in Sunday School; always eat your food in such a way that it won't turn someone else's stomach; on Sundays try to walk like a lady and not like the slut you are so bent on becoming; don't sing benna in Sunday School; you mustn't speak to wharf-rat boys, not even to give directions; don't eat fruits on the street—flies will follow you; *but I don't sing benna on Sundays at all and never in Sunday school*; this is how to sew on a button; this is how to make a button-hole for the button you have just sewed on; this is how to hem a dress when you see the hem coming down and so to prevent yourself from looking like the slut I know you are so bent on becoming; this is how you iron your father's khaki shirt so that it doesn't have a crease; this is how you iron your father's khaki pants so that they don't have a crease; this how you grow okra—far from the house, because okra tree harbors red ants; when you are growing dasheen [yamlike tuber], make sure it gets plenty of water or else it makes your throat itch when you are eating it; this is how you sweep a corner; this how you sweep a whole house; this is how you sweep a yard; this is how you smile to someone you don't like too much; this how you smile to someone you don't like at all; this is how you smile to someone you like completely; this is how you set a table for tea; this is how you set a table for dinner; this is how you set a table for dinner with an important guest; this is how you set a table for lunch; this is how you set a table for breakfast; this is how to behave in the presence of men who don't know you very well, and this way they won't recognize immediately the slut I have warned you against becoming; be sure to wash every day, even if it is with your own spit; don't squat down to play marbles—you are not a boy, you know; don't pick people's flowers—you might catch something; don't throw stones at blackbirds, because it might not be a blackbird at all; this is how to make a bread pudding; this is how to make doukona [spicy plantain pudding]; this is how to make pepper pot; this is how to make good medicine for a cold; this is how to make good medicine to throw away a child before it even becomes a child; this is how to catch a fish; this is how to throw back a fish you don't like, and that way something bad won't fall on you; this is how to bully a man; this is how a man bullies you; this is how to love a man and if this doesn't work there are other ways, and if they don't work don't feel too bad about giving up; this is how to spit up in the air if you feel like it, and this is how to move quick so that it doesn't fall on you; this how to make ends meet; always squeeze bread to make sure it's fresh; *but what if the baker won't let me feel the bread?*; you mean to say that after all you are really going to be the kind of woman who the baker won't let feel the bread?

Consider this . . .

- What writing strategies did this writer use?
- What does the text that is in italics represent? Why do you think the writer chose to use that technique?
- What do you think about the use of questions in this essay?

CHOOSING AN ORGANIZATIONAL METHOD

The organizational patterns most often used in personal writing are chronological, spatial, and conceptual.

☰ Chronological Order

Because most personal writing involves sharing an event, it makes sense to use chronological organization and give the information in the order in which it happened. The following essay by Amy Tan uses chronological order.

CONFESSIONS

Amy Tan

1   My mother's thoughts reach back like the winter tide, exposing the wreckage of a former shore. Often, she's mired in 1967, 1968, the years my older brother and my father died.

2   1968 was also the year she took me and my little brother—Didi—across the Atlantic to Switzerland, a place so preposterously different that she knew she had to give up grieving simply to survive. That year, she remembers, she was very, very sad. I too remember. I was sixteen then, and I recall a late-night hour when my mother and I were arguing in the chalet, that tinderbox of emotion where we lived.

3   She had pushed me into the small bedroom we shared, and as she slapped me about the head, I backed into a corner, by a window that looked out on the lake, the Alps, the beautiful outside world. My mother was furious because I had a boyfriend. She was shouting that he was a drug addict, a bad man who would use me for sex and throw me away like leftover garbage.

4   "Stop seeing him!" she ordered.

5   I shook my head. The more she beat me, the more implacable I became, and this in turn fueled her outrage.

"You didn't love you daddy or Peter! When they die you not even sad." 6

I kept my face to the window, unmoved. What does she know about sad? 7

She sobbed and beat her chest. "I rather kill myself before see you destroy you 8
life!"

Suicide. How many times had she threatened that before? 9

"I wish you the one die! Not Peter, not Daddy." 10

She had just confirmed what I had always suspected. Now she flew at me with 11
her fists.

"I rather kill you! I rather see you die!" 12

And then, perhaps horrified by what she had just said, she fled the room. 13
Thank God that was over. I wished I had a cigarette to smoke. Suddenly she was
back. She slammed the door shut, latched it, then locked it with a key. I saw the
flash of a meat cleaver just before she pushed me to the wall and brought the blade's
edge to within an inch of my throat. Her eyes were like a wild animal's, shiny, fix-
ated on the kill. In an excited voice she said, "First, I kill you. Then Didi and me,
our whole family destroy!" She smiled, her chest heaving. "Why don't you cry?"
She pressed the blade closer and I could feel her breath gusting.

Was she bluffing? If she did kill me, so what? Who would care? While she ram- 14
bled, a voice within me was whimpering, "This is so sad, this is so sad."

For ten minutes, fifteen, longer, I straddled these two thoughts—that it didn't 15
matter if I died, that it would be eternally sad if I did—until all at once I felt a snap,
then a rush of hope into a vacuum, and I was crying, I was babbling my confession:
"I want to live. I want to live."

For twenty-five years I forgot that day, and when the memory of what happened 16
surfaced unexpectedly at a writer's workshop in which we recalled our worst
moments, I was shaking, wondering to myself, Did she really mean to kill me? If
I had not pleaded with her, would she have pushed down on the cleaver and
ended my life?

I wanted to go to my mother and ask. Yet I couldn't, not until much later, when 17
she became forgetful and I learned she had Alzheimer's disease. I knew that if I
didn't ask her certain questions now, I would never know the real answers.

So I asked. 18

"Angry? Slap you?" she said, and laughed. "No, no, *no*. You always good girl, 19
never even need to spank, not even one time."

How wonderful to hear her say what was never true, yet now would be forever so. 20

> ## Consider this . . .
>
> ■ What does the writer want you to learn from her essay?
>
> ■ What does the last sentence of the essay mean? What is more real—what really happened or what we remember?
>
> ■ What organizational methods does the writer use? How are they effective?

☰ Spatial Order

Spatial organization, which is based on physical location, is especially useful for descriptive writing. It is very hard to share an experience without describing aspects of it. In "Will the Real Adult Please Stand Up?" the writer blends spatial organization with her primary method, chronological organization.

☰ Conceptual Order

A writer will often weave points he or she wishes to make relating to the personal experience he or she is sharing with the actual narrative. This is what the writer of "Perry Mason" chose to do. When you choose a conceptual organization, you introduce points related to your topic and then develop and link them.

The final example of personal writing is a selection of entries from the diary of Anne Frank. These passages were written by her in the days preceding her family's move into the secret annex, where they would remain in hiding for two years before being discovered. She shares specific events and explains why those events forced her family into hiding.

FROM THE DIARY OF A YOUNG GIRL
Anne Frank

. . . When we walked across our little square together a few days ago, Daddy began to talk of us going into hiding. I asked him why on earth he was beginning to talk of that already. "Yes, Anne," he said, "you know that we have been taking food, clothes, furniture to other people for more than a year now. We don't want our belongings to be seized by the Germans, and we certainly don't want to fall into their clutches ourselves. So we shall disappear of our own accord and not wait until they come and fetch us."

"But Daddy, when would it be?" He spoke so seriously that I grew very anxious.

"Don't you worry about it, we shall arrange everything. Make the most of your carefree young life while you can." . . . [July 5, 1942]

"The S.S. have sent a call-up notice for Daddy," she [Anne's sister Margot] whispered. . . . It was a great shock to me, a call-up; everyone knows what that means. I picture concentration camps and lonely cells—should we allow him be doomed to this? "Of course he won't go," declared Margot, while we waited together. "Mummy has gone to the van Daans to discuss whether we should move into our hiding place tomorrow. The van Daans are going with us, so we shall be seven in all."

. . . We put on heaps of clothes as if we were going to the North Pole, the sole reason being to take clothes with us. No Jew in our situation would have dreamed of going out with a suitcase full of clothing. I had on two vests, three pairs of knickers, a dress, on top of that, a skirt, jacket, summer coat, two pairs of stockings, lace-up shoes, woolly cap, scarf, and still more; I was nearly stifled before we started, but no one inquired about that. [July 8, 1942]

AP/Wide World Photo

Because Anne Frank kept a faithful journal of her years in hiding, we have a much better sense of how the Holocaust affected Jewish families in Europe.

Consider this . . .

- What writing strategies does Anne Frank use?
- What organizational methods does she use?
- A diary usually has no pertinence for anyone but the writer. Why is this diary an exception to that generality?

IF YOU'RE LIKE MANY students, you may cringe when a teacher asks you to do personal writing. But think about how deeply you have been affected by a song or a movie or a story. All of these types of communication share a personal experience. The difference between good and poor personal writing is the level of significance. A trip you took might not have been very interesting to anyone else, but an experience you had last week might be well worth sharing. The world is full of good stories; add yours to the mix. ▪

COLLABORATIVE EXERCISES

Do the following exercises in groups, and be prepared to share your results.

Group Exercise One

- For either Option One or Option Two of Writing Picks, work as a group to come up with a paper topic.
- As a group, write an introduction and a conclusion for the paper.
- Share your writing with the class.
- As a class, list qualities that characterize good introductions and conclusions.

Group Exercise Two

- As a group, choose the essay in this chapter about growing up that you considered best.
- Make a list of specific reasons why you chose that selection.
- Make a list of specific techniques the writer uses: metaphor, adjectives, sensory description, dialogue.
- Share your lists with the class.
- As a class, write a list of the qualities of good personal response papers.

Group Exercise Three

- As a group, choose an event that one or more of the group members observed first hand: a car accident, an argument, a crime, etc.
- Write a narrative about the event, trying to "show" what happened rather than "tell" what happened.
- Share your work with the class.
- As a class, make a list of the qualities of good narratives.

WRITING PICKS

Option One

Events that shape us

Growing up happens to everyone. Some of us grow up surrounded by a happy family. Some of us grow up in foster care. Some of us never know hunger. Some of us have been homeless. Regardless of how or where we grow up, we are all influenced by events that shape us. These events don't always happen when we are children. How was Anne Frank shaped by her two years in hiding? What events have shaped your growing up? What experiences made you grow up? Write an essay in which you share an experience that affected you in some lasting way. For example, an experience could have caused you to mature, to develop a life-long fear, or to reconsider an important decision.

Breakfast in Bed by Mary Cassatt. The Huntington Library, Art Collections, and Botanical Gardens, San Marino, California./Superstock

Artist Mary Cassatt frequently used mothers and their children as the subjects for her paintings. What kind of relationship do you think this mother and child share?

Option Two

Rites of passage

We've all heard the term *rite of passage*, and we've all read stories and seen movies that are about rites of passage. In the film *Trainspotting*, several urban Scottish teens pay the price of heroin addiction as they watch their lives unravel. In "Will the Real Adult Please Stand Up," the writer explains how a conflict with her son's teacher caused her to grow up. What was your most memorable rite of passage? How did it make you grow up? How do our individual rites of passage make us unique? In this essay, share your rite of passage, or describe that of someone else who is significant to you. For example, how was your best friend's rite of passage different from yours?

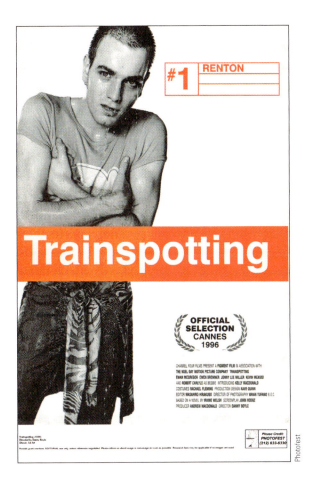

Option Three

How others grow up

Think about the different childhoods that your relatives or your friends may have had. For example, did anyone you know grow up in another country? Was anyone a first-generation U.S. citizen? Did anyone have an identical twin? Choose a family member or close friend who grew up very differently from you. Ask them to tell you a story about how their experience was different from yours. How do you think you would have managed in a similar situation? Do you think the differences determined who that person later became? How does your childhood compare? Compare your own childhood to someone else's. How were your experiences different? How were they the same? Explore this idea in your paper.

Option Four

Image of hunger

For most of us in the United States, hunger, true hunger, is unknown. We casually say we are hungry three hours after we've eaten a large meal, and we say, "There's no food in the house," when we really mean there is no food in the house that we want to eat.

What do you think hunger means for the children in this photograph? Can you imagine what their lives must be like? What do the expressions on their faces tell us? What can you say about these children?

Abbas/Magnum Photos

In your paper, analyze one aspect of what you see in this photo: for example, what hunger really means, what it's like to lose your childhood, or how our lifestyles have made us immune to the plight of others.

APPLYING THE RHETORICAL SITUATION

As always, you must consider the rhetorical situation throughout the process of making choices for a personal essay. Use these questions to guide your decision making.

Audience

- Is your audience motivated to read your story?

- What information does your audience need in order to relate to your story?

- Are you using any language that you will need to define for your audience?

Purpose

- What point are you trying to make?

- What writing techniques can you use to make it?

- How can you organize your paper to emphasize that point?

- What do you want the reader to take away from reading your essay? A shared experience? A new awareness? A resolution to do something? Insight into another human?

Occasion

- How can you make your readers want to read about the event you are narrating?

- Have you given your readers a clear reason to choose to read your essay?

- Have you fully shared the experience you are describing with your readers?

FOCUSING ON PROCESS

Prewriting

Before you can begin writing your essay on a personal experience, you have to have some material with which to work. Where can you find material?

- Your responses to the Writer's Breaks in this chapter

- Your personal life (Do you have any old photos? Letters? Mementos? What do they remind you of? Do you have any old diaries or journals?)

- Your family (What stories does your family tell? Do you have any favorites? Why? Would you like to rewrite any of your family history?)

Drafting

Most of us are more accustomed to telling stories than we are to writing stories. Thus, we sometimes lose some of the flavor of our stories when we put them in writing. The tone and emphasis we add with our body and our voice are missing. In order to keep these elements in your essay, ask a friend to help you draft this time.

- Ask your friend to meet you somewhere quiet where you are free to talk.

- Ask your friend to listen to the story you plan to tell in your essay.

- Write the story down.

- Ask your friend to read the written version of your story, and tell you how it differs from the one you told. Use what you learn from your friend to improve your essay.

Revising

In this chapter, we discussed three techniques you could use when writing to share a personal experience:

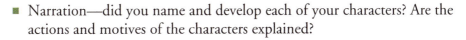

- Narration—did you name and develop each of your characters? Are the actions and motives of the characters explained?

- Description—could someone else draw a picture of each character based on the detail you gave? Did you describe the setting if it was important?

- Comparison/contrast—if you compared two or more things, did you compare the same elements of each topic?

Editing

- When you think your paper is done, underline every subject.

- Go back again, and double underline every verb.

- Did every sentence have both a subject and a verb?

- Was every subject a person, place, thing, or idea?

- Was every verb active? If not, is the passive voice used for a good reason?

Grammar Choices

COMPLEX SENTENCES

A **complex sentence** contains at least one independent clause and a dependent clause. In order to be able to identify complex sentences, you need to add these words to your vocabulary:

A **subordinating conjunction** is a linking word such as *as*, *because*, or *although* that subordinates a clause and makes it depend on an independent clause to complete its meaning.

A **relative pronoun** is a pronoun such as *who*, *which*, or *that* that subordinates a clause.

Here are several examples of complex sentences:

It was a clear sunny day **although** I couldn't see the sun from the windowless room in which I sat.

He was also in danger of repeating kindergarten **because** his teacher claimed he wasn't learning the alphabet and couldn't count.

In the first example, the second clause is a dependent clause. Notice that it begins with the subordinating conjunction *although*. In the second example, the second clause is dependent; it begins with the subordinating conjunction *because*.

A complex sentence can either begin or end with the dependent clause:

When I was in elementary school, material things meant a great deal to me.

I recall a late-night hour **when my mother and I were arguing in the chalet**.

Notice that the first sentence has a comma after the dependent clause, but the second one doesn't have a comma preceding the dependent clause. The reason is as follows:

- When the dependent clause precedes the independent clause, it is followed by a comma.

- When the dependent clause follows the independent clause, it may not be preceded by a comma.

Making It Work

Read through a draft or essay you've written.

- Identify each complex sentence.

- If you didn't find at least three complex sentences, combine other sentences to create at least three.

Style Choices

USING THE ACTIVE VOICE

You can write in either passive or active voice, but active voice is a better choice for most types of writing. The active voice is more concise, and readers expect the subject of a sentence to be the actor.

Passive Voice

Passive voice has these characteristics:

- The **actor** and the **subject** are not the same. In the following sentences, *sandwich* is the subject, but the actor is *him*.

  The **sandwich** was eaten by **him**.

- The verb is a form of the verb to be (*is, am, are, was, were, be, being, been*), plus a past participle. In the example above, the verb is *was eaten*.

- The indirect object is often the actor.

Active Voice

Active voice has these characteristics:

- The actor and subject are the same. In the following sentence, *He* is both actor and subject.

  He ate the sandwich.

- The sentence does not contain a form of the verb *to be* followed by a past participle.

- The object of the verb follows the verb. In the example above, *sandwich* is the object of *ate*.

Reasons to Use the Passive Voice

There are times when the passive voice is a good choice:

■ When the actor is unknown.

The car was fixed.

■ When the action, not the actor, is the focus.

The test was completed.

■ In scientific writing, where the facts or the findings, rather than the researchers, are more important.

Gamma rays have been proven to be harmful to humans.

Making It Work

Read through a draft or a paper you've written, and complete these steps:

■ Identify every sentence as being written in either the passive or the active voice.

■ Change the passive voice to the active voice whenever possible.

■ Justify any uses of the passive voice that remain.

THE WORLD AROUND US

Writing about Observations

In this chapter, you will learn:

- How to make an observation about the world around you the focus of an essay

- How to use the strategies of description and comparison/contrast to write about an observation

- The organizational methods often used for observational writing—spatial, chronological, and logical order

Night Hawks by Edward Hopper. Francis G. Mayer/Corbis.

This painting captured a moment in time—a collection of people looking for comfort at an all-night diner.

W e don't simply see the world; we experience it. As we have experiences, we make observations; we also pass judgments and draw conclusions. How often do you sit with friends in a public place like a sports arena talking about the players and the game being played? How often do you make assumptions based on what you see? Many kinds of scientific research, including the work of animal behaviorists such as Jane Goodall, are based on close and extended observation.

In this chapter, we are going to talk about how to use observations of the world around you to draw conclusions that can become the focus of a paper.

MAKING CHOICES WHEN YOU WRITE ABOUT OBSERVATIONS

Observation is based on our perceptions of the physical characteristics of people, places, and things. This is because we observe with our senses:

- Sight

- Sound

- Touch

- Taste

- Smell

Based on what we are observing, the sense or senses we rely on most heavily will vary. If you are observing people, your purpose for observing them, or the nature of your initial observation, might determine which senses contribute the most information. If you are observing a place, sight, sound, and smell will be very important. Taste might not contribute unless the place is a restaurant. Different places can be recognized by their smells. We all know what hospitals smell like. What about a vet's office? Your favorite restaurant? What is most important about the process of observation is that you use all your senses to help you collect as much data as possible. Then you use your observations to help you make a point.

Drawing Conclusions from Observations

No one wants to read description just for its own sake. We read description because a writer gives it some significance for us. Whether you realize it or not, you draw conclusions from almost everything you experience. Sometimes you probably do it unconsciously; other times you may do it deliberately, but you always do it. By drawing conclusions, you turn what you observe into something worth writing about.

How often have you sat in an airport, a restaurant, or some other public place drawing conclusions about the people you see? "Look at that couple. They're reading books while they eat dinner. Some relationship. That's really pathetic." "Look at those older people holding hands. I think they're in love." "He's reading my favorite book. I bet I would like him if I could meet him." You've probably drawn conclusions like these many times. Most of us have. These are the sorts of conclusions we draw without really thinking about it. However, sometimes these automatic conclusions make us aware of a trend that leads us to begin observing something more closely.

Making an Observation the Focus of an Essay

We make an observation the focus of an essay when we draw conclusions from what we observe based on patterns we notice or patterns of information that support what we suspect. For example, if you open the swimsuit issue of *Sports Illustrated*, you might question the connection between its content and the magazine's title. Although this magazine is supposedly devoted to sports and athletes, this issue is almost exclusively devoted to photos of women in skimpy swimsuits. Of the more than twenty women shown in bathing suits in the 2003 issue, only one is an athlete—Serena Williams. Browsing through this magazine might make a reader wonder exactly what its editors consider valuable about women. To write a paper about your observations of this magazine, you might ask the following questions:

- How many men wearing bathing suits does this magazine feature?

- How often does the magazine feature women athletes who are wearing a team uniform or sports gear?

Asking questions and collecting data allow you to justify the conclusions you reach.

Writer's Break

- Based on your observations of the people around you, describe the current concept of beauty in the United States.
- Give three specific examples to support your opinion.
- Find three specific images that support your opinion.

Maybe you want to explore the idea that people under twenty are politically apathetic. Perhaps you do not believe that this is true. In order to make this argument, you would have to spend time observing people in this age group. You might decide to observe them in a specific location, such as a political science class or a polling place at election time. What you learned from your observations would give you the information you needed to write your paper. However, you still have to convince other people to see things as you did, to reach the same conclusion. For example, after watching the students in the political science class, you might be convinced that people under twenty have very strong political convictions and are politically active. You are certainly entitled to your opinion, but if you want others to agree with you, you have to build an argument that will convince them that you based your opinion on specific observations.

Look at the following student essay about driving habits and what they say about us as people. Does the writer make a good argument?

Road Signs

Haley Hoskinson

"You are tuned into 104.1 KRBE, this is Sam Malone, and we've got Michelle Branch comin' up right after this traffic update brought to you by Maria Todd and sponsored by Radiant Energy." Maria's perky voice cut in: "Well, Sam, traffic is about as bad as it can get this beautiful Friday afternoon; everyone is headed to the shore. Highway 59 is backed up all the way to Kirby. There's an overturned semi on I-10 east outbound that's causing a two-hour delay. This has got traffic backed up all the way around the north loop, lot of rubber neckers out there. . . ." Click. I turned off my radio, and sat in my car surrounded by thousands of other cars, all surrounded by thousands of other cars, all with thousands of bored occupants. Traffic jams are just peachy. To pass the time and distract myself from the incessant honking (Didn't these people realize we'd all be moving if we could?), I began to glance at the people sitting in the stationary cars around me.

> Reason for writing—to share observations about other drivers

> Organizational method—chronological blended with spatial

I'm in the little red car. I may never move again!

First observation

Draws conclusion

To my left, in the "fast" lane, was a black Corvette, license plate KEEP UP. "Hmmph," I snickered to myself--this is hurting him more than me. I wondered how many speeding tickets he had, or maybe he was really one of those slow drivers who just wanted people to think he was a speed junky. No, he was an impatient speed demon. He continuously ran his fingers through his thinning hair, not in an "Oh man I'm sexy" way but in an "I'm going to rip out what little hair I have left if this driver in front of me does not put the pedal to the metal" way. He kept trying to peer out his window to see around the car in front of him. He seemed to think seeing what was two cars ahead of him would make a difference. To top it all off, he kept revving his engine. Did he need a way to pass the time? Did he honestly think he needed to remind everyone sitting around him that we were not moving? This guy just reeked impatience and anxiety. Does that sound like you? Or are you more like the next person I observed?

The guy on my right had his seat leaning so far back that all I could see was his hand dangling out the window, and I could feel the bass of his music vibrating my windows. Just watching this guy lowered my stress level. That hand that was dangling out the window was calmly rotating back and forth. I knew he was enjoying the light breeze that was blowing across his skin. Here he was in the middle of one of the worst traffic jams the city had ever seen, and he was just chillin'. Clearly how far someone lays his or her seat back indicates how laid back he or she truly is.

I glanced into my rear view mirror at the girl behind me. "What a Suzie Q," I thought to myself. Her car was spotless,

Uses specific examples to support conclusion

Second observation

Lists examples

Draws conclusion

Third observation

Draws conclusion

Lists examples

Reconfirms conclusion

Final observation

completely immaculate--inside and out as far as I could tell. She clearly took care of herself the same way she did her car. Her shirt collar was perfectly pressed, and her hands were neatly positioned at 10:00 and 2:00 on the steering wheel. As I chewed on my own ragged cuticles, I admired her perfectly manicured nails. Yes, this girl was definitely a perfectionist. Anyone who actually drives with their hands in the position recommended by their Driver's Ed teacher, in the middle of a traffic jam, must be a perfectionist.

Just then I was rudely interrupted by a woman with a mullet meandering across the lanes in an El Camino. She honked as she tried to steer her way into my lane. From the number of dents in her car, I could only guess that this was how she usually drove--carelessly. She was obviously careless in other aspects of her life as well. Her hair was a mess! She was clearly enjoying the attention she was receiving by honking her horn. Too bad it was negative attention. I've never seen so many fingers shoot up so fast. I couldn't help but wonder, "What is she trying to do?" She appeared to be alone in the car, but I wouldn't have been surprised to find out all her kids were in the car with her--ducking under the seats in embarrassment. I would not have blamed them.

The next time you are sitting at a traffic light, or worse luck, are stuck in a traffic jam, keep your eyes open. You never know who might be sitting next to you analyzing every move you make. There is an adage, "You are what you eat." On the contrary, "You are what you drive." Do you blare your music? Cut people off? Multi-task while trying to drive, or do you let the other cars go first at the four-way stop sign? Take a step back and assess your driving habits. You may be saying more about yourself than you realize.

> Conclusion—clarifies point of essay

Consider this . . .

- What point did the writer hope to make by writing about observations of other drivers?
- Did she establish the significance of her topic?
- How effectively did she justify her conclusions?

CHOOSING STRATEGIES FOR WRITING ABOUT OBSERVATIONS

As with any type of writing, you can use multiple strategies for observational writing. What you should remember is to choose your techniques based on your purpose: Are you making a humorous observation? Are you drawing a conclusion about Americans' obsession with weight? Are you trying to show that children are more judgmental than adults? Choose your techniques accordingly. Every essay based on observation is different, but most use one of these writing strategies:

- Description
- Comparison/Contrast

≡ Description

A large portion of the information you gather through observation will be based on what you perceive. You use your judgment to weigh and balance the evidence of your senses. When you write about what you have observed, you can use either sensory or psychological description.

Sensory description

We use sensory description when we describe things we can perceive with any of our senses. Look at the italicized words in the following passages:

FROM THE GRAPES OF WRATH
John Steinbeck

Sight	When June was half gone, the big clouds moved up out of Texas and the Gulf, *high heavy clouds, rainheads.* The men in the fields looked up at the clouds and
Smell/touch	*sniffed* at them and held *wet fingers* up to sense the wind. And the horses were
Sound	nervous while the clouds were up. The rainheads dropped a *little spattering* and
Sight	hurried on to some other country. Behind them the *sky was pale again and the*

sun flared. In the dust there were *drop craters* where the rain had fallen, and there were *clean splashes* on the corn and that was all.

Sight

FROM NATIVE SON
Richard Wright

"I didn't know I was sho drunk," *she mumbled*.

Sound

He led her slowly up the narrow stairs to the kitchen door, his hand circling her waist and the *tips of his fingers feeling the soft swelling* of her breasts. Each second she was *leaning more heavily* against him. . . .

Touch

She *pulled heavily* on him, her arm about his neck. He pushed the door in and took a step inside and stopped, waiting, *listening*. He felt her hair *brush his lips*. His skin *glowed warm* and his *muscles flexed*; he looked at her face in the dim light, his senses drunk with the *odor of her hair and skin*. He stood for a moment, then whispered in excitement and fear:

Sound/touch
Touch
Smell

"Come on; you got to get to your room."

In these passages, the writers incorporate a great deal of sensory description. In the first passage, John Steinbeck is trying to emphasize the fear and frustration of farmers in the Dust Bowl. In the second passage, Richard Wright is trying to emphasize the physical closeness of the protagonist, Bigger, to the young woman he is helping. This passage effectively describes the intimate contact between the two by using sound, smell, and touch—senses that require closeness or contact. A description that was purely visual would not have created that same sense of intimacy.

Writer's Break

- Choose a place where things are sold—a grocery store, music store, or clothing store—and spend a few minutes watching the customers.
- Write a physical description of the people you observe shopping and what they buy. Involve as many senses as possible.
- After reading your description, what conclusions can you draw about Americans and their buying habits?

Psychological description

In addition to describing what we can perceive with our senses, we can also describe what goes on in our minds—our thoughts and emotions. When we use words to tell a story, we can't tell the whole story without describing our feelings as the events unfolded. In fact, it is often psychological description that is most important to readers. Consider this example:

FROM TO KILL A MOCKINGBIRD
Harper Lee

Surprise

Confusion

Dr. Reynolds's voice was as breezy as his step, as though he had said it every evening of his life, an announcement that astounded me even more than being in the same room with Boo Radley. Of course . . . even Boo Radley got sick sometimes, I thought. But on the other hand I wasn't sure. . . .

"Er—" said Atticus, glancing at Boo. "Heck, let's go out on the front porch. There are plenty of chairs out there, and it's still warm enough."

Confusion

Understanding

I wondered why Atticus was inviting us to the front porch instead of the livingroom, then I understood. The livingroom lights were awfully strong.

In this passage, the writer lets us into the mind of the narrator, Scout. We are able to know what she knows and feel what she feels. Without this psychological description, we would not be able to see the events from the mind of the narrator, which is often the point of a story.

Writer's Break

- Make a list of five stereotypes you believe exist.
- Observe the world around you in order to determine how each stereotype is perpetuated. Are TV shows doing it? Popular jokes? The Internet?
- Make a list of at least three conclusions you can draw from your observations.

☰ Comparison/Contrast

One of the best ways to describe what you observe is by comparing it to something else. This can be done in two ways. First, you can compare something familiar to something unfamiliar, which can give familiar ideas new impact. Second, you can compare the unfamiliar to the familiar, so that your readers have a context for understanding something that is strange to them. For example, if you were describing snow to someone who lives where snow does not fall regularly, you might want to describe snow in a way that would make them understand your negative feelings about it:

> The snow was a wet gray blanket of misery. [metaphor]
>
> Snow is like a bad date. [simile] It seems to last forever.
>
> Snow is a guaranteed traffic jam on a morning when you are running late. [metaphor]

You can also use comparison to describe snow positively to someone who has never seen it:

> Snow is a blanket of cotton wool that covers the ground. [metaphor]
>
> Snow is like a cloak of invisibility. [simile] It makes everything ugly disappear.
>
> Snow covers the world like a layer of white frosting. [simile]

Comparisons that use the structure "*a* is *b*" are *metaphors*, and comparisons that use the structure "*a* is like *b*" are *similes*. You probably use figurative language in speech almost every day. How often do you say things like this?

> That test was a beast.
>
> That party was a riot.
>
> My date was a nightmare.

Writer's Break

Find an ad you consider thought-provoking, and put it in your writer's notebook.

- ■ What conclusions can you draw from it?
- ■ What does it say about our society and what we value?

Statements like these are rather clichéd, and clichés, while fine in conversation, are better avoided in writing. However, metaphors and similes such as those that follow can give you the power to express yourself vividly:

The rain crust broke, and the dust lifted up out of the fields and drove gray plumes into the air like sluggish smoke.

The sun was as red as her lipstick.

It is a damp, drizzly November in my soul.

In the next essay, a student uses a variety of writing strategies to argue that Americans are too obsessed with brand names. Based on your own observations, do you agree?

Argument

What's in a Brand?

A Brand by Any Other Name Would Fit as Sweet

Cody Martin

Someone can sell a red shirt with yellow polka dots and as long it has the right brand logo on it, people will buy it. The public is obsessed with name-brand clothes, and otherwise intelligent people spend their time and money in pursuit of the lifestyle they believe that brand promises.

When did fashion become reduced to "brand"? Why is a person's sense of style so often tied to a brand? Many people are attracted to a particular brand because of the stereotype represented by its ads. J. Crew represents the preppy fashion statement. Hot Topic appeals to those who favor gothstyle, and Abercrombie and Fitch is for the hard-bodied partiers. These brands not only stress these stereotypes in their ads; they reinforce them in their stores. If you want to apply for a job at Abercrombie, don't brush up on your computer skills, but do brush up on your abs. It's all about how you look in the clothes, not what you know about merchandising.

People are so obsessed by their desire to "fit" a brand that they will resort to all sorts of measures to "fit in." Despite the fact that doctors have proven too much sun is harmful to our skin, tanning salons continue to proliferate. You won't see any of the models for Tommy Hilfiger or Ralph Lauren with pasty white skin. On a recent episode of <u>Will & Grace</u>, Will had Botox injections when his friends told him he was too old to wear a shirt

> Description blended with examples of different styles

> Examples

Argument

from Abercrombie and Fitch. Is wearing a brand well more important than good health? And what about the impact on our wallets?

Narration

A good friend of mine has a son who is about to start kindergarten. She told me just the other day, "My son will be starting school this fall with all name brands." He's in kindergarten. Does he need a $26 dollar Tommy brand t-shirt to smear with paint? Wouldn't Fruit of the Loom work just as well for wiping his hands after lunch? What is she teaching him?

The Advertising Archive/The Picture Desk, Inc.

Name-brand obsession is creating a nation of fashion clones. What happened to mixing and matching different brands and styles to create your own look? When did fashion cease to be about creating your own look and become copying someone else's?

I shop in resale stores. From vacation t-shirts to leisure suits, they have it all. I mix old clothes with new to put my own twist on fashion. Unfortunately, too many people see the brand of the clothes, not the person in the clothes. But I don't care. I'm not a hard body; I'm not a preppy; I'm not a goth. I'm just me, and if clothes really do make the man, I'd rather make myself.

Consider this . . .

- ▪ How effective were the writing strategies used in this essay?
- ▪ Did the writer give his topic pertinence for his audience?
- ▪ The essay is fairly short. Did the writer say enough to make his point?

Look at the next essay. How did this professional writer use her observations about a cutlery phenomenon?

ORIGIN AND HOPEFULLY NON-EXISTENT FUTURE OF SPORKS

Lenore Skenazy

1   "Mom!" said my son, poking through our cutlery drawer, "where are the sporks?" Sporks. It was like being stabbed through the heart with a three-tined plastic spoon. Sporks? In my home? Where does he think we live, Taco Bell? But no, to my son, sporks are just a normal part of life, like shoes that Velcro shut and yogurt you suck from a tube. Yeah. It looks just as attractive as it sounds.

2   Anyway, you'll find these plastic spoon-fork hybrids in any school cafeteria. Spoon plus fork equals spork—or maybe it's spock plus mork equals spork. Either way, fast food lovers, jailed felons and kids in public school spork on a daily basis.

3   According to the Culinary Institute of America the spork is the only true American utensil. It is our answer to flatware just as the nugget is our answer to chicken cordon bleu. But however popular it is becoming, the spork's origins remain obscure.

4   From the beginning the spork got no respect, and historians agree why: It doesn't deserve any. Humans developed cutlery and cutlery developed humans. Using evermore complex utensils, we developed as civilized human beings. Once you could slice off a piece of mammoth, you didn't have to yank it out of someone else's paws. That's progress. After knives came even more civilizing spoons. Then in the 1500s Catherine de Medici moved from Italy to France bringing with her that newfangled fad: the fork. It caught on among royals, and pretty soon everyone who was anyone could eat without grabbing food by the fist.

5   Abandoning forks and spoons because we've got the spork is like abandoning reading and writing because we've got video games. By promoting spork culture in prison and school—the very institutions where we are trying hardest to civilize the inhabitants—we are lurching backward.

Consider this...

- What writing strategies did this author choose? Did she make good choices?
- What conclusions does she draw about the importance of cutlery, and sporks in particular?
- How did this writer make her description vivid?

Writer's Break

- Look at your Writer's Breaks from pages 177, 178, and 180, and choose the idea you like best.
- For this topic, choose a point you could make.
- Choose three writing strategies that would help you make that point.
- Choose an organizational pattern.

CHOOSING AN ORGANIZATIONAL METHOD

As with any essay, you have almost unlimited choices for organizing an observational essay. However, three organizational methods are especially applicable to an essay based on observations: spatial, chronological, and logical order.

☰ Spatial Order

When you organize a paper spatially, you base its structure on physical orientation. In other words, if you were describing a building, you could describe each room as you walked into it. If you were describing an object, you could describe it from top to bottom, or part by part. Essays based on observations often use spatial organization because the writer is describing something, someone, or someplace that he or she observed. In the essay "Road Signs," the writer uses spatial organization to move from a description of one nearby driver to a description of the next.

☰ Chronological Order

When we organize a piece of writing, such as a description of an event we've observed, chronologically, we order it based on the passage of time rather than the arrangement of space. Writing based on observations often uses chronological order because the writer presents the details of what he or she observed in the order in which they occurred.

≡ Logical Order

When you use logical order, you either begin with a general statement and then expand it or begin with specific details and then conclude with a general statement of their significance. In the essay on the spork, the writer uses a logical order blended with a chronological order. She begins with specific details: "It was like being stabbed through the heart with a three-tined plastic spoon." Then she develops her thesis by presenting the results of her research on the spork in chronological order based on the origin of cutlery.

In the next essay, the writer observes the influence of hairstyles on who people believe they really are. What organizational methods does she use?

HAIR

Marcia Aldrich

1   I've been around and seen the Taj Mahal and the Grand Canyon and Marilyn Monroe's footprints outside Grauman's Chinese Theater, but I've never seen my mother wash her own hair. After my mother married, she never washed her own hair again. As a girl and an unmarried woman—yes—but, in my lifetime, she never washed her hair with her own two hands. Upon matrimony, she began weekly treks to the beauty salon where Julie washed and styled her hair. Her appointment on Fridays at two o'clock was never cancelled or rescheduled; it was the bedrock of her week, around which she pivoted and planned. These two hours were indispensable to my mother's routine, to her sense of herself and what, as a woman, she should concern herself with—not to mention their being her primary source of information about all sorts of things she wouldn't otherwise come to know. With Julie my mother discussed momentous decisions concerning hair color and the advancement of age and what could be done about it, hair length and its effect upon maturity, when to perm and when not to perm, the need to proceed with caution when a woman desperately wanted a major change in her life like dumping her husband or sending back her newborn baby and the only change she could effect was a change in her hair. That was what Julie called a "dangerous time" in a woman's life. When my mother spoke to Julie, she spoke in conspiratorial, almost confessional,

tones I had never heard before. Her voice was usually tense, on guard, the laughter forced, but with Julie it dropped much lower, the timbre darker than the upper-register shrills sounded at home. And most remarkably, she listened to everything Julie said.

As a child I was puzzled by the way my mother's sense of self-worth and mood seemed dependent upon how she thought her hair looked, how the search for the perfect hairstyle never ended. Just as Mother seemed to like her latest color and cut, she began to agitate for a new look. The cut seemed to have become a melancholy testimony, in my mother's eyes, to time's inexorable passage. Her hair never stood in and of itself; it was always moored to a complex set of needs and desires her hair couldn't in itself satisfy. She wanted her hair to illuminate the relationship

between herself and the idea of motion while appearing still, for example. My mother wanted her hair to be fashioned into an event with a complicated narrative past. However, the more my mother attempted to impose a hairstyle pulled from an idealized image of herself, the more the hairstyle seemed to be at odds with my mother. The more the hairstyle became substantial, the more the woman underneath was obscured. She'd riffle through women's magazines and stare for long dreamy hours at a particular woman's coiffure. Then she'd ask my father in an artificially casual voice: "How do you think I'd look with really short hair?" or "Would blonde become me?" My father never committed himself to an opinion. He had learned from long experience that no response he made could turn out well; anything he said would be used against him, if not in the immediate circumstances, down the line, for my mother never forgot anything anyone ever said about her hair. My father's refusal to engage the "hair question" irritated her.

So too, I was puzzled to see that unmarried women washed their own hair, and married women, in my mother's circle at least, by some unwritten dictum never touched their own hair. I began studying before and after photographs of my mother's friends. These photographs were all the same. In the pre-married mode, their hair was soft and unformed. After the wedding, the women's hairstyles bore the stamp of property, looked constructed from grooming talents not their own, hairstyles I'd call produced, requiring constant upkeep and technique to sustain the considerable loft and rigidity—in short, the antithesis of anything I might naively call natural. This was hair no one touched, crushed, or ran fingers through. One poked and prodded various hair masses back into formation. This hair presented

obstacles to embrace, the scent of hair spray alone warded off man, child and pests. I never saw my father stroke my mother's head. Children ran when my mother came home fresh from the salon with a potent do. Just when a woman's life was supposed to be opening out into daily affection, *the* sanctioned affection of husband and children, the women of my mother's circle encased themselves in a helmet of hair not unlike Medusa's.

4   In so-called middle age, my mother's hair never moved, never blew, never fell in her face: her hair became a museum piece. When she went to bed, she wore a blue net, and when she took short showers, short because, after all, she wasn't washing her hair and she was seldom dirty, she wore a blue plastic cap for the sake of preservation. From one appointment to the next, the only change her hair could be said to undergo was to become crestfallen. Taking extended vacations presented problems sufficiently troublesome to rule out countries where she feared no beauty parlors existed. In the beginning, my parents took overnighters, then week jaunts, and thereby avoided the whole hair dilemma. Extending their vacations to two weeks was eventually managed by my mother applying more hairspray and sleeping sitting up. But after the two week mark had been reached, she was forced to either return home or venture into an unfamiliar salon and subject herself to scrutiny, the kind of scrutiny that leaves no woman unscathed. Then she faced Julie's disapproval, for no matter how expensive and expert the salon, my mother's hair was to be lamented. Speaking just for myself, I had difficulty distinguishing Julie's cunning from the stranger's. In these years my mother's hair looked curled, teased, and sprayed into a wave tossed monument with holes poked through for glasses. She believed the damage done to her hair was tangible proof she had been somewhere, like stickers on her suitcases.

5   My older sisters have worked out their hair position differently. My oldest sister's solution has been to fix upon one hairstyle and never change it. She wants to

be thought of in a singular fashion. She may vary the length from long to longer, but that is the extent of her alteration. Once, after having her first baby, the "dangerous time" for women, she recklessly cut her hair to just below the ear. She immediately regretted the decision and began growing it back as she walked home from the salon, vowing not to repeat the mistake. Her signature is dark, straight hair pulled heavily off her face in a large silver clip, found at any Woolworth's. When one clip breaks, she buys another just like it. My mother hates the timelessness of my sister's hair. She equates it with a refusal to face growing old. My mother says, "It's immature to wear your hair the same way all your life." My sister replies,

"It's immature to never stop thinking about your hair. If this hairstyle was good 6 enough when I was twenty, it's good enough when I'm forty, if not better."

"But what about change?" my mother asks. 7

"Change is overrated," my sister says flipping her long hair over her shoulder 8 definitively. "I feel my hair."

My other sister was born with thin, lifeless, nondescript hair: a cross she has had 9 to bear. Even in the baby pictures, the limp strands plastered on her forehead in question marks wear her down. Shame and self-effacement are especially plain in the pictures where she posed with our eldest sister, whose dark hair dominates the frame. She's spent her life attempting to disguise the real state of her hair. Some years she'd focus on style, pulling it back in ponytails so that from the front no one could see there wasn't much hair in the back. She tried artless, even messy styles—as if she had just tied it up any old way before taking a bath or bunched it to look deliberately snarled. There were the weird years punctuated by styles that looked as if she had taken sugar water and lemon juice and squeezed them onto her wet her and then let them crystallize. The worst style was when she took her hair and piled it on the top of her head in a cone shape and then crimped the ponytail into a zigzag. Personally, I thought she had gone too far. No single approach solved the hair problem, and so now, in maturity, she combines the various phases of attack in hope something will work. She frosts both the grey strands and the pale brown, and then perms for added body and thickness. She's forced to keep her hair short because chemicals do tend to destroy. My mother admires my sister's determination to transform herself, and never more than in my sister's latest assault upon middle age. No one has known for many years nor does anyone remember what the untreated color or texture of either my mother's or sister's hair might be.

10   As the youngest by twelve years, there was little to distract Mother's considerable attention from the problem of my hair. I had cowlicks, a remarkable number of them, which like little arrows shot across my scalp. They refused to be trained, to lie down quietly in the same direction as the rest of my hair. One at the front insisted on sticking straight up while two on either side of my ears jutted out seeking sun. The lack of uniformity, the fact that my hair had a mind of its own, infuriated my mother and she saw to it that Julie cut my hair as short as possible in order to curtail its wanton expression. Sitting in the swivel chair before the mirror while Julie snipped, I felt invisible, as if I was unattached to my hair.

11   Just when I started to menstruate, my mother decided the battle plan needed a change, and presto, the page boy replaced the pixie. Having not outgrown the thicket of cowlicks, Mother bought a spectrum of brightly colored stretch bands to hold my hair back off my face. Then she attached thin pink plastic curlers with snap on lids to the ends of my hair to make them flip up or under, depending on her mood. The stretch bands pressed my hair flat until the very bottom, at which point the ends formed a tunnel with ridges from the roller caps—a point of emphasis she called it. Coupled with the aquamarine eyeglasses, newly acquired, I looked like an overgrown insect that had none of its kind to bond with.

12   However, I was not alone. Unless you were the last in a long line of sisters, chances were good your hair would not go unnoticed by your mother. Each of my best friends was subjected to her mother's hair dictatorship, although with entirely different results. Perry Jensen's mother insisted that five of her daughters per-

Robertstock/Retrofile.com

oxide their hair blonde and pull it back into high ponytails. All the girls' hair turned green in the summer from chlorine. Melissa Matson underwent a look-alike "home perm" with her mother, an experience she never did recover from. She developed a phobic reaction to anything synthetic, which made life very expensive. Not only did mother and daughter have identical tight curls and wear mother-daughter outfits, later they had look-alike nose jobs.

13   In my generation, many women who survived hair bondage to their mothers

now experiment with hairstyles as one would test a new design: to see how it works, what it will withstand, and how it can be improved. Testing requires boldness, for often the style fails dramatically, as when I had my hair cut about a half inch long at the top, and it stood straight up like a tacky shag carpet. I had to live with the results, bear daily witness to the kinks in its design for nine months until strategies of damage control could be deployed. But sometimes women I know create a look that startles in its originality and suggests a future not yet realized.

The women in my family divide into two general groups: those who fasten upon one style, become identified with a look, and are impervious to change, weathering the years steadfastly, and those who, for a variety of reasons, are in the business of transforming themselves. In my sister's case, the quest for perfect hair originates in a need to mask her own appearance; in my mother's case, she wants to achieve a beauty of person unavailable in her own life story. Some women seek transformation, not out of dissatisfaction with themselves, but because hair change is a means of moving along in their lives. These women create portraits of themselves that won't last forever, a new hairstyle will write over the last.

14

Writer's Break

- For a topic that you selected in a previous Writer's Break, find at least three graphics that would help support your point.

- Incorporate these graphics into your draft. Do they strengthen your argument?

Since my mother dictated my hair, I never took a stand on the hair issue. In maturity, I'm incapable of assuming a coherent or consistent philosophy. I have wayward hair: it's always becoming something else. The moment it arrives at a recognizable style, it begins to undo itself, it grows, the sun colors it, it waves. When one hair pin goes in, another seems to come out. Sometimes I think I should follow my oldest sister—she claims to never give more than a passing thought to her hair and can't see what all the angst is about. She asks, "Don't women have better things to think about than their hair?"

15

I bite back: "But don't you think hair should reflect who you are?"

16

"To be honest, I've never thought about it. I don't think so. Cut your hair the same way, and lose yourself in something else. You're distracted from the real action."

17

I want to do what my sister says, but when I walk out into shop-lined streets, I automatically study women's hair and always with the same question: How did they arrive at their hair? Lately, I've been feeling more and more like my mother. I hadn't known how to resolve the dilemma until I found Rhonda. I don't know if I found Rhonda or made her up. She is not a normally trained hairdresser: she has a different set of eyes, unaffected. One day while out driving around to no place

18

in particular, at the bottom of a hill, I found: "Rhonda's Hair Salon—Don't Look Back" written on a life-size cardboard image of Rhonda. Her shop was on the top of this steep orchard planted hill, on a plateau with a great view that opened out and went on forever. I parked my car at the bottom and walked up. Zigzagging all the way up the hill, leaning against or sticking out from behind the apple trees were more life-sized cardboard likenesses of Rhonda. Except for the explosive sunbursts in her hair, no two signs were the same. At the bottom, she wore long red hair falling below her knees and covering her entire body like a shawl. As I climbed the hill, Rhonda's hair gradually became shorter and shorter, and each length was cut differently, until when I reached the top, her head was shaved and glistening in the sun. I found Rhonda herself out under one of the apple trees wearing running shoes. Her hair was long and red and looked as if it had never been cut. She told me she had no aspirations to be a hairdresser, "she just fell into it." "I see hair," she continued, "as an extension of the head and therefore I try to do hair with a lot of thought." Inside there were no mirrors, no swivel chairs, no machines of torture with their accompanying stink. She said, "Nothing is permanent, nothing is forever. Don't feel hampered or hemmed in by the shape of your face or the shape of your past. Hair is vital, sustains mistakes, can be born again. You don't have to marry it. Now tip back and put your head into my hands."

Consider this . . .

- Does this writer justify her evaluation of what she observed? Were you persuaded?
- Which writing strategies did the writer choose and how appropriate were they?
- How effective is the organization of this essay?

In this last essay, the writer draws his own conclusion concerning observations made about a longstanding climbing mystery.

SUMMIT SHOT

Tim Sohn

"I can't see myself coming down defeated," wrote 37-year-old Himalayan pioneer George Leigh Mallory shortly before his third assault on Mount Everest, in 1924. Nearly 80 years later, whether the British explorer was defeated remains the biggest mystery in mountaineering history. Did he and his 22-year-old climbing partner, Andrew Comyn Irvine, reach the summit of the world's tallest mountain 29 years before Sir Edmund Hillary and Tenzing Norgay? [1]

Mallory and Irvine—nattily outfitted in gabardine, the Gore-Tex of their day—departed their high camp early on the morning of June 8. They were last seen by fellow climber Noel Odell at 12:50 p.m. ascending one of the three rocky steps that characterize the upper reaches of Everest's difficult Northeast Ridge. But clouds soon enveloped the top of the mountain, and Mallory and Irvine vanished into the penumbral mist. [2]

Hard evidence in the case is scant. A 1933 British team found Irvine's ice ax below the first step at 27,760 feet, and one of their oxygen cylinders was found nearby in 1991. A 1999 expedition led by American climber Eric Simonson discovered Mallory's bleached and mummified body lying facedown at 26,760 feet. As incredible as that discovery was, there are still no answers. [3]

"The camera would be the definitive clue," says Simonson, alluding to the still-missing Vest Pocket Kodak that Mallory supposedly borrowed from a teammate for his summit bid. "And more evidence could absolutely be found up there." [4]

The final sighting of the two climbers—the starting point for the bulk of the subsequent speculation—became problematic as Odell equivocated in the days after the climb, unable to decide whether he had seen Mallory and Irvine grappling with the Northeast Ridge's relatively benign first step or the far more difficult second step. Climbers on the ridge today bypass the crux of the second step via a rickety ladder. The only group to ascend it in pre-ladder days, a four-man summit team from the 1960 Chinese expedition, did so with the aid of pitons—equipment that Mallory and Irvine did not have. [5]

Dave Hahn/Mallory & Irvine/Getty Images

6   Everest veteran and filmmaker David Breashears, director of the 1987 documentary *Everest: The Mystery of Mallory and Irvine*, says there's no way the duo could have free-climbed the second step—and, thus, they could not have reached the summit. "At over 28,000 feet, in an unprotected lead with a bowline around his waist and hobnail boots, and with Irvine on a marginally anchored or possibly unanchored belay stance, Mallory climbs something as hard or harder than he'd ever climbed at sea level?" asks Breashears. "It is not only ludicrous to think they could do that; it is a flight of fancy."

7   American climber Conrad Anker, the 1999 expedition team member who found Mallory's body, agrees. "Saying that they could have climbed the second step is putting the romantic dream ahead of the factual evidence, and that, in a sense, does a disservice to the climbers," he says. "There's just no way they climbed the second step without gear."

8   But Simonson, who returned to Everest in 2001 for an unsuccessful attempt to find Irvine, refuses to rule out the possibility. "On a good day, sufficiently motivated, people do some amazing things," he says, referring to Mallory's indomitable will. "It's my opinion that it was possible for them to climb the second step."

9   Simonson is contemplating another fact-finding expedition to the mountain, spurred by the recent revelation that Xu Jing, a climber on the 1960 Chinese

expedition, encountered a body—possibly Irvine's—in decaying old clothes, lying supine, arms frozen to his sides, on a section of the Northeast Ridge. If that is Irvine's body, perhaps he holds the final answer to mountaineering's long-standing debate in his icy grip.

Consider this . . .

- What writing strategies did this writer use?
- What organizational method did he use?
- What point did he make with his observations of the mountain, the bodies and equipment found on the mountain, and the reports of other climbers?

MUCH OF THE WRITING you will do—not only the writing for your English classes—will be based on observation. Most scientific writing is based on observation, as is writing in fields such as psychology and anthropology and journalism. Learn to pay attention to what is going on around you, and rather than just letting it flow past you, be aware, draw conclusions, and make notes. ■

COLLABORATIVE EXERCISES

Group Exercise One

As a group, spend some time making observations. To do this, you might go to a local coffee house, go to the library and flip through magazines, or watch TV together. As you observe, try to draw a conclusion based on what you see. Once you reach a conclusion, write a few paragraphs about what you observed and what it means.

Group Exercise Two

Find an example of an essay that is based on the writer's observations. After you read the essay, answer these questions:

- What conclusion did the writer draw from his or her observations?
- How effectively did the writer justify his or her conclusion?
- Were you convinced that the writer made a valid point?

Be prepared to share your answers with the class.

Group Exercise Three

Look at each of the following short essays. Each one was written by a group of students in response to Group Exercise One.

Privileged Athletes

Ever since grade school, athletes have always been known as the special ones. The ones who teachers bend the rules for. They never have to go to class and yet they always somehow pass. A lot of times, the behavior doesn't stop in school. It carries them through college. This happens a lot when athletes are given full scholarships to play some type of sport, relieving the financial burden off of their back. Don't get me wrong, some deserve it, but a lot of them don't deserve it and therefore that money could be given to someone excelling in academics.

Athletes are pampered on and off the field so much until they begin to play a certain role wherever they're at. This behavior consists of them believing they can do whatever they want to do to whoever they choose. Now we see lots of athletes in trouble with the law because they feel above it. This behavior leads to nothing but bad things in the long run.

It's hard to say what it will take to put a stop to this behavior, but it dates back to grade school. So if you wait until they've got far as even high school and try to change things, it could be too late.

Music Lovers

Most of us like some type of music. Depending on how much we like it usually determines how much time we will spend with it, be that listening, creating or searching for. Observing people as they search for "that" CD is quite a sight. Usually when people go into a music store, they fall into two categories: the looking and the known. We observed a man today who knew what he was looking for. This man went straight to the section which he knew the album would be in, and proceeded to flip every disk in search of the "one."

Upon finding it, the emotion of joy and appeasement fell over his face as he was probably already listening to the CD in his head. However, he didn't stop there, he continued looking except he wasn't really looking. There were a few times in the search where he would let out a sensual "Awwww man!" He did this whenever he came across an album that he wasn't expecting to see. There also would be some occasional compromising with himself. What I mean is he would pick up a potential CD and check the price, then look into his wallet and begin to compromise if his money was right to buy the unexpected joy and the known album. After about 5 to 7 minutes, he walked over to the register with just the known album with great dissatisfaction written across his face. The cashier asked "You fine, everything okay?" He replied, "Yes, but I'm seriously coming back later on today to get another CD." The cashier then replied, "Hey, your business is always welcome, so please by every means, come on back!" That was said in a very cheerful persuasive tone. The customer walked out asking what time the music shop closed, so he could be sure to make it back before closing.

Now look at the revised versions of these essays:

Privileged Athletes (Revised Version)

Ever since high school, we have seen athletes receive special treatment in school. More than one "star" football player missed class the day of a big game because he was "working out." This same athlete, who was always absent when the rest of us were taking tests, always passed. A lot of times, this special treatment doesn't stop in high school. It continues in college. When schools recruit athletes and give them full athletic scholarships, they are more concerned with how well the athletes perform on the field rather than in the class. And tutors for the school athletic association report trying to help many students who would never graduate from college because they never studied. Unfortunately, they would never be professional athletes either. Their coaches knew this, but they still continued to encourage them to neglect their classes. Don't take this the wrong way; some athletes deserve scholarships, but a lot of them don't, and that money could be given to someone excelling in academics as well as athletics, who truly deserves the special treatment.

This special treatment that athletes receive on and off the field makes them believe they can do whatever they want to do to whomever they choose. How often do you pick up the paper, or turn on the news and learn about athletes in trouble with the law? Look at Mike Tyson, for example. He served time in prison for sexual assault, yet the Boxing Association still allowed him to continue to fight professionally. What about Michael Irvin of the Dallas Cowboys? He was arrested multiple times for possession of illegal substances, yet the NFL allowed him to continue playing. This sort of special treatment sets a bad example. What sorts of values are children, who admire these players, learning when they see them receive special treatment?

It's hard to say what it will take to put a stop to this behavior, but something needs to be done. Perhaps it is time to reconsider the value we put on sports in our society.

Music Lovers (Revised Version)

Observing people as they search for that "perfect" CD is quite a sight. Usually when people go into a music store, they fall into two categories: the browsers and the seekers. Browsers come to look. They stroll around casually. They flip CDs at random. They wander from one section to the next. They are waiting for the electric jolt you get when your hand makes contact with your day's musical destiny. Seekers have a mission. They ignore the sales staff. They move like guided missiles toward their target. Once they make contact, they retrieve the CD, move to the check-out and complete their mission without ever looking up.

We observed a man today who was a seeker. This man went straight to the section which he knew the album would be in, and proceeded to flip every disk in search of the "one." His face lit up when he found it, and his lips began moving as he started listening to the CD in his head. However, he didn't stop there, he transformed into a browser right before our eyes. He roved slowly around the store, fondling the CDs and letting out a sensual "Awwww man!" when he found one that excited him. Every time he found a potential candidate, he would rummage through his wallet, mentally calculating his money to see if he could afford to take home two prizes rather than one. After about 5 to 7 minutes, he walked over to the register with just the album he'd come in search of, great dissatisfaction written across his face. The cashier asked, "You fine, everything okay?" He replied, "Yes, but I'm seriously coming back later on today to get another CD." The cashier then replied, "Hey, your business is always welcome, so please by all means, come on back!" As he walked out, the customer asked, "What time do you dudes close?" He was once more a man with a mission.

- How do the revised versions of the essays differ from the first versions?

- Make a list of specific changes that the writers made to improve their essays.

- Share your lists with the class.

WRITING PICKS

Option One

Is beauty a myth?

How we dress, how we wear our hair, even how much we weigh is affected by what we see and hear. We are bombarded by images on TV, in magazines, on billboards, on the Internet, and in the movies, telling us how we should look. Society's conceptions of beauty do not develop abstractly. They are based on the stereotypes that are presented in the media. During the seventeenth century, Rubens depicted women as full-bodied and voluptuous, and his paintings set a standard of beauty for his time. Today, these women would be considered overweight; their image has been replaced by that of the gaunt, unisex waif. How do the fashion industry and the media have the power to sell an image to the public? Based on your observations, how do media stereotypes affect how we look at ourselves? At others? How do these stereotypes permeate our everyday lives? Do they hurt us or help us?

The Toilette of Venus by Peter Paul Rubens. Private Collection/Bridgewater Art Library, London/Superstock

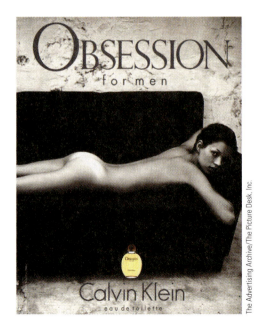

The Advertising Archive/The Picture Desk, Inc.

Option Two

Revelations from buying habits

Pretend that you are from another country and have been sent to the United States to observe the inhabitants. In particular, you are interested in their buying habits and how they make choices regarding what they purchase. In order to do this, you look not only at the people but also at the media that influence their choices. For example, you might notice the large number of ads for weight-loss products. What do these ads say about the people they target? What influence have they had on people's appearance? What about fast food or pet food? Observe some highly visible influence on Americans' purchasing habits, and consider what it says about the people and their beliefs about who they are and what's important.

The Advertising Archive/The Picture Desk, Inc.

Option Three

Places in the heart

The places that are important to us—our homes, our towns, our schools, our farms and forests—say something about who we are and what matters to us. Describe a place that has importance for you, and try to help your readers understand why the place has significance for you. Draw some conclusions about what it says about you as a person.

Photodisc/Getty Images

Option Four

A material world

Look at the eBay home page. What does the information on this page tell us about ourselves? How does it represent consumer society? Analyze the Web site, being careful to observe it closely. Write an essay in which you draw a conclusion about our society based on what you see.

APPLYING THE RHETORICAL SITUATION

As always, you must consider the rhetorical situation throughout the process of making choices for observational writing. Use these questions to guide your decision making.

Audience

- What interest or knowledge does your audience have about what you have observed?

- What information does your audience need about what you observed in order to understand its significance?

- Did you give specific description and examples?

- Do you have enough information, or do you need to do a more thorough observation?

- Are you using any specialized vocabulary that you will need to define for your audience?

Purpose

- What point are you trying to make? What do you want your readers to understand about what you observed?

- What techniques can you use to make your point?

- How can you structure your essay to emphasize that point?

- Have you used figurative language? Have you appealed to all the senses?

Occasion

- How can you describe what you observed in a way that will allow your readers to see what you saw?

- How can you make them share your observations without getting bored?

- How can you make them understand the significance of your conclusions?

FOCUSING ON PROCESS

Prewriting

- Take a sheet of paper and divide it into three columns.

- In the first column, paste pictures that you consider representative of current American stereotypes regarding appearance or eating.

- In the next column, write at least three descriptive words about each picture. Choose words that reflect your feelings about the pictures.

- In the last column, write words that describe the society that produced these pictures.

Drafting

- Choose a time and a place when you can have your computer to yourself.

- Give yourself two hours of uninterrupted writing time.

- Before you start writing, turn down the monitor brightness and the sound so that you can't see or hear anything. For the full two hours, write without being able to see what's on the screen.

- When the two hours are up, turn the brightness back up on the monitor and see what you have.

Revision

- Twenty-four hours after you have written your draft, take a copy of it to your computer.

- Start from the beginning and retype your paper. As you type, make changes where they are needed. Look for opportunities to improve the paper.

- How many changes did you make while you typed?

Editing

- When you think your paper is done, read it out loud and mark every word, phrase, or sentence that sounds funny or off.

- Go back over the marked parts and try to decide why they don't work. Read the paper out loud again, to someone else. What do they think?

- Run a spell check. Have someone else read the paper out loud to you.

Grammar Choices

COMPOUND COMPLEX SENTENCES

Every compound complex sentence contains

- At least two **independent clauses**.

- At least one **dependent clause**.

How you punctuate a compound complex sentence depends on where the dependent clause is placed relative to the independent clause. When the dependent clause comes first, it is followed by a comma:

> **When she went to bed**, **she wore a blue net**, and **when she took short showers, short because, after all, she wasn't washing her hair and she was seldom dirty**, **she wore a blue plastic cap for the sake of preservation**.

> **As I chewed on my ragged cuticles**, **I admired her perfectly manicured nails**, and **I stopped chewing**.

When the dependent clause follows the independent clause, it is not necessarily preceded by a comma:

> **Don't brush up on your computer skills**, but **do brush up on your abs** **if you want to apply for a job at Abercrombies**.
> **I hadn't known how to resolve the dilemma** **until I found Rhonda**, and **I don't know** **if I found Rhonda or made her up**.

Making It Work

- Underline each independent clause in your paper once and each dependent clause twice. Identify sentences that are compound complex.

- Check the punctuation of each compound complex sentence, and make any necessary corrections.

- If your paper has no compound complex sentences, combine some sentences to create a few.

Style Choices

SIMILES AND METAPHORS

You can use two different types of figures of speech to give your writing greater expressiveness. Similes and metaphors are both useful for comparing one thing to another, and these comparisons help you do several things. You can compare an abstract concept to a concrete idea:

My love is like a red red rose. —Robert Burns

You can compare one thing to another thing that is very different:

Lusts were raging fires, and men were the fuel. —*The Jungle*, Upton Sinclair

. . . then the glow faded, each light deserting her face with lingering regret like children leaving a pleasant street at dusk. —*The Great Gatsby*, F. Scott Fitzgerald

Similes

When you write a simile, you say something is like something else:

His eyes are like two bottle caps.

She carried her secret like a mother carries a child.

Chocolate is like love. You can never get enough.

Metaphors

When you write a metaphor, you literally say one thing is another thing:

The sun is a copper penny.

The cold is a brazen monster.

Tourists are all children at history's knee, begging for some snatch of song or scrap of idea to play with. —*Why Stop?* Mary Hood

Use metaphors and similes sparingly, or they will lose their impact.

Making It Work

- Identify any metaphors and similes in your draft or essay.

- Are they interesting or clichéd?

- If you didn't find any figures of speech, add at least one metaphor and one simile.

THE APPEAL OF MUSIC

Writing to Inform

In this chapter, you will learn:

- How writing can be used to share information—to teach, to inform, or to persuade

- The writing strategies often used to share information—definition, process, and interview

- The organizational methods often used to share information—conceptual, logical, and chronological order

Neal Preston/Corbis

Benefit concerts are one means of informing a diverse audience about a worthy cause, as well as raising money for it.

Most students think that all writing is meant to share information, and in a way, this is true. However, as you know from having learned about the rhetorical situation, your purpose will change, depending on whom you are writing for and why. When your purpose for writing changes, so does the type of information you present and the way you present it.

For example, if you decided to write an essay about how music affects teenagers today, you could have several different purposes:

- To persuade—music positively affects teenagers

- To tell a personal story—how music changed your life as a teenager

- To solve a problem—how music helps teenagers deal with emotional stress

Essays written on these topics would all share information, but they would present different information because each has a different purpose. The purpose determines the focus of the essay.

MAKING CHOICES WHEN YOU WRITE TO INFORM

The first step you take when you decide to write a paper to share information is to identify some information worth sharing. In order to determine whether a topic you have chosen is worthwhile, ask yourself these questions:

- Will this information be useful to my readers?

- Who can benefit from this information?

- Is the information accurate?

≡ Evaluating Topics for Informational Writing

We all have a lot of information. You are probably an expert on several subjects, whether you realize it or not. For example, you probably know quite a bit about some of these subjects:

- Tanning
- Music
- Peer pressure
- Sports
- Movies
- Food
- Relationships

Let's say you choose to write about tanning. Which of these more specific topics involves information that is worth sharing?

- Why I like to tan
- Which tanning oil is best
- Young people's obsession with tanning
- How to get a really dark tan
- Health risks of tanning

Writer's Break

Make a list of five topics that you know a great deal about and five topics that you would like to know more about.

- For each topic you have listed, write a brief sentence stating why you would or would not want to write about this topic.
- Rank the topics in order from 1 to 10, with 1 being your first choice.

The information relating to the first topic is probably interesting only to you; it is not information that anyone else can use. When a reader reads to gain information, he or she wants the information to be useful and pertinent and accurate. After all, do you read instruction manuals for fun, or because you need the information they contain? Certainly, you would never pick up the manual for your DVD player unless you had to.

If you wrote about the second topic—which tanning oil is best—you might provide information useful to a few people. Tanning oil is not a major investment, however. Consequently, most people aren't going to look for information on it before they make their purchase, as they would if they were buying a car or some other expensive item. Some specialty magazines, such as *Shape*, *Fitness*, *Cosmopolitan*, and *GQ*, might print an article about the best tanning oil. But keep in mind that such a limited topic has a limited audience.

The third topic—young people's obsession with tanning—involves information that is probably worth sharing. Young people, as evidenced by the number of tanning salons across the country, do seem to consider a tan an essential attribute. As a young person, this trend has the potential to affect you both financially and physically. Because the information that you learned in order to write about this topic would be both pertinent and useful to you and to other young people, it is worth sharing. Even if you don't tan, you might be interested in knowing why so many other people do.

Like the information on different tanning oils, information on how to get a really dark tan might not interest many people. Consequently, that topic has limited appeal. However, information regarding the health risks of tanning is worth sharing because so many people are thus affected by it. Information like this could convince some people to stop tanning and ultimately save their lives. This topic is not frivolous—it could help people in a meaningful way.

So, remember, when you are trying to decide what information is worth sharing, consider whether it is useful, whether it has a potential audience, and whether it is accurate.

Making Information the Focus of an Essay

When you gather information for an essay, you eventually have to decide which information you need to include, because you can't include everything. You have to have all the necessary parts in the right order, or you end up with something unintelligible.

The only way to decide what information to include is to decide what you want your readers to learn. For instance, in a paper about the topic of the health risks of tanning, which of the pieces of information below would you want to include and which ones should you leave out?

- UV rays damage the skin.

- Tanning may lead to skin cancer.

- A tan gives you a healthy glow.

- Tanning causes premature aging.

- Some tanning oils contain pigments that make you tan more quickly.

If you are trying to provide information about the health risks of tanning, you should not include two items in this list: "A tan gives you a healthy glow," and "Some tanning oils contain pigments that make you tan more quickly." Neither of these pieces of information has anything to do with the health risks of tanning, even though they do relate to tanning.

After you have gathered all of your information, or even while you are gathering it, remember to ask yourself, "Does this piece of information relate to what I want my readers to learn?" If not, don't use it.

Look at the following essay written by a student in response to Option Four at the end of this chapter. What sort of information does this writer share? Is it information you can use?

Writer's Break

Make a list of five people you would like to interview. Do not include people who are not living or people you are not likely to be able to contact.

- For each person you listed, write a brief description of what you want to learn from him or her.

- For each person, state what you would have to do in order to contact him or her.

Hey Mom, Who Were the Rolling Stones?

Paula Mathis

Reason for writing—to analyze and compare two music Web sites

Different types of music have always appealed to different age groups, and today, innovative music Web sites are finding creative ways to sell music to their target audiences. Rolling Stone magazine has been a source of musical information for decades, and now it brings information to readers in a new venue--the Web. Radio Disney, a radio station exclusively for kids fourteen and under, started its Web site simultaneously because the newcomer to the radio waves knew today's kids are Internet savvy.

Background information

Radio Disney and Rolling Stone both have Web sites that focus on the music world, but visitors to the two sites come from very different demographic groups, and the designers of the two sites are exceptionally aware of this fact. While Radio Disney caters to the elementary/middle school crowd, Rolling Stone's Web site, like its magazine, targets thirty-something-and-up rockers. A comparison of the two Web sites shows that, although the two share similar features such as advertisements, polls, and sweepstakes, the Web sites are created to attract exclusively the browsers who make up each one's targeted audience.

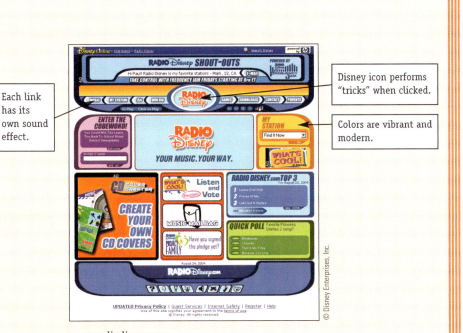

Each link has its own sound effect.

Disney icon performs "tricks" when clicked.

Colors are vibrant and modern.

www.radiodisney.com

The first noticeable difference between the two sites is their links. <u>Radio Disney</u> has these links: Music, My Station, DJs, Win Big, Games, Downloads, Contact, and Parents. Only a site with a target audience that is under fourteen would feature either "Parents," or "Games" as links. <u>Rolling Stone</u> has these links: News, Reviews, Photos, Videos, Community, Politics, and Services. Furthermore, the "Services" offered include dating services and site affiliations, and ticket sales. Only adults have a use for these services.

First point followed by specific examples

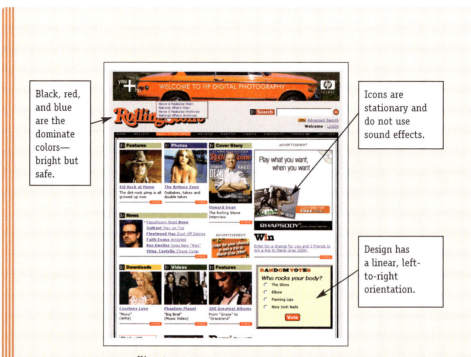

Black, red, and blue are the dominate colors—bright but safe.

Icons are stationary and do not use sound effects.

Design has a linear, left-to-right orientation.

www.rollingstone.com

Second point followed by specific examples

Both sites offer polls as a regular feature, but again, both are uniquely suited to their target audience. <u>Radio Disney</u> has, in the past, asked what its browsers consider the coolest trend. Most folks over thirty could care less about whether they show up to work wearing the ultimate cool shoes, but for a twelve-year-old, lack of such footwear at school could be social suicide. <u>Rolling Stone</u> has asked its readers to consider which bands should release new albums--a question that <u>Radio Disney</u> browsers would be unable to answer because the bands listed all existed years before they were born. Ten- and eleven-year-olds have no interest in which classic bands might decide to reunite for one more song.

The sweepstakes featured by both sites also target their specific audiences very effectively. Both Web sites offer the chance to win great parties, but Radio Disney wants its browsers to party at Disney's Music Awards, while Rolling Stone offers a trip to Mardi Gras. By offering unlimited juice boxes versus unlimited jello-shots, both sites define "party" differently and capture the interest of their target.

Beyond the obvious age-related differences, other factors point to differences between the two sites. Radio Disney encourages its browser to send "a shout out to your friends." Rolling Stone offers no shout out, but it does encourage readers to access the various articles featured in the magazine of the same name. Additionally, while Rolling Stone offers critical reviews of various musical groups, Radio Disney simply offers a list of the songs voted most popular by listeners.

Finally the appearance of the sites themselves is different. The Radio Disney page is bright, colorful, and frenetic. Icons and

Third point

Additional information

Final point

bits of information flash, spin, and bounce--like the kids them-selves. Every link is accompanied by a sound effect. The <u>Rolling Stone</u> site, on the other hand, is more sedate, tending toward a more sophisticated palette of colors and a more linear design. The site is still flashy, but not hyperactive.

Conclusion

The creators of both Web sites had their audiences very much in mind when they created their sites. While the sites may seem initially similar because of their emphasis on music, a closer analysis shows them to be very different sites suited to very different users.

Consider this . . .

- Does the writer of this essay provide enough information to support her argument?
- How does the information provided with the graphics improve the quality of the essay?
- Could providing more information have improved this essay?

CHOOSING STRATEGIES TO SHARE INFORMATION

As with any type of writing, writing to share information tends to use certain strategies. There are several that you can use successfully:

- Definition
- Process
- Interview

Definition

When you define something, you tell your readers what it is. You can define something in any of a number of ways:

- Identifying the class to which it belongs
- Identifying its parts
- Describing how it works
- Comparing it to something else
- Saying what it is not
- Quoting an authority on the subject

Process

Sometimes we share information with our readers so that they can either do something or understand how something is done. For example, if you want to know how to file your tax returns, you need instructions on how to file. If you want to make spaghetti, you follow a step-by-step guide called a *recipe*. Other times we learn about doing something we know we can't do, so that we can understand it better. For example, humans do not have the ability to fly, but we can read about how birds fly in order to understand the process.

When we use process as a writing strategy, we break an overall process down into steps; we usually use graphics also. This is the sort of writing that is often called *technical writing*. When we write an essay about a process, we do it to share information, not necessarily so that readers can carry out the process, but perhaps so that they can simply learn about it in more detail.

☰ Interview

When you are sharing information about a person or a particular group of people, it is often effective to gather the information from the individual or individuals themselves and present it in the form of an interview.

Writer's Break

From the list you made for the Writer's Break on page 217, choose three people to interview.

- For each person, write a thesis statement that specifies the focus of your interview.
- Make a list of ten interview questions for each person, based on the thesis statements you wrote.

Most of you are familiar with interviews that are presented in a question and answer format. Although these can be interesting, they are pure interviews, not essays based on interviews. When you write a pure interview, you usually include every question and every answer; you do not filter the information or draw conclusions for your readers. The interview's organization mirrors the order in which you asked the questions. When you write an essay based on an interview, you use the information you gather from the interview as the raw material; you shape it based on your purpose. You determine the organization of the material, and you choose when to use direct quotes and when to paraphrase.

Look at the following student essay. The writer uses a number of strategies to inform her audience about what she believes is the source of boy bands' success.

Boy Bands--Here to Stay

Kathryn Lee

Around 1987, my cousins introduced me to New Kids on the Block. I was just six years old, but I had to listen to their music. I even slept on New Kids on the Block sheets each night. Why? Why this obsession with a bunch of boys who could sing a good melody? Was it the music they sang or was it their pretty faces? Was it the marketing that placed their faces everywhere a young girl would look? Young girls still listen to boy bands, and now I know why.

Boy bands are not accidents. They are specifically created to appeal to a specific target audience--young women. In his

Reason for writing--to share information

Organizational method--conceptual blended with chronological

Point--creation of the concept

article "Are Boy Bands a Viable Launch Vehicle for Space Tourism?" Richard Perry suggests that "these boy bands are 'manufactured' to meet very demanding commercial criteria, and for an audience which completely repopulates in five years." These bands are usually composed of five members, who are often chosen more for their appearance and ability to dance than their ability to sing. They rarely produce their own music, but sing what is written by their producers.

Point—importance of image

Example

The group's success is tied to its image, and often "each group member will have some distinguishing feature and be portrayed as having a particular personality stereotype--such as 'the baby,' 'the bad boy,' 'the nice boy'" ("Boy Band"). The member's appearance is tied to the personality of that person. For example, Back Street Boys' good boy, Nick Carter, has short blonde hair and blue-eyes—all-American good looks. Bad boy Kevin has long hair, a moustache and beard.

Point—development of boy bands

The boy band trend started with New Kids on the Block--the first successful "white" boy band. It was composed of Donnie Wahlberg, Jordan Knight, Jon Knight, and Joe McIntyre--all from music and/or theater backgrounds. The group released its first

Chronological
organization

album in 1986, but it didn't do well. It wasn't until the group re-released the same album in 1989 that they hit the big time. How-ever, in the 1990s the band broke up to pursue individual careers. The death of New Kids, however, was not the death of boy bands.

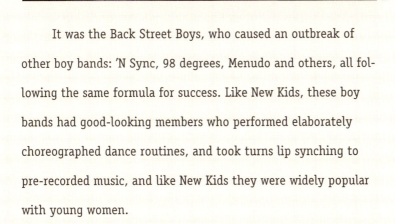

Robin Platzer/Time Life Pictures/Getty Images

Point—influence of boy
bands

It was the Back Street Boys, who caused an outbreak of other boy bands: 'N Sync, 98 degrees, Menudo and others, all fol-lowing the same formula for success. Like New Kids, these boy bands had good-looking members who performed elaborately choreographed dance routines, and took turns lip synching to pre-recorded music, and like New Kids they were widely popular with young women.

Point—length of careers

Despite their popularity, boy bands tend to have relatively short careers. The general opinion among music critics is that boy bands tend to enjoy a short success because the young women who listen to them grow up and lose interest. I asked my cousin Erin, who is 9 years old, if she had ever heard of Back Street Boys. She said, "All you have to do is turn on Radio Disney."

Point—age of target listeners

Clearly young women are the primary fans of boy bands, which explains why boy bands are destined to have short careers. Radio Disney is a highly popular radio station for kids between the ages of 4 and 14. According to Erin, "Radio Disney plays Back Street Boys all the time, and they still play 'N Sync and other new groups such as O-Town," so clearly, boy bands do continue to be popular with the younger crowds. However, after the age of fourteen, Radio Disney listeners move on to other stations.

Conclusion

Because of their looks, their dancing, and the fact that young girls like to see them on lunch boxes, boy bands seem to be here to stay. I listened to them, and now a new generation is listening to them. Whatever it is they do, they must do it well.

Works Cited

"Boy Band." <u>Wikipedia</u>. 2004 <http://www.wikipedia.org/wiki/Boy_band>.

Perry, Richard. "Are Boy Bands a Viable Launch Vehicle for Space Tourism?" *Space Daily* 18 July 2002 <http://www.spacer.com/news/tourism-02j.html>.

Consider this . . .

- Was the information in this essay worth sharing? Did you learn anything?
- Did the writer choose effective writing strategies?
- How could she have improved her essay?

In the following essay, the writer tells us how rock-and-roll became cool.

Birth of the Cool

Michael Satchell

1 We had the teenage attitude—surly lite, with a veneer of indifference. We had the threads—Edwardian-style draped jackets, drainpipe pants, and crepe-soled "brothel creeper" suede shoes. What we didn't have yet, on my side of the Atlantic nor in the States, was the music.

Organizational method—chronological

2 England in the early 1950s was a nation of rigid convention and white-bread culture, enveloped in the lingering depression of the post–World War II era. I lived in the drab and dreary industrial Midlands, and entertainment was mostly whatever mischief you could scare up. High school was Latin verbs and English Lit boring. Food was fish and chips and mushy peas boring. The weather was leaden skies and eternal drizzle boring.

3 Television, still in its flickering infancy, was black and white and talking heads boring. There was no commercial radio, and the BBC wireless diet of news from Whitehall and weather that never changed was boring to the point of stupefaction. As for music, Auntie Beeb offered either classical chestnuts or innocuous American pop—Rosemary Clooney, Doris Day, Kay Starr, Perry Como, Mario Lanza, Nat King Cole—a schmaltzfest guaranteed to induce crashing ennui.

4 And then, outta nowhere, came Bill Haley.

5 It was on the jukebox in a coffee bar called the Casa de Bolero that I first heard it in late 1953 or 1954: "Crazy Man, Crazy," an exuberant, pulsating blend of guitars, sax, and piano, riding the beat of a slap-back bass and a whip-crack snare. It was utterly different from any music we had ever heard. Unlike teens in America,

we had no opportunities to twirl the radio dial and listen to gospel, country, swing, rhythm and blues, boogie, rockabilly, or the other styles that birthed rock-and-roll. We had yawned through "Once I had a Secret Love" and "How Much is That Doggie in the Window?" for the last time. Now, we had music *you could dance to*. It was exciting. It was cool. It was ours.

6   **Cowboy poet.** But who was this chubby chap with a spitcurl who looked like he should be wearing a straw boater and a butcher's apron instead of a tartan tux and a rhythm guitar? We didn't know Bill Haley had been the leader of a Pennsylvania cowboy band who had tired of country, yodeling, and Western swing; who added drums and sax to his lineup, changed the band's name from the Saddlemen to the Comets, and was about to become the first—and one of the most successful—of the early blue-eyed rockers. Like others who soon followed—Jerry Lee Lewis, Elvis, the Everly Brothers, even Pat Boone—Haley borrowed (or stole) styles and beats and licks and tunes from black artists who had a tough time getting airplay and gigs, and then sold millions more records than the "race music" versions.

7   After "Crazy Man, Crazy," for example, Haley's next big hit was "Shake, Rattle, and Roll," a cover of Big Joe Turner's R&B classic. In what was to become a familiar pattern, the earthy lyrics were rewritten to skirt the American censors—and the BBC bluenoses. In 1954, with "Shake, Rattle and Roll" on its way to becoming the first million-selling rock platter, we bounced in front of the Casa de Bolero jukebox, singing: "Wearing those dresses, your hair's done up so nice; you look so warm, but your heart is cold as ice." We had no idea that Haley had bowdlerized the lyrics from: "When you wear your dresses, the sun comes shining though; I can't believe my eyes that all of this belongs to you."

Mirrorpix

8   In 1955 came one of those seminal events that captured the first fusion of rock music and teenage rebellion and dramatized the birth of an era when youth culture

found its identity and expression through its own music. The American movie *Blackboard Jungle*, a switchblade drama of violent high school kids and their passion for rock-and-roll, featured Haley's recording of "Rock Around the Clock," a reworking of a blues number entitled "My Daddy Rocks Me With a Steady Roll." The film was a hit, and the song became history's most successful rock single, selling more than 25 million copies.

Death threats. It helped make Haley a megastar in his homeland, where he toured with black artists like the Platters, the Drifters, and Bo Diddley, drawing teenage crowds but triggering riots, vandalism and death threats in the segregated South. Kids everywhere loved the raw, primitive music that parents, politicians, and clergy saw as harmful, perhaps even a Communist plot to undermine teen morals. J. Edgar Hoover put his FBI gumshoes on Haley to dig for dirt, and Frank Sinatra declared: "Rock-and-roll is phony and false and sung, written and played for the most part by cretinous goons." A Jersey City ordinance banned Haley and the Comets from performing: "Rock-and-roll music encouraged juvenile delinquency and inspired young females in lewd bathing suits to perform obscene dances on the city's beaches." Said Haley, who took to carrying a gun for protection: "Everybody hates us . . . except the kids."

He also inspired fear and loathing in England. When Haley's first movie, the biographical *Rock Around the Clock*, opened in the summer of 1956, we caught the bus to the Trocadero cinema—me resplendent in a hand-me-down, powder-blue Edwardian suit—and bopped in the aisles while gangs of authentic Teddy Boys, with their street punk attitude and straight-razor weapons, tossed light bulbs from the balcony, slashed theater seats and scared everyone half to death. The same thing happened across the country, and the movie was banned in many cities.

Soon after, Fleet Street tabloids were apoplectic when it was announced that the pied piper of rock-and-roll havoc would tour England in February 1957. "Bill Haley, music's Attila the Hun with guitar and drums, plans another path of destruction across Great Britain," thundered one editorial. "Theater owners and police officials quiver as he readies to lead his legions of Teddy Boys on to greater heights of wanton mayhem and civil disorder."

Street-fightin' men. Haley was actually horrified by the violence, and it was to bedevil him the following year with serious riots in France and Germany that cost him a small fortune in damages and canceled dates. In what was dubbed the "Second Battle of Berlin," the Comets were forced from stage as rival gangs fought each other and the police in a massive bloody battle. Once again, the former singing cowboy with the world's most famous cowlick was blamed—this time in a Communist propaganda broadside. "Rock-and-roll gangster Haley produces an orgy of American uncivilization [turning] the youth of the land of Bach and Beethoven into raging beasts," charged a newspaper in East Berlin. Still, his 1957 sellout British concerts were peaceful—although huge throngs of fans besieged hotels and train stations in scenes that weren't to be repeated until Beatlemania erupted some six years later. (John Lennon, then 16, and his pal Paul McCartney were in the audience at the Liverpool concert.)

13　　Biographers have anointed Haley as the Father of Rock and the genre's first international superstar, but his preeminence lasted just four years. After 1958, despite several successful overseas tours, his career spiraled slowly downward in a welter of financial woes, divorce, tax problems, alcohol, self-imposed Mexican exile, and his lonely 1981 death in Harlingen, Texas, at the age of 55.

14　　But all that was in the future. For an English kid who loved his music and could sing the lyrics of every Haley hit, I knew his days

Writer's Break

For each of your top three topics from the Writer's Break on page 215, make an idea map.

- ▪ Write the topic in the center of a sheet of paper.
- ▪ Cluster all the ideas you have concerning this topic on the page around it.
- ▪ Draw lines to connect related ideas. Use color if you like.

were numbered when my cousin Suzanne took me to a youth club in 1957 where the kids were spinning singles on the record player. It was the zenith of Haley's popularity in Britain, but nobody was jiving to "See You Later, Alligator," "Rudy's Rock," or "Rip It Up." They were sitting around mooning over a guy singing about heartbreak in some hotel down at the end of some lonely street someplace.

Consider this . . .

- ▪ Does the writer of this essay successfully define *rock-and-roll*?
- ▪ The writer actually gives two definitions: his own, based on his experience as a teenager, and that of established authorities of the time. How do these two opposing definitions help you understand the point he is trying to make?

CHOOSING AN ORGANIZATIONAL METHOD

When you write to share information, you can use any of the organizational methods discussed in Chapter Two; however, the three most commonly used are: conceptual, logical, and chronological order.

☰ Conceptual Order

When you choose a conceptual organization, you introduce points related to your topic, and then develop and link them. For example, in the essay "Birth of the Cool," the writer introduces several related points: popular culture in early 1950s England, music in early 1950s England, Bill Haley's music in England, Bill Haley's style of music, Haley's music in the movies, Haley's music and violence in America, the spread of the violence to England, Haley's reaction to violence, and Haley's downfall. The writer skillfully and effectively connects these points to explain how Haley's music affected youth culture in England.

☰ Logical Order

When you use logical order as an organizational method, you have two options. You can begin with a general statement and then include specific details to support or elaborate on the statement, or you can begin with specific details and follow with a general statement of their significance.

☰ Chronological Order

When you use chronological organization, you give the information in the order in which it happened.

In the next essay, the writer tells us about the influences that shaped Elvis. He uses primarily chronological order because he is providing background information about the predecessors of and the early influences on the first rock-and-roll sensation.

WHAT MADE ELVIS WIGGLE

Lewis Lord

Reason for writing—to
explain the origin of
Elvis's style of music

Organizational method—
chronological

1 The King of Rock-and-Roll never understood the furor over his pelvis. "Strip-tease behavior," the *New York Times* called the wiggle that shook the world. "Where," asked the *New York Herald Tribune*, "do you go from Elvis Presley—short of obscenity, which is against the law?"

2 Elvis deemed his motions tame, especially compared with the contortions of the God-fearing Mississippians he grew up with. Almost daily in Tupelo, his parents took him to a Pentecostal church where worshippers writhed about in leg-shaking frenzies. When he moved to Memphis at age 13, the congregation there was much the same.

3 And there were other venues: When his favorite white gospel quartet, the Statesmen, took stage at Ellis Auditorium's monthly All-Night Gospel Singings, Elvis kept his eyes on "the Big Chief," bass singer Jim Wetherington. The lower the Chief's voice fell, the more his legs twitched—first his left, then his right, his gaudy trousers ballooning and shimmering with each jiggle. "He went about as far as you could go in gospel music," lead singer Jake Hess told Elvis biographer Peter Guralnick. "The women would jump up."

4 Women also jumped up when Wynonie Harris, a raucous rhythm-and-blues shouter from Omaha, came to town. At one Harris show in the early '50s, a youthful Elvis sat pondering the singer's every move. Harris waved his arms, jutted his hips, and petulantly curled his lips. Years later, blacks would regard Elvis as "the white Wynonie." As Henry Glover, who produced Harris's records, told writer Nick Tosches: "When you saw Elvis, you were seeing a mild version of Wynonie."

AP Photo/RCA Victor

5 Wynonie didn't mind. Blues singers and "hillbilly" musicians had long shared one another's music. In

the early '50s, Harris turned a white man's country song, Hank Penny's "Blood-shot Eyes," into an R&B record. From Harris, Elvis would appropriate a song as well as a motion. Wynonie's 1948 R&B hit "Good Rockin Tonight"—a rouser Elvis would cut for Sun Records in 1954—started a tide of sexually suggestive disks featuring the word *rock*.

Southern man. Long before Elvis helped make it a national rage, the embracing of black music by young whites was commonplace in the South. In 1952, students at the University of Mississippi chose as their favorite deejay the jive-talking Gene Nobles of WLAC in Nashville, who played R&B amid ads for Royal Crown hair dressing ("Just a touch means so much") and live poultry ("Friends, get 100 baby chicks for just $1.98"). 6

"Every Southerner, white and black, heard that music," recalls William Ferris, former chairman of the National Endowment for the Humanities, who, as a white teenager on a cotton farm near Vicksburg, Miss., spent many hours tuned to WLAC. The various forms of music riding the airwaves of Elvis's youth—R&B, black spirituals, white gospel, the Grand Old Opry's country sounds—were "parts of a common culture, sacred and secular," says Ferris. . . . 7

Southern culture alone didn't give Elvis his wiggle and singing style. But time and place clearly shaped the man who reshaped American music. Since boyhood, Elvis had hoped to become a country star, the next Eddy Arnold or Ernest Tubb—a dream first displayed at the Tupelo fair when, at 10, he sang a weeper about a boy and his dying dog. The song, "Old Shep," came from Red Foley of WSM's Grand Ole Opry in Nashville. 8

But on daytime radio in Memphis, Elvis savored not only the country hits of Hank Williams, but also a flood of blues played by deejays who became performers: B. B. King, Howlin' Wolf, and Rufus Thomas. At night, Dewey Phillips—the eclectic Daddy-O-Dewy—spun R&B hits like Ruth Brown's "Mama, He Treats Your Daughter Mean" and such obscure numbers as "Tell Me Why You Like Roosevelt" by Otis Jackson and the National Clouds of Joy, mixed with Muddy Waters and Frank Sinatra. 9

"Mr. Rhythm." The blend of sounds helped make Elvis the sensation that Sun owner Sam Phillips had long coveted—a white kid who sang black—a musical melting pot so rare that listeners initially didn't know what to make of him. In the wake of his first record (a Big Boy Crudup blues song on one side, a Bill Monroe bluegrass tune on the other), the 19-year-old was hailed as "the Hillbilly Cat" and "Country Music's Mr. Rhythm." 10

11   Not that Elvis didn't like pop music. He described Dean Martin, Perry Como, and Patti Page as favorite singers. But no one did more to bring about pop's demise. Before Elvis, romantic ballads hogged TV's *Your Hit Parade*, a pop music showcase with a cast that took turns singing the week's top tunes. In 1957, a year after Elvis became a star, the show folded. Its regulars could not do two vital things at once—wiggle and shout several words on the minds of millions of teenagers: "You ain't nothin' but a hound dog."

Consider this . . .

■ After studying the steps that led to the development of Elvis's signature style, do you have a greater appreciation or understanding of what he did?

■ What types of information did the writer include?

■ What were the sources of the information, and how do you think the writer collected it?

PICK UP almost any magazine, and you'll find articles that share information. That's what most nonfiction writing does. Information helps us keep up with current events; it helps teach us new things; it gives us access to new information. Not only will writing to inform allow you to share what you know with other people, it will allow you to learn something new about a topic that interests you. ■

COLLABORATIVE EXERCISES

Group Exercise One

- As a group, select someone to interview.
- Before you conduct your interview, decide what your focus will be, and write your questions. Be sure your questions will get you the information you need. Each person in the group should ask at least one of the questions.
- After the interview is over, write a brief essay based on what you learned.
- Be prepared to share your essay with the class.

Group Exercise Two

- Someone from each group should read aloud the essay the group wrote based on an interview.
- When each reading is done, the class should answer these questions:
  Did the essay have a clear focus?
  Was the point of the essay worth making?
  Did the group members use the information they gathered during the interview effectively?
  How could they improve the essay?

Group Exercise Three

- Choose a topic that interests the group.
- Determine who knows what about the topic.
- Gather information on the topic from at least three other sources: an article, the Internet, an expert, a book.
- Write the introduction to an informative essay about this topic, and prepare an outline of the remainder of the essay.
- Share your work with the rest of the class, and determine whether the purpose of the essay is clear and there is enough information to support the main point.

WRITING PICKS

Option One

Music moves us

Music affects us everyday. Sometimes we choose the music to which we listen—when we play a CD or listen to a particular radio station. Other times—when we watch movies or TV—we listen to music chosen by someone else. In each case, the music chosen is intended to create or support a particular mood. How does music do this? How do you choose the music you listen to? How do musicians use music to create a mood for a movie? How is music used persuasively in advertisements? For this paper, gather information about some aspect of how music is used to affect people and share it.

Though he is known for his acting, not his musical abilities, Johnny Depp is moved by music.

Option Two

Pick someone's brain

One of the best ways to understand something is to talk to someone who is an expert on that subject. An interview allows you to learn one person's personal perspective regarding a topic, to share the information he or she has gathered about that topic. For example, if you want to know how someone starts a band or becomes a professional musician, one of the best ways to find out is to talk to someone who has done this. For this paper, interview someone who has valuable information to share about music or the music industry, and make your interview the focus of an informative essay. Remember, photos communicate as effectively as words.

Option Three

Feed your curiosity

Humans have enjoyed music almost as long as they have walked the earth. In fact, the first music may have been enjoyed by humans before their linguistic abilities developed. As with most topics, we can understand music more fully if we know something of its history. Perhaps you are interested in the development of a particular instrument, or perhaps you'd like to know when and where archeologists found the first musical instruments. Perhaps you'd like to learn more about a particular type of music. Choose some aspect of musical history to investigate, and then share the significance of your findings in an informative essay.

As this ancient relief carving from a Hindu temple in India illustrates, music has been an important part of human culture for centuries.

Lindsay Hebberd/Corbis

Option Four

Targeting music to specific audiences

Each of the Web sites below is intended to share information about music with its target audience, yet the information that each site includes and the format in which the information is presented are different. How does the target audience influence the design and content of each Web site? In an essay, compare the two sites, and discuss whether they effectively reach the audience for which they are intended.

APPLYING THE RHETORICAL SITUATION

As always, you must consider the rhetorical situation throughout the process of making choices for informational writing. Use these questions to guide your decision making.

Audience

- What does your audience know about your topic?
- What background information do you need to include in order for your audience to understand your essay?
- Do you have enough information, or do you need to do some research?
- Are you using any specialized vocabulary that you will need to define for your audience?

Purpose

- What is your purpose for sharing this information?
- What do you want your readers to learn?
- How can you structure your essay to help your readers understand the material you are discussing?

Occasion

- How can you make your readers share your interest?
- How can you help them learn about your topic without boring them?

FOCUSING ON PROCESS

Prewriting

- Take a sheet of paper and make a list under the heading "Topics I Would Like to Research."
- For each topic, list research methods that you could use to gather information about that topic.
- On another sheet of paper, make a list of people you would like to interview, and note why.

Drafting

Make a writing date with yourself.

- Choose a time and a place—for example, on Wednesday from 2 to 4 at your favorite cyber cafe.
- Make your date at least 48 hours before the paper is due.
- Don't plan for a friend to be there. This is just for you and your notebook.
- Do nothing but write a draft of a paper.

Next time, try a different time and place, and see which works best.

Revising

Twenty-four hours after you have written your draft, take two copies of it to a quiet place. Bring along a pair of scissors and some tape.

- Take one copy of your paper, and cut it apart into paragraphs. If your paper is six paragraphs long, for example, you should have six pieces.
- Next, take your pieces and try moving the paragraphs around; maybe they work better in a different order. Maybe you need a new order and some new paragraphs. Experiment with structure.
- When you have your paragraphs in the best order, tape them together. Compare the new version with the original one. What still needs to be done?

Editing

- When you think your paper is done, read it out loud and mark every word, phrase, or sentence that sounds odd—weird or somehow off.

- Go back and try to decide why those parts don't work. Read the paper out loud again, to others. What do they think?

- Run a spell check. Have someone else read the paper out loud to you.

Grammar Choices

TRANSITIVE AND INTRANSITIVE VERBS

You must know how to distinguish transitive, intransitive, and linking verbs in order to recognize direct objects and subject complements. To do this, you need to learn these terms:

A **transitive verb** requires a direct object to complete its meaning.

An **intransitive verb** does not require a direct object to complete its meaning.

A **linking verb** connects a subject to a subject complement; examples are *be, feel, seem, appear, look.*

A **direct object** is a noun or pronoun that takes the action of the verb.

An **indirect object** is a noun or pronoun that tells to whom or for whom the action is done.

A **subject complement** renames or describes the subject of a sentence.

An **object complement** follows a direct object and renames or describes it.

An **adverb** follows or precedes a verb and modifies it.

Transitive Verbs

A **transitive verb** requires a **direct object** (a word or group of words) to complete its meaning by taking the action of the verb:

He **threw the ball**.

Cowboys **ride horses**.

She **cooked dinner**.

A transitive verb must have a direct object, but it can also have an indirect object. An **indirect object** normally precedes the direct object, and it tells to whom or for whom the action is done:

He **threw Mike** the **ball**.

Show me the **money**.

He **told you the truth**.

The direct object of a sentence is sometimes followed by an **object complement**. An object complement is a word or group of words that completes the object's meaning by renaming or describing it.

Lack of sleep **makes you sluggish**.

Children **consider toys real**.

Some people **call chocolate candy**. I **call it a necessity**.

Intransitive Verbs

An **intransitive verb** does not require a direct object to complete its meaning because nothing is required to receive the action.

You **lie**.

She **slept**.

A fish **swims**.

An intransitive verb can be preceded or followed by an **adverbial modifier**. This adverb or adverbial phrase modifies the verb.

She **slept quietly**.

You **lie constantly**.

A fish **swims in water**.

Linking Verbs

A **linking verb** connects a subject to a **subject complement**, a word that describes or renames the subject.

The dog **appears sick**.

He **seems angry**.

You **look** tired.

The milk **tastes** sour.

Making It Work

- Locate two transitive verbs, two intransitive verbs, and two linking verbs in one of the essays in this chapter.

- For each verb you locate, identify the accompanying object(s), object complement, adverbial modifier, or subject complement.

- Be prepared to share your answers with the class.

Style Choices

REPETITION

There are two kinds of repetition: necessary repetition and unnecessary repetition.

Necessary Repetition

Necessary repetition increases the clarity of communication by repeating information that readers need to read more than once. For example, if a document refers to a graphic within the text, the graphic itself also has to be labeled in order for the reader to know that he or she has found the correct one. This is one kind of necessary repetition. Sometimes we repeat information for emphasis or for stylistic purposes.

> Michael and John both pay rent on the apartment, but only one pays for utilities.

> Of these two writers, Stephen King and Michael Crichton, I like him the best.

> Last year, I went to Europe with my friends Alex and Jacques. I thought we all had a good time, but later I found out that only two of us did. I wish he had said something at the time.

Each of these sentences is unclear because we don't know who the pronoun *one*, *him*, or *he* refers to. Does Michael pay the utilities or does John? Which author does the writer prefer? Who didn't have a good time in Europe? Look at the revised sentences:

> Michael and John both pay rent on the apartment, but only John pays for utilities.

> Of these two writers, Stephen King and Michael Crichton, I like Crichton the best.

> Last year, I went to Europe with my friends Alex and Jacques. I thought we all had a good time, but later I found out that only two of us did. I wish Alex had said something at the time.

These sentences are perfectly clear because of the writer's use of repetition.

Useless Repetition

Some repetition is not useful. It may even get in the reader's way. Look at these sentences:

> I started to bop my head to a beat I had never heard before.

In this sentence, the use of the word *before* is unnecessary. The words *never heard* convey the idea clearly.

> As I became more and more caught up in the Hip Hop culture, I began finding other kids like myself who were addicted to the same drug.

In this sentence, the writer had no need to repeat *more*. We would have understood the meaning just as clearly without the repetition, which added neither meaning nor stylistic effect.

> I watch BET (Black Entertainment Television) or MTV just to get a little bit of music into my bloodstream.

In this sentence, the writer did not need to use *little*. A *bit* is a small amount. Alternatively, *a little music* would convey the same meaning.

Repetition can be necessary or unnecessary. Consider your use of repetition carefully, and make good choices when you write.

Making It Work

- ■ Locate each instance of repetition within your paper.

- ■ Decide whether the repetition is necessary.

- ■ Remove any unnecessary repetition.

ART AS SOCIAL CATALYST

Writing to Solve Problems

In this chapter, you will learn:

- How to identify a problem—
  personal or general—
  on which an essay can
  be focused

- Strategies for writing
  a problem/solution
  essay—definition,
  comparison/contrast,
  cause/effect, and process

- The basic elements used
  to structure many
  problem/solution essays—
  background information,
  problem statement, proposed
  solution, plan
  of action

Works of art often draw attention to social problems and can provoke social change. The Vietnam War Memorial, which sparked controversy at its unveiling, is a reminder of the devastating casualties of that unpopular war.

Stelios Varias/Reuters/Landov

You would have no trouble identifying a number of problems if you were asked to; unfortunately, we all can. And even though personal problems aren't quite the same as writing problems, one can help you solve the other. For example, you may have a problem with your roommate. Even though you agreed to respect each other's space—no borrowing without asking, no messing up the other person's living area, and so on—she keeps on throwing her dirty clothes all over the floor, and your clean socks are always on her feet. At the same time, your teacher has just assigned an essay, and you don't have a topic. How can you combine your two problems?

> Sloppy roommate
> + No topic for my paper
> ———————————————————
> A paper about respecting other people's space

In most cases, you won't write about problems that affect only you—you will want to examine more general problems. However, by identifying personal problems, you can often trace them back to larger ones. For example, you might be concerned about the fact that a good friend was recently harassed by a group of people at a party. You are concerned personally because he is your friend, but in order to understand the wider implications, you might examine the lack of tolerance for gays as a problem that affects U.S. society, not just you and your friend. In fact, you might use writing as a way of exploring and understanding such a problem.

Writer's Break

Art can take many different forms: music, poetry, sculpture, photos, and so forth.

- Make a list of at least ten art forms.

- For each form you identify, list at least three specific examples. For example, list three specific comic strips or three songwriters.

- For each example you listed, name at least one positive and one negative aspect of it based on the message you believe it shares with its audience. For example, if you listed a poet, what sorts of messages do his or her poems share with the world? Are the messages positive or negative?

MAKING CHOICES WHEN YOU WRITE ABOUT A PROBLEM

There are numerous choices to make when you write an essay about a problem. You must first choose a problem to serve as the focus of the essay and then determine how best to use writing to analyze or solve it.

≡ What Is Problem-Centered Writing?

Problem-centered writing is writing that deals directly with a question, an issue, or a concern. When you write about a problem, you can choose to focus on either the problem or the solution.

Focusing on the problem

You might choose to focus on the problem for any of these reasons:

- *You are trying to determine something about the cause of a problem.* When you realize how many of the students from your high school became pregnant before they graduated, you begin to question why this is happening. Is it a lack of sex education or a lack of morals? Are the parents responsible? Are more teenagers actually becoming pregnant, or are we just more aware of it now?

- *You have identified a problem, but you suspect that it has no solution.* A young man was recently diagnosed with multiple sclerosis. He has struggled to deal with this. On one hand, he is desperate for a solution. He is terrified of the disease's hold on his life. On the other hand, he knows there is no cure for his condition and consequently no "solution." He wants to know how others have handled this situation.

Each year, millions of teenage girls become pregnant and are forced to face many difficult decisions.

Robert Brenner/PhotoEdit

■ *You aren't ready to consider a solution.* You may feel very strongly about global warming. You know the best way to address this problem personally is to give up your car so that you can convince others to do the same. However, you aren't sure you are ready to take this step.

There are many ways in which you can write about problems with no solutions. The three examples above suggest possibilities. Here are some more specific ways of focusing on a problem without knowing what the solution is:

■ *Exploring a personal problem.* Writing is an excellent way to explore problems that affect you as an individual. You probably shouldn't write about your recent spat with your boyfriend or girlfriend; you want your topic to be significant. But you can share your personal struggles with meaningful problems in a way that will help both you and your readers. For instance, you could use your own experience to write about the types of communication problems that make intimate relationships so difficult.

■ *Exploring a societal problem that affects you.* You may want to write about a problem that you can't control but that still affects you in some meaningful way. For example, you might want to write about how racial intolerance affects you on a daily basis. Racial intolerance is clearly a problem, and one worth writing about, even if you don't have the ability to solve it.

■ *Persuading others that a problem exists.* You may feel the need to write about a problem to establish that it needs to be taken seriously. If, for instance, you think cruelty to animals is a serious problem that most people try to ignore or explain away, you might want to write a paper that puts that problem right in your readers' faces where they can't ignore it.

■ *Explaining why a problem is significant.* Sometimes you have to convince readers that the problem is significant, that it affects them in some meaningful way. For example, if you want the people on your college campus to help solve the problem of abandoned dogs and cats, you first have to show them how this problem affects them personally.

In the following essay, the writer doesn't offer a solution because he is still determining what the problem is—what is causing an increasing number of Americans to escape to the movies.

BOFFO BUSINESS AT BOX OFFICE

Philip Wuntch

CD sales are winding downward. Air travel has lost altitude. TV ratings are in a long-term dive. And don't even mention the stock market.   1

Yet the movie business is soaring as never before.   2

So far this year, box-office revenues stand at $4.71 billion, up an eye-popping 19 percent over last year's record pace. It seems nearly every weekend sets a new milestone.   3

The summer surge started with *Spider-Man* which opened May 3 to an unprecedented three-day take of $114.8 million and just topped $400 million. Last weekend, *Men in Black II* broke Fourth of July records with a five-day haul of $87 million.   4

The boom in total receipts can't be explained away by higher ticket prices. The National Association of Theater Owners says the number of tickets sold so far in   5

Spider-Man *blew away the competition the week it was released.*

Marvel/Sony Pictures/The Kobal Collection/The Picture Desk

2002 is 15 percent greater than this time last year, when admissions were at the highest point in 40 years.

6   So what gives?

7   No one knows for sure, but a few theories have been proposed. The multiplexes offer a haven after last fall's terrorist attacks, says studio consultant Sam Christensen. College professor Katherine Giuffre believes that audiences respond to the communal experience provided by modern megaplexes. Others maintain that movies simply offer a great escape.

8   Mr. Christensen says he thinks people are doing what they've done in the past—taking flight to the local theater for emotional reassurance during a time of crisis. This time, it's Sept. 11, he says. In the past, it was World War II and the Depression.

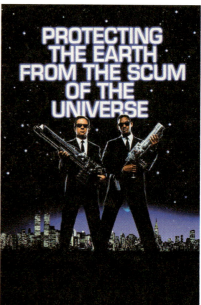

9   "The confusion of stressful times makes people want to seek out endings that reinforce the clarity of good versus evil," he says. "Films can provide that clarity, and being in a group of moviegoers strengthens a sense of identification and relationship. Some movies provide such a strong sense of security that they take us back to our childhood Golden Books. They become a psychological security blanket."

Columbia/The Kobal Collection/The Picture Desk

MIIB, *though less popular than* MIB, *was still a huge hit.*

SAFETY IN NUMBERS

10   The numbers are so astounding and the reasons so murky that even a self-declared "mentalist" is weighing in.

11   "We need to escape more than ever," says The Amazing Kreskin, a frequent guest on TV variety shows who bills himself as a "thought reader." "People feel secure in numbers. A group provides a security blanket, and seeing a movie at a crowded modern movie theater can become an out-of-body experience."

12   Adding a historical footnote, he says: "Winston Churchill slammed down his fist when someone suggested that London cinemas be closed during the World War II blitz. He knew that the cinemas would help the British people endure a time of terror."

Dr. Giuffre, professor of sociology at Colorado College, also subscribes to the safety-in-numbers theory but thinks moviegoing isn't always about finding refuge. 13

"Moviegoing today is not escaping trouble," she says. "It's a sign of people wanting to gather together, as if for a communal campfire in times past, and facing problems together. Small theaters bring people together intimately, but the bigger the multiplex, the bigger the group. It's like a tribal council, a very communal experience." 14

Dr. Giuffre noted that even with the rumored possibility of Fourth of July terrorist attacks, she heard of no one going into hiding. 15

"All my friends were planning on communal situations such as moviegoing," she says. "No one was cowering in a basement." 16

FILLING A NEED

Whatever the reason, screen fare definitely fills a need for movie regulars. Melvonna Crook, photo manager at a Lake Highlands Walgreen's, has three daughters who celebrate their birthdays by "getting a bunch of friends together and going to the movies." 17

"They can watch movies at home anytime, but going out to a theater makes it special," she says. "They all like the glitzy new theaters." 18

"There is a strong sense of family and community in Dallas," says Terrell Falk, vice president of marketing and communications for Dallas-based Cinemark USA. "That makes a shared experience—like going to the movies—an important part of the lifestyle here." 19

Other local exhibitors agree and say that they've seen an uptick this summer in attendance at family movies that are rated G or PG, mirroring a national trend. 20

Dreamworks LLC/The Kobal Collection/The Picture Desk

The family-oriented animated film Spirit: Stallion of the Cimarron *reflected the national trend toward increased movie attendance with its strong opening weekend.*

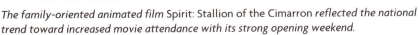

21   Former Dallas residents Jennifer Barr and Kristi Whitt, who now live in Miami, started a moviegoing club in the aftermath of Sept. 11. "Everyone's jobs seemed to have gotten more stressful, so we planned a hump-day movie club for Wednesdays," Ms. Barr says. "Twelve is about the average number we have each week. We have a Web site and vote on what movies we want to see."

22   *Men in Black II* drew the largest attendance of the Miami movie club. The smallest? The terrorist-themed *The Sum of All Fears.*

GOOD TIMING

23   Some films proved to be the right movie at the right time. Russ Leatherman, founder of AOL Moviefone, says attendance dropped on weekdays immediately after the September attack but picked up in time for the weekend.

24   That weekend's No. 1 film was *Hardball*, previously considered a relatively minor Keanu Reeves vehicle about a ne'er-do-well who gains self-respect from coaching an inner-city Little League team.

25   "It was the perfect film for that weekend," Mr. Leatherman says. "Audiences could share laughter and have a good time at a movie with a positive message."

26   Dr. Giuffre believes that *Spider-Man* is also the right movie at the right time.

27   "Part of Spider-Man's success is that it reaches so many demographics," she says. "Grandparents grew up with Spider-Man, and so have their grandchildren. They can talk about it together, which adds to the communal campfire experience of modern moviegoing."

28   Not everyone agrees with the notion that history completely explains the current box-office movie boom. Dallas movie veteran Bob Simonton says the Depression and World War II were just different.

29   "During the Depression, many theaters held Dish Nights and Bank Nights and cheaper ticket prices to lure customers," says Mr. Simonton, a retired film buyer for the United Artists exhibition chain. "And gas was rationed during World War II, which added to the appeal of going to a neighborhood theater or taking the trolley downtown."

30   Kevin Hagopian, lecturer in media studies at the College of Communications at Penn State, cites another difference between moviegoing today and in the 1930s and '40s: In the old days, Hollywood studios owned the majority of movie theaters.

31   "Individual theaters provided a good deal of research to the studios that owned them," Mr. Hagopian says. "With this source of intelligence no longer operating,

and with the extraordinary development periods now common for major films, Hollywood may know less about its audience, and be less responsive to them, than ever before. . . . Hollywood could remain resolutely disinterested in the rest of the world except as scenic backgrounds for espionage stories."

> ## Writer's Break
>
> ■ Make a list of at least three problems related to ethics and the arts. What about the downloading of music off the Internet? Is this stealing?
>
> ■ For each problem, write a three-to-five-sentence explanation of why it has no apparent solution.

Mr. Hagopian may be gloomy about whether the moguls will learn any lasting lessons, but in Hollywood, money talks. And what many analysts are talking about is the ultimate Christmas present—how the all-time one-year box-office record, $8.4 billion set in 2001, should shatter long before Dec. 25.

32

Consider this . . .

■ The people interviewed for this article agree that more Americans are going to the movies, but they don't agree on why. What problem do you think is sending people to the movies in record numbers?

■ Are movies an art form? If so, can they be a solution? What problems can they solve?

Focusing on the solution

Sometimes the solution to the problem may be what you are really interested in. You believe the problem itself is generally acknowledged, and you want to suggest a solution and describe how and why your suggestion will help.

If you have established that a problem really is a problem, you have to offer a viable solution. For example, if you want the campus community to do something about the abandoned pet problem, you have to suggest specific steps that can be taken. These steps have to be practical and possible. It wouldn't do any good to suggest that students within ten miles of campus not be allowed to have pets. No one would support this. You could, however, suggest that all students take responsibility for spaying and neutering their pets and tell them how to get it done inexpensively.

In the next essay, the writer discusses how art can help members of society find a way to express themselves more freely. She uses a cause/effect strategy to identify the problem.

Writer's Break

- List three problems related to art that you believe have solutions. For example, how can the public be taught to appreciate "extreme" art forms like graffiti? Should music be censored when it has controversial lyrics?
- Suggest a solution for each problem you've listed.

Art Is the Solution

Diane Castro

Cause of problem—supression of emotions

Effect of problem—illness

In our restricted society, social norms often force us to repress many strong emotions. For example, most guys aren't comfortable crying, especially in front of women. Consequently, many people feel stifled and unfulfilled and suffer from both mental and physical problems. However, people turn to the arts as a way to fully and freely express themselves. Since ancient times art--dance, music, painting--has offered people a way of

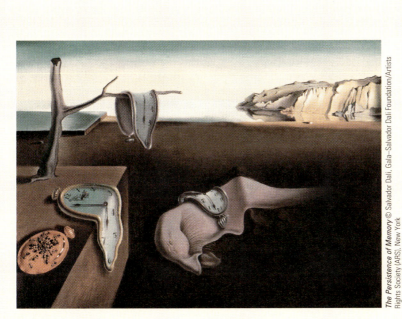

The Persistence of Memory © Salvador Dali, Gala–Salvador Dali Foundation/Artists Rights Society (ARS), New York

The works of Salvadore Dali have puzzled viewers for years.

communicating their feelings to others. Art is the solution that can free society from the chains of convention that prevent them from expressing themselves. And an appreciation of art can make those feelings available to anyone.

Poems and paintings can guide people into the depths of their souls and help them discover new feelings and ideas. Artists and writers such as Salvador Dali and Plato encourage people to search beyond face value and stretch to the farthest reaches of imagination to find meaning in art. Many people may find a brief

Solution–art

respite from reality in different forms of art. For example, many people go to the movies to escape. In many of the current movies, anyone watching can be a hero and save the day, and find a happy ending.

Art can be a revelation for either the creator or the connoisseur. I can curl up and be taken away by a novel that allows me to share an experience I've never had or take a paint brush and express emotions I can't put into words. Art is therapeutic because it gives you a way of expressing what can't be put into words. Different mediums can be used such as clay, paints, crayons, or just pencil. It is a very productive form of therapy that is even used professionally.

Learning about other artists can also be therapeutic because you can appreciate their art rather than producing your own. For example, you may not be able to write a song, but you can listen to the ones sung by your favorite artists. Listening to music can provide you with a cathartic experience when the music expresses what you are feeling. From writers, we can experience what would otherwise be foreign to us. By looking at a painting, we can see what we might never have seen. By reading a poem, we can capture an emotion. By studying architecture, we can enter a new world.

Cave paintings are thousands of years old.

Art has no rules and no restrictions. Writers write, dancers dance and painters paint from pure emotion. Yet these emotions are influenced by the forces that shaped the artist's life. We can understand something of ancient culture by studying ancient art, and we can appreciate the power of a political movement by understanding the art it spawned.

Art is the solution. The different forms of art help us to expand our minds both intellectually and emotionally. Art itself has been and always will be freedom of expression. We can be artists, or we can study art. Open your mind. Open your heart. Art is all around you.

Why the solution works

Conclusion—restatement of solution

Consider this . . .

- What problem does this writer identify? Do you agree that it is a problem?
- How do you define *art*?
- Based on your definition, do you think art has the potential to be a solution to a problem you can identify?

Deciding Whether a Problem Is Significant

Basically, *significant* means "important." Not all problems are significant, and if they aren't, no one will want to read about them. However, distinguishing significant problems from trivial ones is not easy.

Like most of us, you might be inclined to substitute *significant* for *big* or *momentous*. For example, if your teacher asked you to write about a significant event, you might choose your wedding, your graduation, or your basic training. All of these are definitely significant events. However, events that might seem less momentous might be just as significant. Getting married is an important event, but what about your first date? First glance? Without that first glance, there would never have been a first date or a wedding. What about those random events that change the course of our lives? For example, Lance Armstrong was a professional bike racer for several years without any notable success. It wasn't until he was diagnosed with cancer, was treated, and had recovered that he began winning the Tour de France.

We have to consider the question of significance just as carefully when we are thinking about problems to write about. Having to do your own laundry may feel like a problem to you. None of us likes to do laundry. But it's not an important problem. Growing up—the reason you have to do your own laundry—is a much bigger problem. We all have to deal with many problems, but you only want to write about the ones that have significance for yourself and others. Generally, you need to ask yourself these questions when you're evaluating the significance of a problem:

- Could it have a permanent effect on someone?
- Will my readers be able to relate to my problem?

Writer's Break

Choose one of the problems you listed for the Writer's Break on page 257 or page 258.

- Could this problem change you or your life in some way?
- Explain why or why not.

Is the problem likely to have a permanent effect?

Not all problems are life altering. For example, your dissatisfaction with your minimum wage job is not a problem that will change your life. On the other hand, the difficulties of growing up could change your life. At some point, we all have to decide whether we want to grow up and become independent or spend our lives looking for people who will take care of us. You may know some people who have faced the difficulties of growing up by moving back home and choosing not to grow up. Others may have decided to face the challenge head on, and they may be different people because of that.

Significant problems usually change us in some permanent way. It could be the problem itself, the solution, or the process of finding a solution that causes the change. In any case, sharing our experience with such a problem could have the power to change others.

Deciding where to go to college is also a problem. Will it permanently change you or anyone else? Probably not. Years from now, even weeks from now, you will probably not be reminiscing about how you couldn't decide where to go to college. On the other hand, your problem in choosing a major could have a permanent effect on you. The major you choose is likely to determine the job you do later on. Since working is a big part of most people's lives, what you do will affect your life in a significant way. However, your job as a writer is to show how a personal problem like

Writer's Break

For the problem you selected for the Writer's Break on page 263:

- List several other people who could relate to it?
- Identify issues surrounding or contributing to the problem to which others can relate?

choosing a major can have a broader impact. For example, the fact that fewer students are choosing to major in education does have a broad impact because it means that there will be fewer teachers. This problem will affect everyone in the United States.

Will my readers be able to relate to the problem?

Have you ever passed someone on campus and said, "How are you?" only to have them stop and actually *tell* you how they are? If the person is a good friend or has a funny story to tell, you might not mind. But none of us likes being trapped by people telling stories we don't care about. The same is true of the papers you write. A friend is probably willing to listen to you whine or grumble occasionally—that's what friends are for—but readers aren't that nice. If a piece of writing doesn't offer them something to which they can relate, they won't read it. Thus, as a writer, you need to choose a problem to which readers can relate or find a way to make the problem you're interested in pertinent to your readers. For example, consider these problems:

> My roommate smokes, and I don't.
>
> Smoking-related illnesses among young people are increasing.

Which topic can you relate to more? If you happen to have a smoking roommate, maybe the first one. If not, probably the second. The fact that people under twenty now make up the largest group of smokers affects us all. If you are in this age group, it affects you directly. But what if someone really wants to write about his or her smoking roommate? How could he or she make this topic matter to other people? The writer needs to ask himself or herself what larger problems are represented by this smaller problem:

- Respecting personal freedom
- Negotiating differences
- Developing tolerance

All of these problems are related to the smaller problem, and the writer could talk about the personal problem in ways that would give it broader significance.

CHOOSING STRATEGIES FOR WRITING ABOUT PROBLEMS AND SOLUTIONS

Once you've identified a problem and determined its significance, you need to begin thinking about the techniques you can use to write about it. Here are strategies you can use when writing a problem/solution essay:

- Definition
- Comparison/contrast
- Cause/effect
- Process

Writer's Break

Words are art. Words also have the power to solve problems.

- List three situations when words somehow helped you in a specific way.
- List three historical examples of times when words helped someone.
- List three problems you are currently facing that could be solved or at least helped by words.

☰ Definition

When you use definition as a strategy for a problem/solution essay, you clearly explain what the problem is and what it isn't. This helps you and your readers decide whether the problem really is a problem. You can define a potential problem in several ways:

- Say what it is, and compare it to similar things.

  Lack of privacy is a direct violation of a person's rights. Privacy is just like freedom of choice or your right to own property.

- Say what it is not, and compare it to dissimilar things.

  Lack of privacy is not a life-threatening condition. It's not like being denied food or water or other basic necessities of life.

- Classify it as part of a larger group, or category, and then cite other parts of that group.

  Privacy is a personal right. Personal rights include the right to make personal choices, the right to own things, and the right to voice your opinions.

☰ Comparison/Contrast

When you write about a problem, you have to begin by establishing that there is a problem. The writing strategy of comparison/contrast can help you do this. For example, if you chose to write about the increasing emphasis on violence in movies, you might establish that the amount of violence is increasing by comparing the movies of one year to the movies of a previous year. If you were writing about the decreasing quality of public education, you might compare test results over a span of time to prove that children seem to know less.

Writing about problems frequently involves writing about solutions, and if you are going to consider more than one solution, or even the possible benefits of a proposed solution, you will need to compare solutions or benefits. You might suggest several ways in which the movie industry could decrease the amount of violence in films. In order to be able to choose between these options, your readers will need you to compare and contrast them. When you use compare and contrast as an organizing pattern, you can compare all of one thing to all of another, or you can use a point-by-point organization. Both are effective.

In the next essay, poet Andrei Codrescu uses comparison/contrast to criticize our failure to make art a part of our lives.

COMMENTARY: ART SHOULD BE TAKEN ADVANTAGE OF BY PEOPLE

Andrei Codrescu

Quietly, quietly, the artworks and the poems and the stories keep being made in small towns and big towns and middle-sized ones, storms of beauty like butterflies migrating past one's hoary head. You'd think that by now, every wall in every house in the world would be covered by works of art, and that there would be a stack of poems by every chair being read dawn to dusk loudly or to oneself by lovers of words.

But no, most walls are bare, sporting at best religious icons, and at worst, mass-produced pictures from yard sales and Wal-Mart. And the people read the crawlers at the bottom of the TV news and the thin newspapers with even thinner words and zero matter for reflection. People complain of excessive mediatization, of too much TV, too loud advertising, too many sensationalistic news stories, but I don't believe it. I think that a great big silence surrounds and suffuses us and that all the noise the world makes barely penetrates it, and that most people's inner lives are muted craters, gurgling forth only the loopy monotony of one's own voice discussing misconnections and mortality in non-stop prose.

And yet, over there, by the trees in the Vermont hills, lovely magical theater has been made for decades by the Bread and Puppet Theater. And there by the rushing river, living in years in a house beneath the redwoods, poet Pat Nolan projects in lovely lines the issues of a consciousness intensely immersed in nature and irony. And a little up the ocean in Prague Vincent Farnsworth makes the cacophony of the band rehearsal next door into a manual for gracefully aging. And no further than the city of New York, Simon Pettet makes lyrics worthy of the troubadours.

4   When you look for it and listen for it, art surges everywhere, spilling its cornucopial spirit from and into every place humans inhabit. So why is it that all most people hear is that lonely sorrow drowned in TV noise, and all they see is their insignificance barely kept at bay by shopping? The answer is that there are two devils: the devil of conformity that keeps us from seeing and hearing what artists make and thus condemns us to sterile solitude, and the devil of art and joy who is fighting the devil of conformity as we speak. Today in the deep laziness and profound tedium of summer, go out and buy an artwork and a book of poetry, and keep it talismanically around, or take it with you into the waves. You must quit boring yourself.

☰ Cause/Effect

All problems have a cause—a root source. Sometimes the cause of a problem might be obvious: "I want to go to college, but I have no money." Sometimes the cause might be less obvious: "I want to go to college, but I can't seem to commit to starting. Maybe I'm afraid I'll fail. No, I'm not sure what I want to study. No, maybe I'm not motivated. I'm not really sure why I don't just start." Regardless of whether the cause is obvious or still in question, you might explore it in a problem/solution essay. If so, you can use cause/effect as a way of organizing the information within the essay: First, you describe the cause and the effect of the problem; then, you discuss how the solution addresses either or both of these.

Whether the cause or the effect of a problem should receive more emphasis in an essay depends on the situation. For example, some scientists believe the cause of the greenhouse effect is the emissions produced by burning fossil fuels. The effect is the warming of the global climate and the melting of the polar ice caps. If you were studying the ecological health of the planet, the

Peter Calamai/ Toronto Star*/Zuma Press*

Scientists studying global warming are looking for causes of that serious problem.

effect would be more important to your paper than the cause because you would be focusing on the damage that has been done. However, if you were writing about possible solutions to global warming, the cause would be more important because it indicates what must be fixed.

If a woman is being physically abused by her spouse, she may only know the effect, or result—being hit. She clearly knows who is hitting her, but she may not know why; she may feel uncertain about the cause. Ultimately, the cause may be less important in this case than the effect. If you were to write a paper about the issue of domestic violence, you might want to consider possible causes as part of your exploration of the problem. Certainly, you need to know the cause in order to suggest a solution. You could simply suggest that a victim of abuse leave the situation, but this addresses the effect, not the cause of the problem.

In the next essay, a student questions claims that the media's recent embracing of gay culture indicates an increased acceptance of gay culture by mainstream American society. She identifies a different effect of the media portrayal.

America's Queer Eye

Pearla Marquez

As incidents like the 1998 murder-execution of Matthew Shepherd have revealed, the persecution of gays through violence and other types of hate crimes remains a deep-seated problem in society. While many would argue that the media's recent embracement of gay culture means that Americans are taking a

Thesis statement— the perpetuation of gay stereotypes by television shows

step toward acceptance of homosexuals, the truth is that the media's portrayal of homosexuals also perpetuates the very stereotypes that fuel intolerance. Shows such as <u>Will & Grace</u> and <u>Queer Eye for the Straight Guy</u>, for example, exploit the "dandy" stereotype about gay males that have existed for centuries, and not only in American society. These shows might claim to "break down the barriers" of prejudice regarding homosexuals, but they also deal in the demeaning representations that maintain those barriers.

The most problematic example of this double-edged sword is, interestingly, also the most often-cited example of how the media (and America) have embraced gay culture: <u>Will & Grace</u>. The popularity of this show is especially surprising, since Ellen Degeneres's "coming out" basically spelled doom for her sit-com just a few years before <u>Will & Grace</u> began airing on NBC. Therefore, it is easy to understand why many see the show's success as a marker of gay tolerance in America. Most people who claim that the character Will serves as a positive role model have a point. Will is a "normal guy"--a successful lawyer who often serves as the "voice of reason" in the midst of insanity. In this

Cause and effect—effect of embracing of gay culture

sense, the show does debunk common stereotypes about gay men. However, the character of Jack topples what progress the show makes with Will's character. He is a virtual caricature of the gay male: lisping, flamboyant, limp-wristed, at times catty, and always quick with one-liners (mostly for the sake of sexual innuendo). While Will is at the office working on case files, Jack prances carelessly about the town, trying to fit in every stereotypically gay activity that the writers can cram into an episode: dancing, singing, flirting, and imitating Cher. The show both debunks and affirms prejudices about gays.

Other shows that have followed this "gay trend" in the media, such as <u>Queer Eye for the Straight Guy</u> and <u>Queer as Folk</u>, do much the same thing. In fact, the entire premise of <u>Queer Eye</u> is not only that heterosexual males are hopeless slobs, but also that gay males are fashion, culture, cuisine, and beauty savvy. The new term "metrosexual"--a straight man who is conscious of his looks and manners--indicates just how deeply these stereotypes have infested society. A "metrosexual" is basically a straight man who "acts gay"; it has nothing whatsoever to do with sexuality at all. <u>Queer as Folk</u> plays on even more dangerous

Cause and effect—perpetuation of stereotypes has negative effects

Definition—what a metrosexual is

stereotypes about homosexual men and promiscuity. A few of the characters are indeed involved in standing relationships, but many of the men on this show have casual, anonymous, and public sex in the back rooms of dance clubs. While some would argue that this sort of sexual license is also characteristic of the heterosexual world, the show's creators must be aware that it has a particularly negative resonance for mainstream society when portrayed as a gay phenomenon. A common stereotype, after all, is that homosexuals are oversexed and even predatorial. The result of this double-sided representation is that Americans receive a mixed message about gay stereotypes.

Conclusion—solution to problem is elimination of gay stereotypes

Though it is indeed a sign of some progress that gay culture has become something of a trend in contemporary mainstream media, people must also acknowledge the degree to which this trend exploits prejudice and cultural clichés about homosexuals. True acceptance and tolerance can only come about when these stereotypes are out of the picture completely. As long as they exist and continue to be part of mainstream ideology, hatred and violence against gays will continue to plague American society.

Effect of stereotyping of gays

Consider this . . .

- ■ What problem does this writer identify? Do you agree that it is a problem?

- ■ Does she convince you that this problem has significance? Can even those readers who aren't familiar with the television shows mentioned relate in some way?

- ■ How effective were the strategies used by the writer?

≡ Process

A *process* is the method we use to accomplish something. For example, there is a process for writing a paper, for buying a car, and for baking a cake. Process descriptions are important because they tell us how something is done, and frequently, we do not want to commit to a course of action until we know what the process involves. For example, getting a tattoo might seem like a good idea until you find out how long it will take, how many needles are used, and how much pain you will feel.

Processes are often important parts of problem/solution essays because readers may need to know the process that caused a problem to develop or that is involved in making a proposed solution a reality.

CHOOSING AN ORGANIZATIONAL METHOD

Unlike many types of essays you will write, problem/solution essays have a fairly consistent pattern of organization. They almost always contain these elements:

- ■ *Background information.* In order for your readers to understand the problem you are going to discuss, you may need to give them some background information. This will help them understand the context of the problem that you are presenting.

- *Statement of the problem.* Once you have provided your readers with all the background information they need, you can begin stating the problem. In order to do this, you need to

  Define the problem.

  Discuss the cause of the problem.

  Show how the problem affects your readers.

- *Proposed solution.* Next, you offer your solution to the problem you have outlined. In order to do this effectively, you must

  Explain the solution.

  Show how the solution will solve the problem.

- *Plan of action.* No solution is useful unless it is possible. In the plan of action, you discuss specific steps that can be taken to make the proposed solution a reality.

PROBLEM/SOLUTION ESSAYS come in many forms and serve many purposes, but they share a common element. They identify a significant problem that affects the writer and/or the readers, and usually discuss a possible solution to that problem. Because problem/solution essays allow us to better understand the problems that affect us, they help us make informed decisions about the world around us.

COLLABORATIVE EXERCISES

Group Exercise One

As a group, complete the following tasks:

- Identify a local problem that affects most members of the class.

- Write an essay in which you identify the problem and suggest a solution and a plan of action.

- Swap papers with another group.

- Read the other group's paper, and determine whether the problem is clearly stated and the proposed solution is possible and persuasive.

- Be prepared to share your evaluation with the class.

Group Exercise Two

As a class, complete the following:

- Create a list of criteria for peer evaluation of problem-solving essays.

- Write the list in your writer's notebook.

Group Exercise Three

- As a group, find a piece of problem/solution writing.

- Identify the different parts of the piece and the techniques the writer used.

- Determine whether the piece is well-written, and explain why or why not.

- Share your findings with the class.

WRITING PICKS

Option One

The problem of prejudice

Prejudice and intolerance are significant problems in the United States. Many people believe that art can be both the cause and the solution for such problems. For example, can music with racially derogative lyrics enforce racial stereotypes? Do words have the power to heal? Identify a work of art, and discuss how it is either contributing to the problem of prejudice or helping to solve it.

Photick/Index Stock Imagery

While some think graffit is art, its message can contribute to the problem of prejudice.

Option Two

Writing as a solution

Have you ever been in a position where your inability to express yourself became a problem for you or others? Have you and a friend ever been unable to communicate? Writing is art, and art can help us express ourselves. Has writing ever helped you solve a problem? Could a letter to a friend save a friendship? Does having the courage to put an apology in words give it more significance? How did the Declaration of Independence solve a problem for the citizens of the new nation of the United States? What about the Emancipation Proclamation, which freed the slaves? Identify a problem that you believe could be solved with writing, and demonstrate how writing could help solve it.

Bettmann/Corbis

The Declaration of Independence is the document that founded democracy in the United States.

Option Three

Controversial images

Disturbing images captured by photojournalists are published every day. Why are some, such as the photo of the mangled car in which Princess Diana died, considered inappropriate? What are the ethical considerations concerning photography and publishing such images? Should such images be censored? Explore this problem.

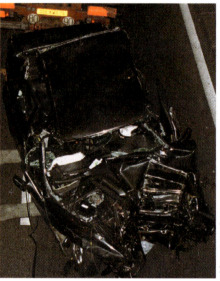

AP Photo/Jerome Daley

Images such as this one can be controversial.

Option Four

Personal appearance as artistic expression

People often attempt to define who they are by the clothes they wear, the hairstyles they choose, or the body art they display. Can a person's appearance be viewed as a work of art? Do you find it troubling that your appearance can have a strong influence on what people think of you? Do you deliberately try to project an image to others through your appearance? What are some consequences of judging people solely on physical appearance? Write an essay exploring one of these questions.

APPLYING THE RHETORICAL SITUATION

As always, you must consider the rhetorical situation throughout the process of making choices for a problem/solution essay. Use the questions here to guide your decision making.

Audience

- How does your audience feel about your problem?

- Is your audience motivated to read about your topic?

- What information does your audience need in order to understand the problem?

Purpose

- What point are you trying to make?

- What effect do you want to have on your readers?

- What do you want the readers to take away from your essay?

Occasion

- How can you make readers understand the significance of the problem without lecturing?

- How can you explain the role they may play in the problem without making them angry?

- How can you make them share your feelings without getting bored?

- When you consider other viewpoints, are you offering opinions or passing judgments?

FOCUSING ON PROCESS

Prewriting

Before you can begin writing an essay, you have to have some material with which to work. Where can you find material for a problem/solution essay?

Collecting Material

- *Your Writer's Breaks for this chapter.* Each of these exercises has helped you amass useful material.

- *Your personal life.* What personal problems are you currently struggling with? Are any of them appropriate for a problem/solution essay?

- *Articles and news reports on current events.* What interesting local or national problems can you learn about from published sources?

- *Your school or place of work.* Are you or your colleagues being affected by any problems at work or school? Would you like to participate in solving them?

Creating Material

- Collect blank paper (poster size works well), scissors, a glue stick, and assorted magazines.

- In the middle of the paper, paste a picture that represents your problem in some way, or if you prefer, write a phrase that identifies your problem.

- Go through the magazines you've collected and cut out pictures and bits of text that are related to your problem.

- Paste these pictures and excerpts on the paper to create a collage effect. You can overlap related items, create designs, or just glue at random.

- When you are done, write a page in your writer's notebook that describes your collage and what it shows about your topic.

Drafting

- Schedule four consecutive days that end at least one day before your paper is due. Be sure to block out two hours on each day.

- On the first day, write the problem portion of your paper.

- On the second day, write the solution portion of your paper.

- On the third day, write about the plan of action.

- On the fourth day, write the introduction and conclusion.

Revising

- Read each sentence in your draft carefully, and determine whether it is a complete sentence.

- If you identify any fragments or run-ons, correct them.

Editing

- Ask a couple of friends to sit and listen while you read your paper out loud.

- Provide each friend with a noisemaker of some kind (a buzzer, two wooden spoons, etc.).

- Ask each friend to use the noisemaker whenever he or she hears you read something he or she doesn't like.

- Mark the spot to go back to later.

Grammar Choices

SENTENCE ERRORS

The three most common sentence errors are fragments, fused sentences, and comma splices.

Fragments

A *fragment* can be one of two things:

A **phrase** is a series of words that may have a noun and a verb form, but they do not act as a subject and a verb.

A **dependent clause** has a subject and a verb but cannot make sense alone.

Phrases

A phrase is a group of words that does not have both a subject and a verb. For example, these are phrases:

running down the street **[participial phrase]**

walked around the block **[verb phrase]**

into the night **[prepositional phrase]**

to run the marathon **[infinitive phrase]**

To correct a fragment, you simply add the missing **subject** and/or **verb**:

He was running down the street.

The cat disappeared into the night.

Dependent Clauses

A dependent clause has a subject and a verb but begins with a word that subordinates the clause and makes it dependent. Common subordinators include the following:

Time—*after, before, once, since, until, when, whenever, while*

Reason—*as, because, since*

Effect—*in order that, so, so that, that*

Condition—*if, even if, provided that, unless*

Contrast—*although, even though, though, whereas*

Location—*where, wherever*

Choice—*than, whether*

When one of these words comes before the subject of a clause, that clause is dependent. If you try to use it as a sentence, you will have a fragment.

Fused Sentences

A *fused sentence* is two or more independent clauses that have been joined without the use of a coordinator or the appropriate punctuation. For example:

It is important to vote in each election **you have** no right to criticize the government if you do not participate in the election process.

I need a car in order to get to work **I worry** that I am contributing to the problem of air pollution.

Because these sentences have two independent clauses that have not been coordinated, they are fused. The writer should place a period or a semicolon after *election* and a comma followed by *but* after *work*.

Comma Splices

Like a fused sentence, a *comma splice* consists of two independent clauses, but in this case they are combined with only a comma. Consider these examples:

Dogs make good companions because of their loyalty, **cats make** good companions because of their independence.

I served in the military for two years before starting college, this **experience helped** to prepare me.

The commas after *loyalty* and *college* could be replaced with semicolons or periods, or the writer could insert a conjunction such as *but* or *and*.

Making It Work

- Identify each independent and dependent clause in your draft or essay.

- Make sure that each sentence has at least one independent clause and that no sentence consists of just a phrase.

- Correct any punctuation errors in your sentences.

Style Choices

TOPICS AND COMMENTS

Every sentence has a subject and a verb. Another way of saying this is to refer to the parts of the sentence as the topic and the comment. The topic is what the sentence is about and is usually the grammatical subject of the sentence, and the comment is everything else in the sentence, what is being said about the topic.

He **[topic]** works for the telephone company **[comment]**.

The restaurant **[topic]** is closed for renovation **[comment]**.

You can use the idea of topic and comment to create coherence in your paragraphs in the following way: After the first sentence, the topic should refer to previously introduced information, and the comment should be what you have to say that is new. Compare the following two paragraphs:

Version One

Dogs and cats **[new]** were probably the first animals to be domesticated **[new]**. Smaller livestock **[new]**, such as sheep and goats, followed **[new]**. Next **[new]** were cattle, pigs, and horses **[new]**. It **[new]** is believed that many animal control problems began immediately after animals were domesticated, including:

- Animal bites
- Territorial conflicts
- Feral animal communities
- Disease transmission, and
- Nuisance animals. **[new]**

Version Two

Dogs and cats **[new]** were the first domesticated animals **[new]**. Domesticated dogs and cats **[old]** were followed by domesticated livestock: sheep, goats, cattle, pigs, and horses **[new]**. Domestic animals **[old]** are the cause of many animal control problems, including:

- Animal bites
- Territorial conflicts
- Feral animal communities
- Disease transmission, and
- Nuisance animals. **[new]**

As you can see, the first paragraph lacks coherence because the writer uses a new-new order; consequently, the reader cannot put the information into a context or see how the ideas relate. In the second paragraph, the writer uses an old-new order. Consequently, each topic is a restatement of the new information in the previous sentence, causing the sentences to build upon one another.

Making It Work

- For each sentence in your paper, identify the topic and the comment.

- Determine if you are you using an old-new order.

- Rearrange information to create coherence.

CHAPTER EIGHT

THE PARADOX OF TECHNOLOGY

Writing to Evaluate

In this chapter, you will learn:

- What evaluation is and how to make it the focus of an essay

- What strategies you can choose when writing to evaluate—comparison/contrast, description, and definition

- The organizational methods commonly used for evaluative writing—topical, conceptual, and chronological order

Zuma Press

The Terminator *series predicts a future in which the machines that humans have created to improve life threaten to end it.*

valuate means "to place a value on" or "to appraise." In the poem that follows, the writer evaluates the qualities of two men, in order to choose between them.

THE LOVER NOT TAKEN (1984)

Blanche Farley

1   Committed to one, she wanted both
And mulling it over, long she stood,
Alone on the road, loath
To leave, wanting to hide in the undergrowth.
This new guy, smooth as yellow wood

6   Really turned her on. She liked his hair,
His smile. But the other, Jack, had a claim
On her already and she had to admit, he did wear
Well. In fact, to be perfectly fair,
He understood her. His long, lithe frame

11 Beside hers in the evening tenderly lay.
Still, if this blond guy dropped by someday,
Couldn't way just lead on to way?
No. For if way led on and Jack
Found out, she doubted he would ever come back.

16 Oh, she turned with a sigh
Somewhere ages and ages hence,
She might be telling this. "And I—"
She would say, "Stood faithfully by."
But then who would know the difference?

21 With that in mind, she took the fast way home,
The road by the pond, and phoned the blond.

This writer's criteria are not as objective as they might be, but it is *her* evaluation, on which she is basing her choice. You might not agree with her choice. Maybe you think she should have stayed with Jack, who understood her. On the other hand, maybe you were convinced by her live-for-the-moment argument. Either way, you have to agree that she did share her process of evaluation with us. We could easily make a list of the attributes of her two lovers.

What this poet did—comparing the value of two different things in order to make a choice between them—is one way people use evaluation. However, you can use evaluation in other ways:

- To choose between available options

- To prove the value of something that you believe has been undervalued

- To determine whether something does have value

- To compare the value of two or more things

- To question the value that someone else places on something.

WHAT IS EVALUATION?

Evaluation requires more than just offering a quick opinion based on a gut response. An evaluation is based on careful observation and study and the use of specific criteria.

When you are making an important decision—what car to buy, what job to accept, where to live—you need more than just someone's opinion. For example, your friend might say that living in an apartment is much better than living in a dorm. However, if she can't give you specific reasons why it is better, based on a careful evaluation of the two options, her opinion won't mean much to you. When an opinion can have serious ramifications for someone else—for example, your review of someone else's job performance could determine whether or not that person keeps the job—your evaluation needs to be based on factual evidence.

Writer's Break

- Take a piece of paper, and draw a line down the middle.
- Label the left side "Positive effects of technology."
- Label the right side "Negative effects of technology."
- List at least ten items under each heading.

The first step toward evaluating anything is developing criteria, or standards for judging that type of thing. This is especially important if you will be comparing one thing to another.

If you were asked to review local restaurants for your school paper, you would have to develop criteria to guide your evaluation. You would begin by asking yourself these questions: What types of restaurants will I review? Will I choose by location? Type of food served? Price range? Quality? Clearly, it would not be fair to compare the quality of food at a local fast-food franchise to the fine cuisine at a five-star restaurant, so you have to decide what your readers need most. If you determine that good-quality food at a reasonable price within a convenient area is most important, you could choose to evaluate only non–fast-food establishments within walking distance of campus. Next, you could develop your criteria:

- Quality of food—taste, presentation, freshness
- Price—per serving, size of serving
- Service—speed, atmosphere, friendliness
- Options—number of selections available
- Health consciousness—availability of low-fat and vegetarian options

Without specific criteria, you might find yourself taking a hit-or-miss approach—evaluating one aspect of this restaurant and a different aspect of that one. This approach will not lead to a useful evaluation because your readers will not be convinced that you have fairly or completely judged each restaurant. Look at the following report, which evaluates different types of fish. Clearly, the fact that we are unable to control the pollution levels in certain types of commonly eaten fish is a serious problem. Is it just a matter of time until these fish are inedible?

RIGHT FISH, LEAST RISK

Consumer Reports

Fish is rich in omega-3s and other nutrients. But some species may contain excessive amounts of certain pollutants. The most comprehensive data on those pollutants involve mercury. The amounts of that heavy metal in some fish can harm the nervous system of a fetus or young child; whether they do so in adults isn't clear. While studies show that eating fish generally reduces the overall death rate, it's wise to minimize any potential risks from pollutants.   1

YOUR CHOICES

- Most people should eat a variety of fish, frequently choosing the species in the table below that don't have any asterisks. (Fish marked with one asterisk may be high in mercury.) Most people should eat no more than 8 ounces a month of the species marked with two asterisks, which contain the most mercury—shark, swordfish, and king mackerel. Note that prepared breaded and fried fish are generally poor choices, since they tend to be high in heart-unhealthy trans fat and low in omega-3s.   2

- Women who are nursing or pregnant or who may become pregnant should avoid the species with two asterisks and eat no more than 8 ounces per week of those fish with one asterisk. They should heed any warnings from their state, posted on the Internet, about locally caught fish that may be contaminated.   3

- Children under age 5 should eat none of the asterisked fish, except white tuna. That should be limited to 1.5 ounces per week. State warnings generally apply to young children as well.   4

KEEPING FISH FRESH

- Choose fish that looks neither dry nor slimy and that doesn't smell excessively "fishy."   5

- Refrigerate fresh fish as soon as possible. If you won't be eating it within a day, wrap it tightly and put it in the freezer.   6

3-oz. serving (steamed or baked, except where noted)	Omega-3 content (EPA & DHA, in g)
SALMON, ATLANTIC	1.8 g
HERRING, ATLANTIC	1.7
SALMON, PINK, CANNED	1.4
WHITEFISH	1.4
TUNA, BLUEFIN *	1.3
MACKEREL, ATLANTIC	1.0
TROUT, RAINBOW	1.0
BLUEFISH	0.8
SARDINES, OIL-CANNED	0.8
MUSSELS, BLUE	0.7
SWORDFISH **	0.7
TUNA, WATER-CANNED, WHITE *	0.7
BASS, FRESHWATER *	0.6
SHARK (fried) **	0.6
POLLOCK, ATLANTIC	0.5
CRAB, ALASKAN KING	0.4
HALIBUT *	0.4
SOLE/FLOUNDER	0.4
MACKEREL, KING **	0.3
OYSTERS (raw)	0.3
PERCH, OCEAN	0.3
SHRIMP	0.3
CATFISH, FARMED	0.2
CLAMS	0.2
COD, PACIFIC	0.2
TUNA, WATER-CANNED, LIGHT	0.2
TUNA, OIL-CANNED, LIGHT	0.1

The recommended intake of EPA plus DHA omega-3s for most adults is at least 2 grams per week.
* May be high in mercury; see text for precautions.
** Contains the most mercury.
Sources: For omega-3s, USDA; for mercury, FDA, Environmental Protection Agency, and Consumer Reports tests.

Notice that the author of this article made clear the criteria used for the comparison: For the most commonly eaten fish, the relative level of mercury is provided, and specific recommendations are made for different categories of people. Anyone reading this article would be able to determine which fish are safe to eat in unlimited quantities and which should be limited or avoided.

≡ Making Evaluation the Focus of a Paper

When you write to evaluate, you make your appraisal or judgment of something the focus of your paper—in other words, the point is to give your opinion regarding the relative value or merit of that thing. You might evaluate two or more things in order to make a decision: You might evaluate three different cars, for example, and then compare them in order to determine which one is the best buy. Many magazines such as *Consumer Reports* offer evaluations of this sort. You might evaluate a published article or a book in order to recommend that other people read it as well. You might evaluate a historical decision, such as the acceptance of Hawaii as a state of the union, in order to show how that decision adversely affected the native population.

Evaluation is a very useful writing tool that helps you justify your opinion of something in order to help your readers draw their own conclusions. A well-written evaluation can save readers a great deal of time and money. For example, movie and restaurant reviews allow us to make wise choices so that we don't waste our money on something that is not worth the price being asked. Other people's considered opinions can save us from having to learn the hard way.

You can focus on evaluation as the writer of the following essay does—to question the value generally placed on something and ask whether it's justified.

Technology Rules the World

Aaron Anderson

Organizational method—
conceptual

Most people think it is ridiculous to believe that technology could ever control humans simply because we created the technology in question. However, there are those who not only fear technology but also suspect that it may have sinister intentions, a.k.a. the matrix. I don't believe that machines will someday rise up and overthrow the human race, but the question of who is in control is an interesting one. Although technological advances were originally intended to make life easier, it could be argued that the technological gadgetry with which we surround ourselves only clutters our existence. Have we become too reliant on technology to perform tasks we once trusted to our own hands and minds? No matter where we go, technology is our constant companion. And in more ways than one, we are technology's slave.

Purpose of evaluation—to question the value we place on technology and its effects

First criterion—technology strains our finances

First of all, technological gadgetry costs money. Every year new technology makes our televisions, VCRs, DVD players, stereos, etc. obsolete. While we can praise the human ingenuity that keeps improving these products (which we seem unable to live without), we have to question the financial toll it takes on our wallets. In the 21st century "keeping up with the Joneses" has taken on a whole new meaning. Best Buys, Circuit Cities, and Radio Shacks litter the landscape. We are a society of consumers, and technology is in demand. Why don't we just say no? People could work less and read more if they weren't constantly making payments on a new home computer or a fully loaded entertainment center.

Unfortunately, technology itself often makes this difficult. Gone are the days of records, eight tracks, cassettes, BETA, and soon, even VHS. The common thread that connects these outdated media is that all of them were once technological giants in their respective fields. Anyone who thinks he or she has the definitive, top-of-the-line anything is a fool. Give it a year and the technology industry will have developed something new that will leave yours in the dust. Before you know it you'll be running to Best Buy, credit card in hand. If you're lucky, you will have finished paying off the equipment already taking up space in your house.

Aside from putting people in the poor house, technology can also make a person dumber. No one balances check books anymore. A person simply logs on to his or her account and checks the bank statement. Because these figures magically appear on the computer, we assume that they are correct. Of

Second criterion— technology is soon outdated

Third criterion— technology makes us dumber

course banking technology could never let us down. Since so many of us have lost our ability to do the math required to check the balance, let's hope this is true. Once upon a time it was considered normal to know the multiplication tables from the 1×1s through the 1×12s. No more. Why remember anything as mundane as multiplication when you can use a calculator?

Fourth criterion—cell phones have enslaved us

Of all the ways in which technology has enslaved us, cell phones have the tightest hold. I never leave home without my cell phone. I'm not anticipating any emergencies--I just don't want to miss any calls. Despite the fact that very few people seem to have completely controlled that piece of technology we call the car, now people commonly attempt to drive while talking on a cell phone. My math is rusty, but I think that is two times the usual danger. We used to go on vacations to get away from the demands of work and home. Not anymore. Cell phones let us take worries with us no matter where we go.

Fifth criterion—technology is even invading our bodies

Technology is even invading our bodies. I'm not talking about pacemakers or prosthetic devices--I'm talking nanotechnology. In all fairness, nanotechnology may offer a way to remedy various malfunctions of the brain, but it may also tempt us to begin installing chips in people's heads that contain huge amounts of information. Imagine having a complete set of encyclopedias installed in your brain.

Make a list of every piece of technology that you own, and every form of technology you use each day. You will be surprised at the length of the list. While you're working on that, I'm going to make some microwave popcorn and watch a DVD. I'll leave my computer on in case you want to send me an email.

> Result of evaluation—we depend too heavily on technology

Consider this . . .

- What is this writer evaluating?
- What factors does the writer choose to evaluate?
- Did the evaluation provide you with useful information?

Writer's Break

Ask ten people of different ages and backgrounds the following questions:

- How far do you walk every day?
- How often do you exercise?
- Are there any physical activities that you used to do but have given up?
- Why did you stop?
- Are people as active as they were 20 years ago? Why or why not?

Based on the information you collect, what conclusions can you draw?

CHOOSING STRATEGIES WHEN WRITING TO EVALUATE

When you write to evaluate, you can use any of the strategies for development we discussed in Chapter Two, but the ones you will use most often are these:

- Comparison/contrast
- Description
- Definition

Comparison/Contrast

Comparison/contrast is a very useful strategy when you write to evaluate because it allows you to show similarities and differences between things. It also gives you a way to present people's differing opinions about something you are evaluating.

Description

When you write to evaluate, you often need to describe. You might need to describe the thing or things you are evaluating or the criteria you are using. You might need to describe people's reactions to whatever you are evaluating or your own experience with it.

Definition

Until you tell your readers what something is, you can't establish what its value is. Consequently, you may want to begin by defining what you are evaluating. You might also have to define the criteria you use to evaluate.

In the next essay, the writer evaluates the names of historical eras based on the technology that marked those periods and questions what we should call the current era.

What's in a Name?

Terry Smith

What's in a name? A rose by any other name would smell as sweet. Yet, we all know that names do matter because they define who and what we are. Throughout history, we have been defined by technology: Stone Age, Bronze Age, Iron Age, Industrial Age. Each of these ages was influenced, and in part determined, by the technology that controlled it. The practical application of the technology discovered in each era was responsible for shaping lifestyles. If this is true, how do we define the 21st century? Are we the Computer Age, the Cyber Age, the Internet Age? If historical ages have always been named for the technology that revolutionized the lives of the people who lived in that era, maybe we are the Computer Age because the common thread that weaves together the technological advances of the 21st century is the computer. However, before we adopt this moniker, we must carefully evaluate its appropriateness.

Organizational method— topical blended with chronological

The Stone Age

Archivo Iconographico, S. A./Corbis

Description of Stone Age

During the Stone Age, humans used sharpened stones and sticks to dig roots and round stones to grind those roots into a pulp. The use of stone tools separated humans from other animals, so the name "Stone Age" is uniquely appropriate to name this phase in human development.

The Bronze and Iron Ages

Description of Bronze and Iron Ages

It was the discovery of fire that led to the development of bronze tools. When humans used their stones tools in conjunction with fire, they learned that some stones contained metal such as copper and tin that could be smelted from rocks and shaped into new tools. Many centuries later humans learned to mix alloys to create new metals such as bronze (hence the Bronze Age) which were harder.

Cause/effect

Humans did not move from the Bronze Age to the Iron Age because of the shift from making tools from bronze to making tools from iron. The shift occurred because of the discovery of a revolutionary process-- the making of iron, which allowed humans to make things bigger, better and faster. It was from the processes developed when people began making iron, that steel was discovered. Steel

Archivo Iconographico, S. A./Corbis

was the foundation of the industrial revolution. And even today, steel is the metal most commonly used to build everything from cars to skyscrapers. Does this mean we are still in the Iron Age? Many people disagree.

The Computer Age?

Today, the tool that controls and shapes our lives is the computer. Computers are the agents which we use to create, store, and share information. As of yet, computers have no intellect of their own; computers are intermediaries--they are not yet sources of information. However, computers were the catalyst for the information boom we call the Internet. The Internet, a world

Definition of computers

wide web of information, supplies us with more information on a daily basis than we can read in a lifetime. Furthermore, because the information

Richard Orton/Index Stock Imagery

is dynamic--changed, altered, and added to almost every minute--there is no likelihood that we will ever be able to keep up with the flow of information being generated. Given the fact that it is the flow of information that seems to shape our world, and computers which help create and control it, perhaps we are now in the Computer Age.

Why Now?

Comparison/contrast— previous ages to current age

Clearly the creation and proliferation of information is not a completely new invention. Before recorded history humans used smoke to send signals, and plant and animal dyes to paint on rock. Later more advanced technologies were discovered: paper, ink, pens, pencils, type, typewriters, etc. With each and every advance, the speed with which information could be sent, and the distance which it covered dramatically increased. Yet we didn't name any of the eras in which these discoveries were made the Information Age. Why?

As I stated earlier, each age was named for the technology that controlled it. Certainly, the invention of technologies such as paper and ink were important, but they were not the technological discoveries that controlled those eras. Those discoveries were overshadowed by other discoveries. In the 21st century, the computer technologies that have been developed to create and control information truly have defined our age.

Computers--Paving the Way for the Future

Are we in the Computer Age? Centuries in the future, will it be known by this name? Have we truly been defined by this technology? Or is it defining us? Will we find new ways to manage this information or will it bury us under its mass? Are we foolish to think that we are controlling either computers or the information they proliferate?

We assume that because computers cannot think for themselves, they do not have the ability to control themselves. It may seem egotistical to think that if an entity does not have the ability to think or learn for itself, it cannot control the lives of

Writer's Break

From previous Writer's Breaks, choose the topic you find the most interesting. What criteria could you use to make an evaluation based on that topic? List those criteria.

humans. In fact, many people believe we have been enslaved by technology. But however convenient technology might make our lives, we could live without it--we have lived without it. Evidence shows that humans have historically used technology to improve their lives, but not to control it. From the discovery of fire to the invention of nuclear energy, humans have paved the way for technology not vice versa.

In the next brief essay, the writer evaluates a newly developed hearing aid for children who are profoundly deaf.

THE SOUND AND THE WORRY

David Bjerklie

1   The cochlear implant is a technological miracle that has restored hearing to thousands of children with severe to profound hearing loss. But according to a study conducted by the FDA and the CDC, children who receive implants are more than 30 times as likely to develop bacterial meningitis infections. These infections, even when treated with antibiotics, are lethal in some 10% of cases.

2   This certainly doesn't mean parents should give up on implants. The risk of infection is still tiny. The study advises that all children getting implants have the shots (pneumococcal and Hib) that protect against meningitis. Also, parents should watch for warning signs of infection, such as a high fever and a stiff neck.

Writer's Break

You've chosen a topic and made a list of possible criteria. Now:

- ■ Write an evaluative thesis statement.
- ■ Determine what information you still need to collect.
- ■ Create an outline of your essay.

CHOOSING AN ORGANIZATIONAL METHOD

You can use any of the methods of organization outlined in Chapter Two when you write to evaluate, but your best choices are these:

- ▪ Topical order
- ▪ Conceptual order
- ▪ Chronological order

Topical Order

When you use topical organization, you present several related points about a topic and then develop those points. In the case of an evaluation, you might organize your paper topically based on either the criteria you are using to evaluate your subject or the subjects themselves if you are discussing more than one.

Conceptual Order

When you use conceptual organization, you introduce points related to your topic and then develop and link them. In the case of an evaluation, you might make specific points regarding whatever you are evaluating and then link those points to draw your conclusion regarding its relative value.

☰ Chronological Order

When you use chronological organization, you order the information on the basis of time. The previous essay used chronological organization in discussing the historical eras from earliest to most recent. The next essay uses a blend of chronological and conceptual organization to evaluate computer chess playing.

MAN VERSUS MACHINE

Ross Bentley

1   He is probably the most famous chess champion in history, and certainly the most successful grandmaster of recent times. But lately Garry Kasparov has been cast in an even loftier role—standard-bearer for the human mind in the battle with computer-generated intellect. As *Newsweek* put it, he embodies "the brain's last stand."

2   Kasparov made his name in a series of classic battles with Anatoly Karpov in the 1980s, but a new generation of chess fans know him as the frowning Russian who pits his wits against the most sophisticated chess software around.

3   The latest of these contests took place at the New York Athletic Club last month when Kasparov drew a six-match encounter with a PC-based computer program called Deep Junior.

4   Winner of the world computer chess championship three times and noted for its aggressive attacking style and tremendous tactical ability, Deep Junior is the creation of Israeli programmers Amir Ban and Shay Bushinsky.

5   Computer chess software has a rich heritage stretching back to IBM's Deep Blue computer, which Kasparov first played—and beat—in 1996, and IBM's Deeper Blue, which famously defeated the Russian in 1997.

6   But, according to Ban, this latest creation marks a quantum step in the evolution of chess software. "Compared with Deep Blue's awesome powers of number crunching, almost 300 million calculations per second, Deep Junior is a babe," he says. "The strength, however, of Deep Junior is that it processes in more abstract human terms. Deep Junior's capability of three million moves per second may not sound like much, but it also analyses and assesses the best future moves at the same time," he says.

Supporters of Deep Junior say its humanoid qualities were best illustrated in game five of last month's tightly fought contest, when it took the speculative step of sacrificing a bishop in order to further its progress. "What it did was audacious and unprecedented in the history of man versus machine—its seemingly human-like cunning took everyone's breath away," says Bushinsky. 7

ASCENDANCY

But while Kasparov admits he had to muster all his powers of concentration after this unconventional manoeuvre, he denies that the contest signifies the ascendancy of the computer over the human mind. "What this tournament has shown is why a computer, in my view, cannot be more like a human, at least not in the immediate future. Whatever Shay and Amir say about Junior's ability to run through millions of possible strategies, I, by contrast, might consider only a few strategies in any one game. But you can bet your life they will be the very best ones," says Kasparov. 8

With several titanic struggles against high-powered chess computers under his belt, Kasparov is keen to expand on his theme. "The mind's essence is creativity and the ability to improvise—this is what demarcates humans' brains from computer software. Chess computers have something I call a 'black limit'. Based on its pre-programmed algorithms, a chess computer will calculate six, seven or maybe eight moves ahead. The problem is that once the computer has decided upon a course of action, it is very hard for the machine to change that instantaneously. We humans—even when playing a strategic game like chess—will nearly always feel the danger even before it happens." 9

But if chess computers are always going to play second fiddle to the human mind, do they have any use in the wider world? 10

While academics have, for the most part, rubbished the idea of chess programs being important testing grounds for the future development of artificial intelligence, Bushinsky says he is in negotiation with a number of parties to develop the commercial potential of Deep Junior. 11

At IBM where the original Deep Blue program was developed on an RS/6000 Unix server, the high-powered, number-crunching technology honed for the Kasparov contests is now being used to compute large quantities of data in areas such as molecular modelling and oil exploration. 12

"Deep Blue may make big headlines but the real work of Deep Blue's RS/6000 technology takes place quietly," says Mark Bregnan, general manager of IBM's RS/6000 division. "Day after day, the IBM RS/6000 helps pharmaceutical com- 13 panies develop innovative drug therapies, auto makers design cars and petroleum companies explore for oil under the ocean. It also helps forecast the weather."

14   But whatever the context, computers have one habit that places them below humans in the food chain, as Kasparov is quick to point out. "People think that chess is a calm and gentlemanly game. But in fact it is a sport that can, on a psychological level, be very aggressive and dynamic," he says. "I like to joke that I managed to psych out Deep Blue in our second tournament in 1997. Not a lot of people know that Deep Blue actually crashed three times—something IBM's PR department initially tried to deny."

Consider this . . .

- Did this writer choose an effective organizational pattern?
- How did he make his evaluation pertinent to his readers?
- Did you find the article interesting? Why or why not?

The next two brief reports evaluate techniques for combating and diagnosing physical problems. Is technology helping us win the fight against disease and disability? Or is it taking over our bodies?

PARKINSON'S DISEASE AND PAIN RELIEVERS

The quaking, shaking symptoms of Parkinson's disease afflict $1\frac{1}{2}$ million Americans. It can be slowed but not cured, which makes prevention all the more appealing. A new study, released in the *Archives of Neurology*, suggests that regular use of nonsteroidal anti-inflammatory drugs (NSAIDs) such as ibuprofen offers some protection. About 44,000 men and 99,000 women were followed for 14 and 18 years, respectively. Researchers found that the risk of developing Parkinson's was 45% lower among men and women who regularly use nonaspirin NSAIDs than among nonusers. Also last week a Parkinson's patient was treated with an experimental gene therapy. Results probably won't be known for months.

BETTER X-RAY VISION

Fenella Saunders

Medical X rays are so penetrating that they pass right through the soft tissues that can reveal diseases the bone does not. But a novel X-ray imager, developed by anatomist Carol Muehleman of Rush Medical College in Chicago, physicist Zhong Zhong of Brookhaven National Laboratory, and numerous colleagues, brings tendons and ligaments, even skin and blood vessels, into view.

The new method, called diffraction-enhanced imaging, takes advantage of the intense X-ray beam generated at the National Synchrotron Light Source, a particle accelerator at Brookhaven. Once filtered and collimated [aligned], the beam passes through the body part being studied and onto a silicon crystal, which bounces the X rays onto film. Each type of soft tissue bends the X rays by a slightly different amount, allowing it to show, for instance, the way the surface of cartilage turns rough in the early stages of osteoarthritis.

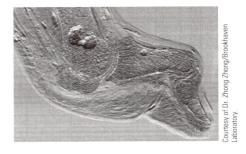

Courtesy of Dr. Zhong Zhong/Brookhaven Laboratory

In tests on cadaver toes, researchers could clearly see skin, nails, tendons, and the fat pad in the ball of the foot. "We are picking up different tissue characteristics than MRI can pick up, and the imaging times are much shorter. We're taking seconds as opposed to sometimes 45 minutes," says Muehleman. The research team is now adapting the technique to smaller, more practical X-ray sources.

EACH DAY, we make many choices. We choose the food we eat. We choose how to spend our money and our time. We choose our attitudes. Evaluation is a tool that can help us to make successful choices. Without evaluation, we might find ourselves not only regretting our choices, but failing to understand why they were poor. Evaluation will not allow you to avoid making bad choices, but it will maximize your chances of making good ones. And writing to evaluate will give you the ability to share what you learn with others so that they can benefit from your experience. ▪

COLLABORATIVE EXERCISES

Group Exercise One

■ As a group, choose a common example of technology (for example, a toothbrush, a blow dryer, an electric razor, a can opener, or a can), and write a brief essay based on the following criteria:

> You must write to an audience who is not familiar with the item you picked. For example, you might write to a Stone Age person or someone from another planet.

> You must explain the thing and its purpose to the person, and evaluate its usefulness as a tool.

■ Be prepared to share your work with the class.

Group Exercise Two

■ As a group, choose three varieties of one product to compare and contrast. For example, you might compare three brands of pizza or three energy drinks.

■ Develop three criteria that you will use to compare the versions of the product you chose.

■ Write a brief essay presenting the results of your evaluation and suggesting the best product based on the criteria you developed.

■ Share your material with the class.

Group Exercise Three

■ Exchange copies of the essays that you wrote for Group Exercise Two. Each group should get another group's essay.

■ As a group, read the essay you received and determine how effectively the writers evaluated the product they chose. Make a list of specific ways in which the essay was successful and specific ways in which it should be revised.

■ Present your findings to the class.

■ As a class, make a list of criteria for evaluating the essays you write in response to this chapter's Writing Picks.

WRITING PICKS

Option One

The good old days

Have you ever heard anyone talk about the good old days? Those simple bygone times when people read books, families gathered around the piano for sing-alongs every night, and children actually knew the multiplication tables? For most of us, it's hard to imagine life without television, computers, and DVD players. We are so surrounded by technology that we no longer do many of the tasks we once did. How often do you work a math problem with pencil and paper? Isn't that what calculators are for? How often do you sit around and talk with your friends or play a game like cards or charades? Isn't it more fun to watch a DVD or listen to music? When was the last time you read a book? On the other hand, do pacemakers prolong lives? Have new medications improved the quality of life? How has technology affected our lives? Do you consider the changes positive or negative? Evaluate the effect of some form of technology on our lives, being sure to give evidence to support your conclusion.

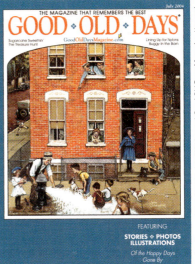

Option Two

I walked three miles uphill to school each day

Many scientists believe that one of the reasons that obesity and heart disease are on the rise is because technology has made it possible for us to turn into couch potatoes. We no longer grow our own food. We no longer walk to our destinations. Cleaning our houses is less physically demanding. We can ride elevators rather than climb stairs. Is technology to blame for the poor physical condition of Americans, or are we simply choosing to be couch potatoes? Evaluate the situation, and determine where to place the blame for those extra pounds—on humans or on technology.

Children playing outside was once a common sight. Why has that changed?

Option Three

Lost without technology?

There are people alive today in the United States who remember life before electricity, cars, telephones, television, and other forms of technology that are now considered a standard part of life. Once people made their own bread and killed their own meat. They sewed their own clothes and washed them by hand. How would we survive if all our technology disappeared tomorrow? Could we manage, or have we lost all our survival skills? In your essay, evaluate the likelihood that average Americans could live without technology, and offer specific suggestions to support your viewpoint.

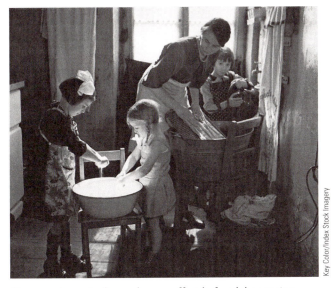

Housework required more human effort before labor-saving technology was developed.

Option Four

The future of humankind

The premise of many movies is the destruction of humans by technology. In *2001: A Space Odyssey*, Hal, the computer, takes over the ship and tries to destroy the occupants. In *Star Trek: First Contact*, the Borg, half-human, half-machine life forms controlled by a central computer, attempt to take over the universe. In the *Terminator* series, the very androids created to save humankind attempt to destroy it. Do you believe that this is what the future holds for us? If we continue to create bigger, smarter machines, will those machines eventually enslave us? Will machines take over the world? Evaluate this premise, and offer your own opinion based on the available evidence.

Zuma Press

Photofest

Warner Bros. Pictures/Zuma Press

APPLYING THE RHETORICAL SITUATION

As always, you must consider the rhetorical situation throughout the process of making choices for an evaluative essay. Use the questions here to guide your decision making.

Audience

■ Is your audience likely to have strong opinions about what you have chosen to evaluate?

■ How can your audience use the information you are providing?

■ What information does your audience need in order to consider your evaluation fair and accurate?

■ Are you using any specialized vocabulary that you will need to define for your audience?

Purpose

■ What is the purpose of your evaluation? To change people's opinions? To help them make a decision?

■ What techniques can you use to make your point?

■ How can you structure your essay to emphasize that point?

■ What do you want readers to take away from reading your essay?

Occasion

■ How can you provide readers with the information they need in an interesting manner?

■ How can you use tables, charts, or other graphics to make your evaluation clear to readers?

■ When you consider other viewpoints, are you offering opinions or passing judgments?

FOCUSING ON PROCESS

Prewriting

- Identify at least five forms of technology that you use every day.

- For each item, list the positive benefits of that piece of technology.

- For each item, list the negative effects of that piece of technology.

- Based on your evaluation, would you recommend that people use that piece of technology?

Drafting

- Outline your essay.

- Use your outline to create the major headings and subheadings for your paper.

- Use a different font size for each level of heading.

- Write a draft using these headings for your guide.

Revising

- Make two copies of your paper.

- Give one copy to a friend, who will read your paper out loud to you while you listen.

- As he or she reads, mark your own copy. Use question marks, circles, underlining, whatever marks will help you remember where you need to do more work.

- Ask your friend's opinion when you are done.

Editing

- Run a grammar checker on your draft.
- What errors did it flag?
- Did you agree with every change that the program suggested?
- How many changes did you accept?

Grammar Choices

PRONOUNS

Pronouns are words that substitute for nouns or other pronouns. There are several types of pronouns:

Personal—*I, you, he, she, it, we, they, me, him, her, us, them*

She gave **me** a book.

Possessive—*my, mine, his, hers, its, our, ours, your, yours, their, theirs*

My home is **your** home.

Demonstrative—*this, that, these, those*

This dog is his, and **that** dog is hers.

Indefinite—*all, any, anyone, anybody, anything, both, each, either, everyone, everything, many, neither, no one, none, nothing, one, some, someone, something*

Everyone tried to do his or her best.

Relative—*that, which, what, who, whom, whose, whatever, whoever, whomever, whichever*

The vacation **that** we planned so carefully was a huge success.

Interrogative—*who, which, what, whose, where*

Who would like to go to the movies?

Reflexive—*myself, ourselves, yourself, yourselves, himself, herself, itself, themselves*

The girls fixed the car **themselves**.

Reciprocal—*each other, one another*

The horses chased **each other**.

When you use a pronoun in a sentence, it must agree in number with the noun or pronoun it is renaming and the verb that follows it:

> **They** should heed any warnings from **their** state, posted on the Internet, about locally caught fish that may be contaminated.

In this sentence, the plural personal pronoun *they* is the subject of the sentence and is followed by the plural possessive pronoun *their*.

> **No one** balances checkbooks anymore. A person simply logs on to **his or her** account and checks the bank statement.

In the first sentence, *no one* is an indefinite pronoun that serves as the subject of the sentence. The verb *balances* has the singular form because *no one* is singular. In the second sentence, the singular subject *person* is followed by the singular possessive pronoun *his or her*.

> When humans used **their** stone tools in conjunction with fire, **they** learned that some stone contained metal such as copper and tin that could be smelted from rocks and shaped into new tools.

In this sentence, the plural subject *humans* is followed by the plural possessive pronoun *their* and the plural personal pronoun *they*.

Sentences that contain indefinite pronouns are especially prone to agreement errors. Remember, even though they may seem to imply that they refer to more than one person, the following indefinite pronouns are singular:

> Is **anyone** going?

> Does **anybody** have his or her class notes?

> If **anything** can go wrong, it will go wrong.

> **Everyone** is working hard.

> **Everything** is fine.

> **No one** was willing to volunteer his or her time to help.

> **Nothing** is wrong with me.

> **One** can never spend enough time with his or her friends.

Some is more than none.

Someone is responsible for this mess.

Somebody left his or her car keys at my house.

Something always prevents us from leaving on time.

Making It Work

- Circle each pronoun in your draft or essay.

- Draw a line from the pronoun to the noun to which it refers.

- Make sure each pronoun agrees with each noun.

Style Choices

CONCISENESS

Many writers clutter their writing by using words they don't need. Writers do this for a number of reasons:

- Because they are afraid their essays will be too short

- Because they are attempting to sound "academic"

- Because they are trying to use colorful language

Student writers often worry that they have too few words. This can be a valid concern, but fillers won't fool your readers. It is fine to experiment with different styles, but adding unnecessary words is not the way to achieve effect.

In order to write concisely, avoid these common problems:

- Repetition

- Fillers

- Unnecessary phrases

Repetition

You do not need to say the same thing twice. This problem arises when you use certain phrases:

> Whatever Shay and Amir say about Junior's ability to run through millions of possible strategies, I, by contrast, might consider only a few strategies in **any one** game.

The phrase *any one*, is redundant because *any* and *one* mean the same thing in this context.

> With **each and every** advance, the speed with which information could be sent and the distance which it covered dramatically increased.

Because *each* and *every* mean the same thing, there is no reason to use both.

Fillers

Fillers are words that take up space but add no meaning.

> First **of all**, technological gadgetry costs money.

The words *of all* do not add any further information that *first* did not already give.

> Yet, we all know that names do matter because they define **who and what we are**.

In this sentence, the writer could have simply said *who we are*. The words *and what* are fillers.

> Most people think it is ridiculous to believe that technology could ever control humans simply because we created the technology **in question**.

The readers do not need the words *in question* to identify which technology is being discussed.

Unnecessary Phrases

Phrases often add valuable information to a sentence, but they sometimes serve no purpose and should be deleted.

> No matter where we go, technology is our constant companion. **And in more ways than one**, we are technology's slave.

In this sentence, the phrase *And in more ways than one* is unnecessary. It can be deleted without losing any relevant information.

> **Given the fact that** it is the flow of information that seems to shape our world, and computers which help create and control it, perhaps we are in the Computer Age.

Here the writer should have avoided using the phrase *Given the fact that*. It would be better to begin this sentence with *Because*.

> While we can praise the human ingenuity that keeps improving these products (which we seem unable to live without), we have to question the financial toll **it takes on our wallets**.

Clearly, a financial toll will affect our wallets; therefore, the writer could delete the final modifying clause.

Making It Work

- Underline each phrase in your draft or essay.

- Determine whether any of the phrases are unnecessary.

- Remove the unnecessary phrases.

CHAPTER NINE

THE POWER OF NATURE

Writing to Persuade

In this chapter, you will learn:

- To recognize persuasive communication

- How to develop a persuasive thesis

- Strategies for writing persuasively—Aristotelian, Rogerian, and Toulmin arguments

- How to organize a persuasive essay—classical, inductive, and deductive arrangements

Chuck Doswell/Visuals Unlimited

Natural disasters make headlines and draw federal funds, but scientists and writers still struggle to persuade people to recognize more subtle environmental problems such as global warming.

TYPES OF PERSUASIVE COMMUNICATION

What types of communication are persuasive? In order to answer this question, you first need to consider the definition of persuasion. *Persuasion* means using arguments or reasons to influence someone. Persuasive communication attempts to move you to action, to change your opinion, or to consider another option. For example, advertisements try to persuade you to purchase products.

"Time to Come Out of Hibernation." Photo by Anthony Redpath represented by Robert Bacall. Graphics by Copacino. Courtesy, REI.

Political speeches persuade you to support a political agenda. President Abraham Lincoln's famous "Gettysburg Address" sought support for the abolishment of slavery:

> The world will little note nor long remember what we say here, but it can never forget what they did here. It is for us the living rather to be dedicated here to the unfinished work which they who fought here have thus far so nobly advanced. It is rather for us to be here dedicated to the great task remaining before us— that from these honored dead we take increased devotion to that cause for which they gave the last full measure of devotion—that we here highly resolve that these dead shall not have died in vain, that this nation under God shall have a new birth of freedom, and that government of the people, by the people, and for the people shall not perish from the earth.

Propaganda posters persuade you to support a policy or a cause.

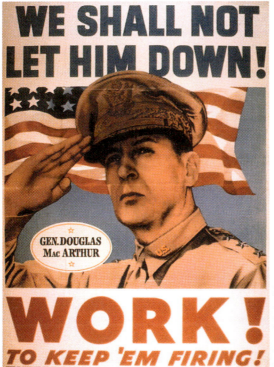

The Granger Collection, NY

Editorials persuade you to consider someone's viewpoint.

FROM "WHERE IS THY STING?"
Nicholas D. Kristof

Pssst. Wanna live to the age of 600?

This may not be as absurd a question as it sounds. Genetic medicine is making enormous strides, and it may hold the promise—or maybe it's the peril—of eventually making us something closer to immortal. . . .

We are now blundering . . . toward genetic manipulations, a technology that we should embrace—but prudently. It will reshape humanity far more than fire, electricity, space exploration or any other branch of science we have encountered. We might remember the wisdom of Odysseus, who was offered immortality by a luscious goddess, Calypso, but turned her down to grow old and die with his wife, Penelope.

These are only a few examples of the types of persuasive documents we encounter every day. In fact, all written communication is persuasive to some degree—we write in order to be read; in order to be read, we must persuade a reader to read. We use a number of techniques to make our writing persuasive, including these:

- We make it interesting.
- We make it correct.
- We make it informative.
- We create an effective design.

However, if all communication is persuasive, how is an essay in which you take a stand different from any other essay? An essay in which you take a stand begins with an arguable thesis and that thesis is supported in the remainder of the essay. This is primary persuasion. Your goal as a writer in this case is to persuade someone to accept your position on the issue.

MAKING CHOICES WHEN YOU WRITE TO PERSUADE

When we argue for a position, we choose one side of an issue and argue in support of it. For example, if we take an issue such as banning cigarettes in all restaurants, four people could argue four different viewpoints:

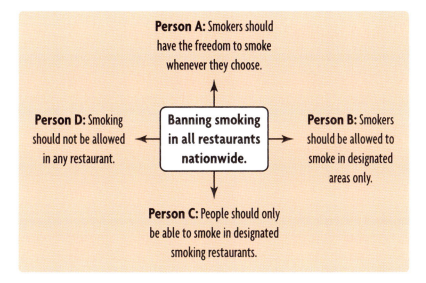

Person A: Smokers should have the freedom to smoke whenever they choose.

Person D: Smoking should not be allowed in any restaurant.

Banning smoking in all restaurants nationwide.

Person B: Smokers should be allowed to smoke in designated areas only.

Person C: People should only be able to smoke in designated smoking restaurants.

Each person could formulate an argument to support his or her viewpoint, but only if he or she could understand both verbally and visually what it means to take a stand. Furthermore, in order to support a position on a topic, each person must also consider the opinions of others about the topic. Normally, when you pick a topic on which to take a stand, you will not have a clear sense of who your opponents are. However, this does not mean that you can dismiss other viewpoints. Part of your job as the writer of a persuasive essay is discovering what other viewpoints exist, so that you can develop arguments to refute them.

Writer's Break

Look through magazines and other sources of information to find an article concerning humans or their property being hurt by nature:

■ In the article you identified, who do you believe was at fault? Humans or nature?

■ What opinion did the writer of the article have?

Thus, when you write an essay in which you take a stand, you have to complete several steps:

- Choose a controversial topic.
- Develop a persuasive thesis.
- Develop supporting arguments.
- Refute opposing position(s).

≡ Recognizing When a Topic Is Controversial

The first step toward writing a persuasive essay is to choose a controversial topic. This might seem like a simple task, but you need to consider these questions:

- Is the topic arguable?
- Is it pertinent to a broad audience?

Is it arguable?

Your first instinct might be that every topic is arguable. Some people act as though this is true. However, would you want to argue about these topics?

- Who makes a better hamburger, McDonald's or Burger King?
- Which is better, VHS or DVD?
- Which is better, a ski vacation or a beach vacation?

You might argue topics like these if they had personal relevance for you—perhaps you are trying to decide where to go for spring break—however, these topics have no real significance. So, perhaps the question we should ask about a topic is not whether it is arguable, but whether it is worth arguing. In order to determine if a topic is worth arguing, consider these questions:

- Are you willing to devote time and energy to creating a good argument?

- Is the topic significant or trivial?

- Is it of passing or lasting importance?

Is it pertinent to a broad audience?

Sometimes, in order to determine if a topic is worth arguing, you have to determine who it affects. In other words, if the topic has pertinence only for you or a handful of people, it is not a good choice for an essay. Which of the following topics have pertinence for a large audience?

- Tax cuts for the wealthy

- The superiority of dogs to cats

- The war in Iraq

- Why co-ed dorms are better

Only two of these topics have significance for a large audience: tax cuts for the wealthy and the war in Iraq. Each of these topics affects every person in the United States. The other two topics might be important to you or other college students or to people choosing pets, but only in a superficial way.

Writer's Break

- Identify several specific examples of how we try to outsmart nature: for example, implants or cosmetic surgery.

- How effective are these remedies in terms of the problem they claim to cure? For example, can a facelift prevent you from aging?

- Do the benefits outweigh the costs?

Obviously, the writing situation can affect how we judge the significance of a topic. For example, if your university was considering changing the dorm you live in to a co-ed dorm, you would be personally affected, and you might feel compelled to speak out in the student newspaper. This topic would be significant for many people on your campus, but not to a wider audience than that.

Look at the following essay. Does it have pertinence for a large audience?

My "Short" Essay

Katie Gornik

Deductive arrangement—begins with specific examples

"Hey shortie, how's the weather down there?" "You're not short; you're just vertically challenged!" As someone who is only five feet tall, jokes like this are a daily part of my life. I am called names, harassed, and often simply overlooked. From the time I began kindergarten I was labeled as "short" by the other children. The larger children thought it was a good time to pick me up and carry me around as though I were a doll. Needless to say, I didn't agree. On my eleventh birthday, I took some friends to Six Flags for the day. They had a great time. I wasn't tall enough to ride any of the cool rides, so I sat on a bench while they lined up for the Rattler and the Cliff Hanger. When I was sixteen, I was turned down for a job at the Gap because I was too small to wear the clothes and reach the upper shelves. I never asked to be short. In fact, like millions of other people in the world, I think Mother Nature gave me the short end of the stick when she was passing out the tall genes.

Conclusion drawn from examples

The sad thing is, not a lot has changed. Last week a woman at the Driver's Registration Office asked me, "How old are you sweetie, fifteen?" I wanted to shout back at her, "No, you moron. I'm nineteen." Many people assume I am younger than I am because I am short; therefore, I am treated like I am younger. It is very upsetting to have someone cooing at you like you are an eight-year-old, especially when the person doing the cooing is the same age you are.

Short people suffer from more than age discrimination. We spend hours shopping for age appropriate clothing. Yes, there are specialty shops for people who are petite; unfortunately, most are for older women and the clothes styles are dull and out of date. As a college student, I really don't want to dress in flowered pants suits, or Capri pants covered in little doggies. When I buy clothes at the shops I prefer, Gap and Abercrombie, I have to spend almost as much on alterations as I do on the clothes themselves.

Many people in our society believe that being taller is better than being shorter; therefore, shorter people are often treated with a lack of respect. The taller population seems to believe that if you are the size of a child, you have the mentality and abilities of a child. I recently volunteered to help clean a local park. When I started to pick up large pieces of trash with a friend of mine, the person in charge came over and suggested I concentrate on the "smaller waste, like the gum wrappers," because she didn't want me to get hurt. However, this sort of daily humiliation is trivial compared to the larger issues short people face.

Support for conclusion

Many short people are denied jobs, even when they are qualified. Apparently all managers believe that short people are not strong enough or capable enough. This problem is especially prevalent for men, who are often judged by their height. Also, short people are paid less money than taller people. Taller people make 1,500 dollars more per inch than short people (Sanders). It is discouraging to enter the job market knowing that a physical characteristic that you can't change has the ability to hinder your chances for success before you ever get started.

Restatement of conclusion

"Eat your green beans so you can grow up big and strong." Why does our culture put so much importance on height? In our society, short people are discriminated against. However, unlike sex, age, race, religious, and weight discrimination, height discrimination is being ignored. Our society needs to become aware

of the issue of height discrimination. Short people everywhere

need to fight for the rights they deserve.

Work Cited

Sanders, Doug. "Going for the Tall Money." <u>Augusta Chronicle</u>

1 Apr. 2002. 13 Apr. 2003 <http://

www.augustachronicle.com>.

Consider this . . .

- ■ Is this writer's topic pertinent to a large audience?
- ■ Is the writer's use of qualifying language effective?
- ■ Should the writer have considered opposing arguments?

Writer's Break

- ■ Identify several articles, cartoons, or movies that discuss the attack on a human by an animal.
- ■ Why do we have such a morbid fascination for such stories?
- ■ Why is the animal frequently made out to be some sort of intelligent killing machine rather than just an animal?

When you consider the topic of the preceding essay, you might initially believe that it has no pertinence for a broad audience. Perhaps you are not short and can't empathize with the writer. On the other hand, because her essay deals with a form of discrimination, it does affect everyone—short or tall, you are part of the problem that she describes. Granted, rather than talking about her personal difficulties as a short person, she could give more factual information, such as the pay statistics she includes. Information like that would clearly support her contention that short people are discriminated against. However, her trials and tribulations as a short person are entertaining, and they do capture her audience's attention as well as serving as specific examples from which she builds her argument inductively. In this case, it is not that the topic lacks significance—it is the writer's approach that diminishes the topic's significance.

☰ Developing a Persuasive Thesis

A *thesis* is a statement or statements that indicate to the reader what the focus of your paper will be. A thesis is important, especially in an argumentative essay because it prepares your readers for the argument that follows. In order to ensure that your paper has an effective focus, you need a persuasive thesis. Look at the thesis in the previous paper:

> Many people in our society believe that being taller is better than being shorter; therefore, shorter people are often treated with a lack of respect.

This thesis introduces the general topic of the essay, which is based on specific examples provided by the writer. This thesis is a general conclusion that the writer draws from her specific examples. The thesis is the topic of her essay. It is the conclusion that she is trying to prove.

Once you have chosen your topic, you are ready to write a thesis. Not every essay begins with a thesis, but for less experienced writers, beginning with the thesis is a good way to ensure that an essay has a strong starting point.

When you write a thesis, keep in mind one very important point: your thesis must be arguable. In other words, as stated earlier:

- It must be on a topic worth arguing.
- It must have pertinence for a broad audience.
- It must be something on which people can take more than one position.

Determine which of these sample theses meet these criteria:

Everyone should have health insurance.

The world is tough for left-handed people.

Despite many ethical concerns, human cloning has the potential to aid scientists in finding cures for many diseases.

Any enlisted woman who wishes to be in combat should be allowed to do so if she is able to pass the same fitness test enlisted men do.

Whether women should be involved in combat is a controversial issue.

The first example is a poor thesis because very few people would argue against this statement. Of course, everyone should have health insurance. On the other hand, the writer could revise the thesis to state:

> The government should provide health insurance for every citizen of the United States.

It is certainly possible to argue the pros and cons of this topic.

The second example is also weak. Although the writer has chosen an intriguing topic, the thesis is too vague. It could be revised to this:

> In the 1700s many innocent people were hung as witches simply because they were left-handed, and even today, the world does not adequately understand the plight of the left-hander.

The last two examples of theses are much better. Example three suggests the other side of the issue (ethical concerns) and then specifies the writer's position (the benefits that outweigh the ethical concerns). Example four clearly states a specific position that the writer will support within the essay.

CHOOSING STRATEGIES FOR WRITING PERSUASIVELY

Aristotelian Argument

Aristotle was a fourth-century B.C.E. Greek scholar of rhetoric who wrote a book called *The Rhetoric*. In this book, he teaches his readers how to state a claim and prove it using three forms of proof: logos, pathos, and ethos.

Logos is an appeal to readers' sense of reason or logic. As a form of proof, it relies on common assumptions and beliefs, as well as factual information and data. According to Aristotle, logos was the most important type of proof.

Pathos is an appeal to readers' emotions. An audience's emotions are aroused by the use of emotional language, images, examples, or personal narratives. An emotional appeal is very effective, but it is ethical only when it is used to support the logical basis of the argument rather than to manipulate the audience.

Ethos is an appeal to readers' sense of ethics and credibility. An ethical appeal is intended to convince the audience of the credibility of a source of information, of the argument itself, or even of the writer. For example, in order to be persuaded by an argument, the readers must be convinced that the writer is an ethical person, who knows what he or she is talking about. No one is persuaded by someone he or she doesn't trust.

Rogerian Argument

Rogerian argument is a strategy for conflict resolution that was developed by Carl Rogers, an early psychotherapist. The use of Rogerian argument in writing allows you to reduce conflict and create empathy between yourself and your readers—a very useful strategy when dealing with sensitive topics that are likely to inspire strong emotions. The use of Rogerian argument allows you to render your audience receptive to your positions by helping you to show them that you understand and appreciate their point of view. Rogerian argument involves the use of three steps:

1. *Summarize the opponent's position using neutral language.* By summarizing the position of your opponent, you are establishing that you understand and recognize that viewpoint. Furthermore, by using neutral language, you avoid the perception that you are passing judgment on that viewpoint. This establishes a precedent for listening objectively to different opinions.

2. *Demonstrate your understanding of the opposing opinion by showing you accept at least part of that position.* If you completely reject the reader's viewpoint, you will encourage the same response to your own viewpoint. Conversely, if you show that you find at least a portion of the reader's view-

point acceptable, you encourage your reader to be equally open to accepting your views.

3. *State your opinion in the context of the values, beliefs, and experiences that both sides share.* If you place yourself in the reader's position and consider the aspects of his or her life that led to his or her opinions, you can find the common denominators that you share as humans and use those to present your argument as the product of a shared experience. This allows you to include your reader in your argument rather than excluding him or her by responding judgmentally.

☰ Toulmin Argument

The *Toulmin model* for structuring an argument has six parts. The first three are essential to any argument:

- Claim—statement of writer's position
- Support—data that supports the claim
- Warrant—conclusion drawn from support that confirms claim.

The other three parts are nonessential but often included:

- Backing—additional support for the warrant
- Rebuttal—a response to opposing arguments
- Qualifier—restatement of the claim in order to make it more acceptable to more members of the audience.

Claim

The *claim* is the main point the writer is trying to make in his or her argument—we sometimes call this the *thesis*. A claim can be either explicit (clearly stated) or implicit (the reader has to figure it out for him or herself). A claim can also be ironic. An ironic claim is one that is clearly overstated or exaggerated. The writer doesn't really believe an ironic claim—he or she is overstating the claim in order to emphasize the point.

The claim sets the tone of the argument and can be placed at the opening of the essay or later, depending on the writer's purpose. A claim that appears early in an essay is straightforward and draws readers in quickly. A claim that is deferred until later in the essay allows the writer to string readers along and keep them in suspense.

Support

All claims require additional support. This support can come in the form of facts, opinions, or examples.

- *Facts*—factual support is verifiable. In other words, rather than saying that many Americans are functionally illiterate, you quote a source that states that 9% of all Americans are functionally illiterate. Readers might not agree on the interpretation of a fact, but they can agree on its existence and its source.

- *Opinions*—opinions are not verifiable, and though they may be based on the interpretation of facts, they are not facts themselves. Because opinions are not verifiable, their credibility is tied to the credibility of the person who holds the opinion. Obviously, someone who is an expert on the subject being discussed will have a more valid opinion than someone who is not.

- *Examples*—examples can be real or made up, though examples based in reality are more convincing. Examples help writers to explain and clarify, and they make writing more interesting. They provide readers with a more tangible way of understanding the writer's claim.

Writer's Break

Choose the option you like best from the Writing Picks at the end of this chapter.

- Write an argumentative thesis.
- Present your thesis to the class and ask for feedback.

Warrant

Warrants are based on commonly held opinions and beliefs, and they are part of every argument. For example, consider this argument:

Claim: The president of the United States is doing a poor job.

Support: He declared war on another country without approval from the United Nations.

Warrant: A good president does not engage in a war that does not have UN support.

The warrant is based on the commonly held belief that part of a president's job is maintaining a good relationship with the United Nations. Because they are based on commonly held beliefs, warrants are rarely stated explicitly.

Backing

Even though warrants are based on commonly accepted beliefs, they still often require backing, or support. This is especially true if the audience might be inclined to reject the warrant. For example, some people might reject the previous warrant regarding a president's obligation to refrain from engaging in warfare without the support of the United Nations. Consequently, the writer would need to provide further evidence to support this warrant.

Rebuttal

A writer must acknowledge arguments that have already been stated and anticipate arguments that readers might make and must counter them, by showing them to be invalid. This is rebuttal.

Qualifier

No argument is expected to be proved absolutely. In fact, most arguments are based on probability and likelihood. Therefore, arguments often are restated in language that qualifies: *sometimes*, *many*, *in some cases*, *probably*. These words do not indicate the sort of certainty that no argument can claim.

Look at the following essay. It follows the Toulmin model.

Stepmother Nature and Her Redheaded Stepchildren

Paula Mathis

Sergio Moraes/Reuters/Landov LLC

We humans often view Mother Nature not as a benevolent mother who loves us unconditionally, but as a raging stepmother who apparently resents our existence. This mother is occasionally nice to her children, as when she provides us with a beautiful fall weekend filled with cool air and sunshine. But mostly, as when she pummels us with the rain, hail, and tornadoes of spring, she seemingly can't wait for us to grow up and leave home. However, if nature is our stepmother, then we are her naughty stepchildren who often try to push our luck to see what we can get away with before we are soundly punished. In this relationship

Claim—the writer's point

between humans and nature, we might occasionally get our way, but in the end, nature always wins.

John Gibbins/*San Diego Union*/Zuma Press

Support for claim

People are often mesmerized by nature's beauty: the hypnotic sights and sounds of the ocean, or the peace and tranquility of a wooded hillside. But it never fails to amaze me when peo-

Warrant for previous support

ple who build their homes in these environments appear on the evening news, shaken and traumatized by nature's fury. Perhaps a hurricane has come and washed their homes into the sea for the third time in as many decades, or one of the annual west coast fires has burned their homes to the ground--yet again. But their responses remain the same: "We will rebuild!" Why? Don't these people realize that they should never have built their homes in these places in the first place, much less continue to rebuild after Mother Nature has reclaimed "their" land as her own? Clearly they do not. Even as a small child in school, I learned that the "wise man built his house upon the rock, and the foolish man built his house upon the sand." Unfortunately, that lesson was one many people have either forgotten or never learned. Those people apparently live by a different point of view--one that simply must include breathtaking land-scapes, no matter the cost.

Alan Kearney/Taxi/Getty Images

Most people's lives are boring, and we often look to Mother Nature for fun. Some people long to climb snow-capped peaks or go hiking in the woods. Some people even

Backing for warrant

Backing for warrant

Support for claim

feel the urge to swim with the dolphins. These people are foolish. The reason that people don't live on Mount Everest or deep in the ocean is because these places are incredibly dangerous for humans. While many of us might enjoy testing our skills in these harsh environments, most of us are not equipped to survive when these fun vacations don't go as planned--and Stepmother Nature resents our planning.

For hundreds, perhaps thousands of years, humans have done their best to try to tame Mother Nature, but our attempts at correction have blinded us to the dangers of trying to subdue that which we do not control. We build dams and straighten winding rivers to control flooding, then are shocked when the floodwaters climb higher and faster than before. We train tigers and snakes to keep as pets, then we are stunned when they attack us in our homes. Most recently we have seen the phenomenon of women trying, with the help of modern science, to control their biological clocks. Alas, we are saddened when the numbers of babies born mentally retarded, or otherwise disabled, increase. The harsh truth is that no matter how hard we keep trying to manipulate the world around us and outwit

Support for claim

Warrant for previous support

Mother Nature, she still reserves the right to be petulant and unyielding.

Reuters/Corbis

We humans have an inherent flaw: the need to make everything around us conform to our own desires. And what we perceive as Mother Nature's betrayal of us, her impudent stepchildren, is usually just the result of our arrogance. In our stubborn attempts to force nature to submit to our will, we create situations in which Mother Nature must give us a swat on our behinds now and then to remind us who's in charge.

Warrant for opening claim

Consider this . . .

- Was this writer's choice of strategy effective, or should she have used something besides a Toulmin argument?
- Did the author do an effective job of persuading you to accept her viewpoint?
- How could the writer strengthen her argument?

In the following excerpt, the writer attempts to persuade himself, and his readers, that safety supercedes a man's pride—even his livelihood—and that eventually we are all betrayed by our bodies' limitations.

FROM JUMPING FIRE
Murry A. Taylor

1   I pulled up alongside Mitch Decoteau. Mitch hates the PT test, too. Not because it's that difficult, really, but somehow combining physical distress with the threat of losing your job produces an inordinate amount of anxiety. Mitch was panting hard and soaked with sweat. I felt my pace falling off. Even though I was still ahead of several others, I knew I had to pick it up. Listening to my feet strike the ground, I concentrated on maintaining the rhythm and not on the pain building in my left knee.

2   My chest felt like it had been hit by lightening. I had visions of my oxygen-starved body diving into a snowbank. But there was nothing to do but just keep running. Then around the corner appeared a lovely sight—Kelton in his cool, hot-pink T-shirt, the van, and the finish line. Jim's eyes were glued to his stopwatch as he called out the time. A wave of pain and nausea rose inside me as I ran past. "Taylor," he yelled, "22:05."

3   My vision pulsed with a matrix of black dots, and my lungs gasped for more air as I watched Mitch and Fergy come in. The fatal 22:30 came and went with ominous finality. A couple of old veterans barely missed it. They crossed the finish line, then crumpled in disappointment. One was Trooper Tom, a veteran of two com-

bat tours with the marines in Vietnam and twenty-two seasons smokejumping. At forty-six, Troop had more fire jumps than any other jumper in history. He also had two injured knees and a hip he'd fractured in Montana in 1989.

The other was Gary Dunning, the second-oldest jumper in the fifty-two-year history of smokejumping. In 1986, on a windy jump east of Fort Yukon, he'd suffered a smokejumper's nightmare, when a spear-pointed black spruce punctured the middle of his left thigh, leaving him skewered thirty feet in the air. A gust of wind grabbed his chute and toppled jumper and tree to the ground. Gary was unconscious when the other jumpers found him. Last year he had extensive surgery on his left foot. Like most old-timers, our beloved "Secret Squirrel," as we called him, had a pair of jumper's knees as well.   4

When Troop and Dunning failed to meet the time limit, no one said a word. Side-glancing at Troop I saw a pleading sadness in his kind, brown eyes as he looked over at me. To a man we all felt defeated. Their loss was ours.   5

You can be strong. You can be dedicated. You can have run thousands of miles down those long country roads in the winter cold just before nightfall, alone, hurting, pushing, with no one to notice, no one to care. Run in the rain, run in the snow, against the wind and with it, through the injuries and pain. A smokejumper's commitment to physical fitness is year-round. It has to be. I'd run more than eight thousand miles to remain a trooper; Troop and Gary probably more. You can have done it all in the best of faith and still the day will come when   Thesis
you will no longer be able to keep up. On that day your life as a smokejumper will end.   6

Consider this . . .

- What strategy did this writer use? Was it effective?
- What evidence did he use to support his claim?
- In this excerpt, the writer places his thesis last. Is this use of reverse order effective? Why or why not?

CHOOSING AN ORGANIZATIONAL METHOD

There are three methods of organizing an argumentative essay from which you can choose: classical, inductive, and deductive arrangement.

Classical Arrangement

The method of organizing an argumentative essay with which you might be most familiar comes from classical rhetoric. The classically arranged argument has six parts: introduction, narration, partition, argument, refutation, and conclusion.

1. *Introduction*—introduces the subject, gets the reader's attention, and establishes the writer's ethos.

2. *Narration*—provides any background information that the reader needs.

3. *Partition*—states the thesis or claim on which the argument will be based.

4. *Argument*—provides evidence to support the writer's claim.

5. *Refutation*—refutes any opposing arguments anticipated by the writer.

6. *Conclusion*—summarizes the arguments and reiterates the writer's claim.

Inductive Arrangement

An argument arranged inductively begins with a specific example or examples and then draws a general conclusion based on those examples. For example, in the next excerpt from an argumentative essay, the writer begins with this example:

FROM LICENSE TO KILL
Cathy Young

Late one night in August 1991, a Tacoma, Washington, woman named Brenda Lee Working called her estranged husband, Michael, and told him that her car had broken down, stranding her and their two preschool daughters in a wooded area on a military base. When Michael Working came to her aid, it turned out to be an ambush. Brenda shot him several times, hitting him in the arm and the shoulder. Then she beat him in the face with the handgun as he tried to wrench it from her hands and stalked him through the woods for hours after he managed to get away.

Brenda Working's sentence for the attempted murder of her husband: one day in jail.

From that example and a few others, the writer draws the following general conclusion:

Nonetheless, the pattern does exist. Two Justice Department studies in the late 1980s found that male offenders were more than twice as likely as women charged with similar crimes to be incarcerated for more than a year, and that even allowing for other factors, such as prior convictions, women were more likely to receive a light sentence.

To be effective, an inductive argument must be based on a sufficient number of examples. For instance, it would be ineffective to claim that women receive lighter sentences for violent crimes on the basis of one example. The writer has to use many examples to prove her case. Inductive arguments based on insufficient examples are fallacious, and they result when someone "jumps to a conclusion."

In the following article, the writer uses inductive reasoning to argue that the media exaggerate the risk of shark attacks. She presents specific statistics to support her argument that unprovoked attacks are rare and fatalities even rarer.

GREAT WHITE SHARK ATTACKS: DEFANGING THE MYTHS

Jennifer Hile

1   There is good and bad news for surfers regarding the great white shark (*Carcharodon carcharias*). The bad news, according to shark scientists, and contrary to popular opinion, is that great whites are sharp sighted, curious animals, prone to taking "taste tests" of unfamiliar objects that catch their eye.

2   The good news is they generally don't like to eat people.

3   "In the 20th century, there were 108 authenticated, unprovoked shark attacks along the Pacific Coast of the United States," said Ralph Collier, president of the Shark Research Committee in Canoga Park, California, and author of *Shark Attacks of the Twentieth Century*.

4   Of those, eight attacks were fatal. "When you consider the number of people in the water during that hundred year period, you realize deadly strikes are very rare," said Collier.

5   Films like *Jaws* propagate the image of great whites as mindless hunters prowling dark, coastal waters for hapless swimmers—an animal whipped to frenzy by the scent of human blood. Yet not only do most people survive their encounters, many suffer only moderate injuries. Swimmers dragged underwater by great whites are sometimes left with puncture marks, but the animals often don't inflict more severe wounds.

6   A great white shark can reach 20 feet (6 meters) in length and weigh up to 5,000 pounds (2,270 kilograms); survivors' explanations of their escapes amplify misconceptions about the nature of this beast.

MISTAKEN IDENTITY

7   The most common myth is that great whites, with their poor vision, attack divers and surfers in wet suits, mistaking them for pinnipeds (seals and sea lions), their main prey. In this scenario, once the animal realizes its mistake, it releases the victim and swims away.

"Completely false," said R. Aidan Martin, director of ReefQuest Centre for Shark Research in Vancouver, Canada. A shark's behavior while hunting a pinniped differs markedly from its demeanor as it approaches people—suggesting that the animal does not confuse surfers for seals.

"I spent five years in South Africa and observed over 1,000 predatory attacks on sea lions by great whites," said Martin. "The sharks would rocket to the surface and pulverize their prey with incredible force."

By comparison, sharks usually approach people with what he calls "leisurely or undramatic behavior."

CURIOUS ANIMALS

On August 15, 1987, Craig Rogers, a landscape contractor then living in Santa Cruz, California, paddled out to go surfing at a nearby break. It was 7:30 a.m., Rogers was sitting up on his board, legs dangling over each side, searching the horizon for the next set of waves. Abruptly, he noticed his board stopped bobbing in the water.

"I looked down and my eyes filled with a sight of instantaneous horror," said Rogers. A great white shark was biting his board just in front of his left hand; the head was almost three feet (one meter) across. "I could have touched its eye with my elbow."

The shark had surfaced so quietly, Rogers hadn't heard a thing. He flung up his hands, accidentally grazing two of his fingers along the shark's teeth. "I yelled in terror and slid off the board to the opposite side," Rogers explained in a written report made just after the attack.

He was bleeding when he entered the water.

Submerging to his shoulder, he watched the shark gently release his board and sink like a submarine, disappearing beneath him. Later analyses of the puncture marks on his board suggest the shark was 17 feet (5 meters) in length.

"It is typical for a great white to swim up to someone at a relaxed pace, take a bite, then swim off," said Collier. This contrasts with the torpedo-like attacks on the seal, suggesting that the shark's goal is not predation.

TEETH LIKE HANDS

"Great whites are curious and investigative animals," said Martin. "That's what most people don't realize. When great whites bite something unfamiliar to them, whether a person or a crab pot, they're looking for tactile evidence about what it is."

18   A great white uses its teeth the way humans use their hands. In a living shark, every tooth has ten to fifteen degrees of flex. When the animal opens its mouth, the tooth bed is pulled back, "causing their teeth to splay out like a cat's whiskers," said Martin.

19   "Combine that with the flexibility of each tooth, and you realize a great white can use its jaws like a pair of forceps. They're very adept at grabbing things that snag their curiosity."

20   Great whites are also sharp sighted, further evidence that they do not mistake humans for other prey. Scientists believe that sharks see as well below the surface as humans do above it. And they see in color.

21   "I've seen these sharks swim 70 feet (21 meters) to the surface to investigate a piece of debris no bigger than the palm of my hand," said Martin. They are also known to take bites of buoys, paddle boards, brightly colored kayaks, zodiac boats, and other man-made objects floating in the ocean.

22   "Everyone wants to think sharks just search out seals, but they bite a lot of things that don't resemble any of their known prey," said A. Peter Klimley, an expert in marine animal behavior at the University of California, Davis, and author of the *Secret Lives of Sharks* and co-author of *Great White Sharks: The Biology of Carcharodon carcharias*. "They don't tear these things to pieces. They take a bite, feel them over, then move on."

THE TASTE TEST

23   If sharks bite to figure out the nature of various objects, then why do they usually spit out people rather than adding them to the menu?

24   "They spit us out because we're too bony," said Martin.

25   Great whites have extremely slow digestive tracts; if they eat something less than optimal, it slows down their digestive tract for days, prohibiting them from eating other things. "That makes them selective about what they eat," said Klimley.

26   The insulation that keeps seals warm is pure fat, which provides twice the calories of muscle. That makes them a favorite of great whites. A high fat diet is mandatory for the great white to maintain its body temperature and keep its brain warm in cold water.

27   Still, sharks do attack people along U.S. coasts and around the world, even if the nature and number of encounters belie expectations.

28   There are steps society can take to reduce the number of incidents.

29   Cities often use beaches as burial grounds for marine mammals that wash up dead—like beached whales. "There is a possibility that when those animals are

buried, some of the decaying material washes out to sea and attracts sharks," said Collier.

A healthy avoidance of pinniped colonies is another way to minimize human fatalities. A more subtle point is to steer clear of river mouths dumping spawning fish into the sea. Fish runs attract pinnipeds, which attract great whites. They feast on both seals and salmon, also a favorite shark snack.   30

"What we need to remember is that if great whites really liked to eat people, there would be a lot more fatalities," said Collier. "And I wouldn't interview so many survivors."   31

Consider this . . .

- ◼ Can you identify this writer's thesis? Is it arguable?
- ◼ How did the writer develop her argument?
- ◼ Were you persuaded to agree with her?

☰ Deductive Arrangement

When you argue deductively, you begin with a general principle and then apply it to a specific case. When a writer begins with a statement that incorporates all of a category and then moves to a specific entity within that category, he or she is arguing deductively. The following essay uses a deductive organization.

MONOGAMY KILLS

Jocelyn Selim

Monogamy may be a virtue for people, but it's a fast track to extinction for other large mammals, says biologist Justin Brashares of the University of British Columbia. He examined 30 years of monthly censuses for 42 mammal species on six separate Ghanaian wildlife reserves, analyzing them for factors that increased   1 the likelihood of local extinctions. Loyal mating behavior ranked second, behind isolation of animal populations, as a death sentence for primates, ungulates, and large carnivores.

2   The study is the first to identify a link between mammal mating behavior and extinction patterns. "It's a pretty striking correlation. Baboons live in large harems, and there's a robust population now, even though it had dwindled in the 1970s. Meanwhile, the more monogamous colobus monkey has gone downhill," Brashares says. "Likewise, you'd think that wild dogs, which form pair-led packs like wolves, would fare better than lions, which require more food but form harems. In fact, the opposite is true."

3   Monogamy evolved over millions of years, but it is a strategy poorly suited to the main dangers of modern times—human and hunting and loss of wilderness areas. "There are a lot of studies showing that hunters tend to take males, the same way deer hunters go after bucks. If you're a female in a harem situation, you just look to the next spare male that steps up to the plate, but if you're a pair-bonding female, you'd soon find yourself with no single guys around" Brashares says. Hunters may also be more effective at killing animals in small groups because they are easier to sneak up on.

Consider this . . .

- What general conclusion does this writer begin with?
- Does she provide adequate examples to support her argument?
- Was deductive arrangement a good choice?

The writer begins with this general statement:

Monogamy may be a virtue for people, but it's a fast track to extinction for other large mammals, says biologist Justin Brashares of the University of British Columbia.

As the essay continues, the writer gives specific examples:

> "It's a pretty striking correlation. Baboons live in large harems, and a there's a robust population now, even though it had dwindled in the 1970s. Meanwhile, the more monogamous colobus monkey has gone downhill," says Brashares.

The premise behind deductive reasoning is that any claim that is true of the whole must also be true of the part. However, remember that most deductive arguments are based on statements of probability. In fact, the deductive method is the basis of scientific research. For example, scientists have probably identified some large mammals who have thrived despite their monogamous mating habits. However, because this writer found several examples to support her claim, she was able to write an argument based on them. A good writer remembers that there are exceptions to every probable belief and anticipates arguments based on those exceptions in his or her rebuttal.

PERSUASIVE WRITING is one of the most difficult but most gratifying forms of writing. It is difficult because we all struggle to see viewpoints other than our own, and we all have difficulty questioning our own beliefs. It is gratifying because a well-written piece of persuasive writing allows you to affect someone else by opening his or her eyes to a new viewpoint. And when you change one person, you change the world. ■

COLLABORATIVE EXERCISES

Group Exercise One

- As a group, identify a controversial issue that affects all of you.

- Outline the information you would include in a persuasive essay in three ways: using an Aristotelian argument, using a Rogerian argument, and using a Toulmin argument.

- Share each version with your class, and determine which is most effective and why.

Group Exercise Two

- As a group, locate a persuasive essay in a newspaper or magazine or online.

- Analyze the essay to determine what form of argument it uses.

- Identify what pattern of organization the essay uses.

- Decide whether or not you find the essay persuasive, and tell why.

- Share your results and the original essay with the class.

Group Exercise Three

- As a class, read the outlines that were written for Group Exercise One.

- After reading each outline, consider these questions:

  Do the writers use an effective organizational pattern?

  Do the waters provide enough evidence to support their argument?

  Was the issue that the writers chose worth arguing about?

- Based on your feelings, develop a list of criteria to use when evaluating persuasive essays.

WRITING PICKS

Option One

Taking responsibility for our choices

As the writer of "Stepmother Nature and her Redheaded Stepchildren," suggested, we have a tendency to ignore possible natural repercussions of our acts and then feel betrayed by nature when our plans fail. Should we be surprised when our beachfront homes are destroyed by hurricanes? Should we be shocked when someone is injured or killed climbing Mt. Everest? Have we been betrayed by nature, or have we made poor choices? In a persuasive essay, explore this aspect of humans' relationship with nature.

A beachfront house is a risky investment.

Option Two

You can't fool Mother Nature

Each year, scientists find new ways to fight the laws of nature. When we grow old, we have plastic surgery. When our joints fail, doctors install replacements made of plastic and metal. If we are born with certain genetic flaws, science can now correct them. But can we really defeat nature? And at what cost do we make the attempt? In this essay, argue for or against further attempts to outsmart nature.

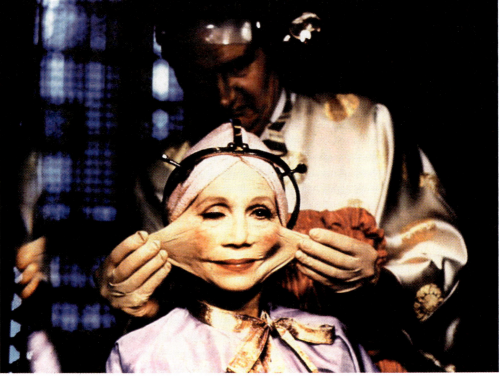

The movie Brazil *asks viewers to consider the dangers of obsessive cosmetic surgery.*

Option Three

Preventable or inevitable?

Almost every major ecological phenomenon—global warming, holes in the ozone, extinction of species—can be seen from two perspectives: Humans are to blame, or it is the natural order and would have happened anyway. Which side do you take? Do you believe our pollution of the atmosphere has caused global warming, or do you believe that like previous ice ages, this period of warming is part of a natural cycle? Choose one side of this issue and argue in favor of your opinion. Be sure to do necessary research and provide solid facts to support your opinion.

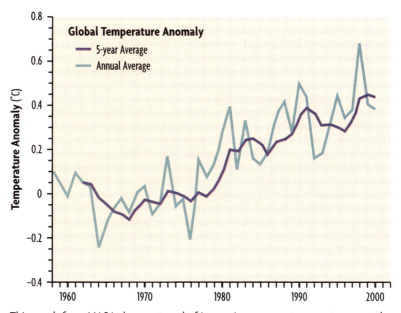

This graph from NASA shows a trend of increasing average temperature over the second half of the 20th century.

Option Four

Humans versus animals

Attacks on people by animals of any kind—bears, dogs, sharks—are big news. And while we all feel horror (that could have been me), sympathy (that poor person), shock (how could such a thing happen), we may also feel some anger. Sharks do live in the ocean. However, sharks have inhabited the ocean for millions of years. Sharks do not have the intellectual ability to target humans or feel any remorse for randomly attacking whatever makes their brains react. So why do we blame the animals? Aren't the animals just as much victims as the humans they attack? What does the cartoon below say about this issue? In your essay, explore the topic of culpability. Who is the real victim? The human or the animal?

APPLYING THE RHETORICAL SITUATION

As always, you must consider the rhetorical situation throughout the process of making choices for a persuasive essay. Use the questions here to guide your decision making.

Audience

- Does your audience agree or disagree with your opinion?

- If your audience disagrees with you, how can you motivate them to read your argument?

- What information does your audience need in order to understand your argument?

Purpose

- Have you considered both sides of the issue you are writing about?

- What techniques can you use to make your argument?

- How can you structure your paper to emphasize your argument?

- What do you want the reader to take away from reading your essay? A changed opinion? A new awareness? More tolerance for another viewpoint?

Occasion

- How can you get readers to consider your argument without getting defensive?

- How can you make them appreciate your viewpoint without lecturing?

- When you consider other viewpoints, are you offering opinions or passing judgments?

FOCUSING ON PROCESS

Prewriting

Before you can begin writing your paper, you have to have some material with which to work. Where can you find material for a persuasive essay?

- *Your Writer's Breaks for this chapter.* The exercises you've done have helped you to amass useful material.

- *News reports on current events.* What local or national issues would you like to write about? What can you learn about them from other published sources?

- *Popular culture sources.* What issues have been featured in current films, songs, or sit-coms?

Drafting

- Write your thesis statement.

- Choose the form of argument you want to use: Toulmin, Rogerian, or Aristotelian.

- Choose the organizational method you want to use.

- Outline your essay.

- Write your draft based on your outline.

Revising

- Ask a friend who does not share your opinion on your topic to read your essay.

- When he or she is done reading, ask him or her if the essay was persuasive.

- Ask your friend to justify the answer given.

- Make changes based on his or her response.

Editing

- Identify the type of each sentence in your paper.
- How many of each of the different types of sentences did you use?
- Does your paper have sentence variety?

Grammar Choices

VERB TENSES

Verbs not only give our sentences action, they also let readers know when that action happened—the past, the present, or the future. In order to help your readers clearly understand the timing and the sequence of actions in your essays, you must be careful to use the correct verb tenses.

Present Tense

The present tense of a verb indicates an action or condition in the present. The dictionary lists all verbs in base form, which is the same as the present tense in most cases.

They **are** in a hurry.

I **write** in my journal every day.

We **run** in the mornings.

The only exception to the rule that the base form expresses action in the present is when a verb is used with third-person singular subjects: singular nouns (proper or common) and singular pronouns such as *he, she, it, someone,* and *everyone.* Present tense verbs in the third-person singular end with *s* or *es*:

He **sings** very well.

Alma **takes** care of everyone.

That man **speaks** with conviction.

Everyone **deserves** more time off.

Present Participle

The present participle describes actions that are still occurring. You form a present participle by adding *ing* to the base form. Verbs in present participle form can also be *gerunds*: words that act as nouns. Verbs in this form can also act as adjectives.

Present Participle

He is **getting** better everyday.

The birds are **migrating** south for the winter.

CDs are **becoming** very expensive.

Gerund

Smoking is harmful to your health.

Swimming is good exercise.

Sleeping is my greatest pleasure.

Adjective

The eagle was tossed by the **howling** wind.

Jesse couldn't find her in the **failing** light.

As I cut up the onions, I had to stop and wipe my **streaming** eyes.

Past Tense

The past tense describes an action that happened in the past. This verb tense is usually formed by adding *d* or *ed* to the end of the base form of the verb:

He **walked** to school yesterday.

I **waited** for you last night.

We **wondered** where you were.

The dog **chewed** the tennis ball.

Some verbs have irregular past tense forms. You can find these in a dictionary.

Past Participle

The past participle indicates that an action was completed at some time before the present. The past participle form is used three ways:

▪ With *have* or *has* to form the perfect tense

Since you ask, I **have seen** that movie before.

You **have ruined** your chances by losing your temper.

Ella **has written** to her congressional representative to express her concerns.

▪ With forms of *to be* in the passive voice

The car **was stolen**.

The experiment **was completed**.

They **were informed** of their rights.

▪ As an adjective

Pleated pants are out of style.

I like **smoked** turkey better than plain turkey.

Do **bleached** blondes have more fun?

Future Tense

You use the future tense when you are writing about something that hasn't occurred yet. You form the future tense by adding the word *will* before the verb. You can use future tense three ways:

▪ To indicate that something is going to happen at some point in the future

I **will arrive** in the morning.

He **will be** the next great artist of the 21st century.

Many animals **will become** extinct if we don't take action.

■ As the future perfect tense to express a completed future action, by using *have* with *will*.

I **will have completed** my college education by 2007.

Within the next decade, scientists predict global warming **will have** seriously **affected** our climate.

Next week, Bryon **will have made up** the hours he took off last week.

■ To express continuing future actions, with *will* and *be* and an *ing* form of a verb

By tomorrow night, I **will be swimming** off the coast of Mexico.

Over the next decade, a second baby boom **will be occurring**.

By next year, Thelma **will be running** her own business.

When you are editing your papers, get in the habit of checking the tense of each verb you use. Make sure all verb tenses are correct and consistent.

Making It Work

■ Determine the sequence of action in each section of your draft or essay.

■ Are the verb tenses in each section appropriate to the sequence of action?

■ Change any verb tenses that do not fit.

Style Choices

LEVELS OF FORMALITY

When you write, one of the choices you have to make concerns the level of formality you use, ranging from low to high.

When you write at a low level of formality your tone is more conversational. You might use contractions, the first person, slang, and colloquialisms. In the following example, the writer uses **first person**, **colloquialisms** and **contractions**.

> At a moment when **we're** all **fretting about** whether **we'll** be **blown up** tomorrow by nuclear terrorists, it may seem odd to worry instead that **we'll** someday survive forever. But just to give you something new to **bite your lip about**, let **me** tell you about roundworms.

When you write at a middle level of formality, you try to maintain a balance between informal and formal. This is the level at which you will normally write. When you write at this level, you might still use contractions and first person, but you will avoid most slang and most colloquial phrases in favor of more standard forms of English. In the next example, the writer uses first person and a contraction, but no colloquialisms or slang:

> The larger children thought it was a good time to pick **me** up and carry **me** around as though **I** were a doll. Needless to say, I **didn't** agree.

When you write at a high level of formality, you avoid the use of the first person, contractions, slang, and colloquialisms. This is the level of writing found in academic publications. The next example is written in third person, and the writer uses intentionally inflated language for effect:

> Four score and seven years ago our fathers brought forth upon this continent a new nation, conceived in liberty and dedicated to the proposition that all men are created equal.

Which level of formality you use is generally determined by the audience you are writing for. Consider these audiences:

- *Friend.* When you write to a friend, it is appropriate to use a low level of informality. Just as you wouldn't speak to a friend using stilted formal language, you wouldn't write to him or her using that kind of language.

- *Potential employer.* When you write a letter of application, your letter must make your first impression. Consequently, it is important to use a high level of formality in order to make the right impression.

- *History professor.* When you write in academic settings, you might use either a middle or a high level of formality, depending on the instructions you receive. You would never use a low level.

- *Parents.* When you write to your parents, you certainly wouldn't use a high level of formality, but you might not use a low level either. Even though you have a close relationship with your parents, you might also use a middle level of formality in order to show your respect for them.

- *Yourself.* Your journal or diary is meant to be private. You can develop your own secret code if it suits you because no one else is meant to read it.

Making It Work

- What level of formality is appropriate for the essay you are writing?

- Have you consistently maintained that level throughout the essay?

- Make any changes that are needed to keep the level of formality consistent.

GLOBAL ICONS

Writing to Respond

In this chapter, you will learn:

- How to analyze a text by focusing on its effectiveness, by agreeing or disagreeing with its main idea, or by interpreting some aspect of it

- How to support a response with a personal experience and evidence

- Strategies for responding—argumentation, example, and definition

- Methods for organizing a responsive essay—conceptual, logical, and alternating order

Le Fils de l'Homme by René Magritte. © 2004 C. Herscovici, Brussels/Artists Rights Society (ARS), New York

For millions of people, this image represents the facelessness of the modern businessman. Others associate it with the film The Thomas Crown Affair, *in which the image represents one man's refusal to accept society's laws.*

We live in a world of texts, which come in many forms: paintings, music, poetry, essays, short stories, photographs. The creator of any of these forms of expression has a message to share, and when we write to respond, we share our opinion of that message.

You will do a great deal of writing in response to other people's work as part of your academic career; however, learning how to analyze and respond is more widely useful. When you read a poem or a novel or see a movie or an advertisement, you will be able to understand it in a less superficial way, and you can share this deeper appreciation with someone else. For example, if you are especially fond of a CD by a particular singer, you can write in response to that music and help others understand it. By doing this, you can give someone else the opportunity to appreciate the music you love.

When you write to respond to something, you have to have a method for analyzing some aspect of that thing. We all have opinions, and it is easy to read or view something and quickly decide what it might mean, but this sort of rushed analysis is very different from the sort of reasoned analysis that is the basis of a good paper.

WHAT IS ANALYSIS?

When you analyze something, you take it apart in order to understand how it works. For example, if you were going to analyze a poem, you might consider these aspects of it:

- Meter
- Rhyme scheme
- Use of figurative language
- Use of imagery
- Theme

Depending on the length of the paper you were writing, you might analyze one or more of these features of the poem as part of your response. In the next essay, a student responds to the play *Trifles*, by analyzing the playwright's use of symbolism.

Free from the Cage: Symbolism in <u>Trifles</u>

Cassandra Estep

Susan Glaspell deals with the mystery of why people are motivated to kill others in her play, <u>Trifles</u>. The investigation of the murder of an upstanding citizen named Mr. Wright begs the question of motive--revenge, taking a soul for a soul. Mr. Wright's wife is the prime suspect, and investigators are looking for proof of motive. Meanwhile, Mrs. Wright's friends, Mrs. Peters and Mrs. Hale, fumble through the Wright's house to bring the comforts of home to the accused wife in jail. While the investigators grow impatient in their search, Mrs. Peters and Mrs. Hale uncover a mysterious piece of evidence they are afraid to interpret: a broken bird cage, and a dead canary. In the play, <u>Trifles</u>, Susan Glaspell uses the symbolism of the dead, caged canary to allude to the motive behind Mrs. Wright's murder of her husband.

Mrs. Wright kept a caged bird as a companion--a symbol of her own confinement. Though Mr. Wright paid his bills and fulfilled his role in society, he did not provide the comfort and love that Mrs. Wright needed. After a long day of tending to the house and the farm, Mrs. Wright could have used the enjoyment of an entertaining husband to offset the hardships of a life of labor. Mrs. Hale acknowledges Mr. Wright's harshness as man, noting "... he was a hard man ... Just to pass the time of day with him. Like a raw wind that gets to the bone. I should think she would a 'wanted a bird'" (Glaspell 307). A lonely, childless wife, Mrs. Wright needed the canary as company in the empty house. As Mrs. Hale considers Mrs. Wright's situation, she comments, "Not having children makes less work, but it makes a quiet house, and Wright out to work all day, and no company when he did come home" (411). Without either children or an attentive husband, Mrs. Wright undoubtedly did feel lonely and secluded from the rest of the world. Her house and her marriage became her cage. Therefore, she could identify with her caged companion, the canary.

Mrs. Wright's canary also symbolized the beauty and talent Mrs. Wright once possessed before her marriage. As Mrs. Hale recalls, "She used to wear pretty clothes and be lively, when she was Minnie Foster, one of the town girls singing in the choir. But that--oh, that was thirty years ago" (325). Now that Minnie Foster was Mrs. Wright, there was no more time for or acceptance of choir singing and looking beautiful. Mrs. Wright's marriage was a sacrifice of dreams for duties. The canary's beauty and voice provided the only outlet through which she could recapture the pleasures of her youth. In fact, "She--come to think of it, she was kind of like a bird herself--real sweet and pretty, but kind of timid and fluttery" (308). Like the canary, she was once a beautiful singer, but her "timid" nature would not allow her to stand up to Mr. Wright's disapproval of her prior interests. The canary not only serves as a reminder to Mrs. Wright of where she is now in her life, but also of who she used to be, and who she gave up when she took Mr. Wright's name.

Mr. Wright's disapproval and murder of his wife's canary symbolize his disapproval and murder of his wife's spirit. What was once a quiet house that Mr. Wright came home to, free from children and his wife's song, would be highly disrupted by the introduction of a singing canary. Imagining Mr. Wright's reaction to finding the canary, Mrs. Hale deduces, that "No, Wright wouldn't like the bird--a thing that sang, she used to sing. He killed that too" (309). Mr. Wright's disapproval over the noise caused by a canary resembles his disapproval with his wife's singing. Since their marriage, Mr. Wright has silenced Mrs. Wright's love for song. Upon finding the canary's cage and its broken hinge, Mrs. Hale states the obvious assumption that it

"Looks as if someone must have been rough with it" (307). After further prodding through the kitchen, Mrs. Peters finds the dead canary, wrapped in silk inside a beautiful box. In complete horror, Mrs. Peters realizes that "Somebody--wrung--its neck" (309). With Mrs. Wright's need for the companionship of the bird, the obvious murder suspect would be Mr. Wright. Although neither woman could be sure that Mr. Wright murdered the bird, both admit their suspicions. Mrs. Wright could see from the loss of her beloved companion the degree to which her husband disapproved of the beauty and talent that both she and the bird possessed. Upon the death of the canary, Mrs. Wright realized that her husband's silencing of the bird was no different from his silencing of her.

Therefore, because of the parallels between the canary and Mrs. Wright, the death of the canary symbolizes an end of Mrs. Wright's tolerance of her caged marriage. The companionship of the canary, which also represented Mrs. Wright's youth, provided an outlet from her impersonal marriage. Mrs. Hale, attempting to imagine Mrs. Wright's reaction to the loss of the canary, speculated that "If there had been years and years of nothing, then a bird sang to you, it would be awful--still, after the bird was still" (310). With the sudden return to the reality of caged loneliness, and the loss of hope that resided in companionship, Mrs. Wright was reduced to the instinct of self-protection. In defending herself against death and captivity, Mrs. Wright brought death to her captor. Mrs. Peters recalls that ". . . what was needed for the case was a motive; something to show anger, or--sudden feeling" (306). The dead canary provided the proof and justification behind Mrs. Wright's anger, and her sudden need to free herself from her own cage.

Through the use of symbolism, Susan Glaspell depicts Mrs. Wright and her state of mind. She is a caged soul--still alive and able to sing, but with no room to grow or fly. Mr. Wright killed his wife's spirit by caging her up in an empty house with nothing. When she found something to fill the void, he killed it. Mrs. Wright, seeing herself as that caged bird, also saw her own spiritual death in the death of the bird. This tangible sight led Mrs. Wright to a vengeful state where only a soul for a soul would settle the matter.

Work Cited

Glaspell, Susan. <u>Trifles</u>. <u>The Prentice Hall Anthology of Women's Literature</u>. Ed. Deborah N. Holdstein. Englewood Cliffs: Prentice, 2000, 301-11.

Consider this . . .

- ▪ Can you identify this essay's thesis? Is it a valid thesis?
- ▪ What point is the writer trying to make? Does she use sufficient evidence from the play to make her point?
- ▪ How could the writer improve her essay?

More generally, analysis can focus on how well a text is structured or argued. Thus, you might write an essay that

- ▪ Analyzes the effectiveness of the text
- ▪ Agrees or disagrees with the main idea of the text
- ▪ Interprets some aspect of the text

Analyzing the Effectiveness of the Text

When you analyze the effectiveness of a text, you look at how successfully it meets basic criteria such as organization, use of supporting arguments, tone, style, and voice. For example, you might analyze an editorial in order to determine how well it addressed its target audience, or you might analyze how certain advertisements contribute to the national obsession with weight.

Agreeing or Disagreeing with the Main Idea

When you choose to respond to a text by agreeing or disagreeing, you create an argument in which you attempt to prove why the main idea of the text is wrong or right. Maybe you are tired of hearing critics claim that the lyrics of the band Back Street Boys are superficial. You could write a paper in which you argue that the lyrics of their songs have deep meaning and address many issues important to their listeners.

≡ Interpreting Some Aspect of the Text

When you choose to interpret some aspect of a text, you choose a portion of the text, a particular technique the author used, or the underlying message of the text. You might also examine the major theme of the work: coming of age, heroic quest, loss of innocence, family, alienation, relationships, or prejudice. These are just a few examples of common themes; you can identify many more in the texts you will examine. If you are fond of the works of Stephen King or J. K. Rowling, you might argue that many of King's characters, and certainly Rowling's protagonist, Harry Potter, are alienated by society. You could make this premise the focus of an essay by first proving that the alienation exists, and then by illustrating why it is an important aspect of the author's works.

Writer's Break

In order to respond to a text by interpreting some aspect of it, a writer must do three things:

- Identify the specific aspect of the text to be discussed.
- Show that it exists in the text.
- Explain why it is important to the text's meaning.

Find an essay written in response to a text, and determine whether it meets each of these three goals.

All of these choices require you to engage in close reading of a text. Close reading is a process of analysis. When you read a text closely, you look at these elements:

- *Symbolism.* If a character is eating an apple, for example, what might the apple symbolize? If the director of a film consistently surrounds an actor in a halo of light, what is he or she trying to symbolize?

- *Character development.* What does a character's body language reveal about him or her? What about the person's appearance, speech mannerisms, or name? What are the characters wearing?

- *Plot.* What happens in the story? Is this a familiar tale? Does it have a moral? What is the point?

- *Scene.* Where does the story take place? How do the physical surroundings add meaning to the text? For instance, in the movie *The Shawshank Redemption*, the walls of the prison represent confinement, while the library the inmates build symbolizes freedom. Why are the walls of the library different from the other walls of the prison?

- *Figurative language.* Look for the use of metaphor and simile. What sort of description is included? What colors are mentioned or shown?

By looking for these elements as you study or read a text, you can identify patterns worth exploring in more detail.

MAKING CHOICES WHEN YOU WRITE TO RESPOND

When you respond to a text, you are creating an argument, and all arguments must be supported with evidence. When you write in response to a text, you can choose from three types of evidence:

- Personal experience

- Evidence from the text itself

- Evidence from other sources

≡ Using Personal Experience

When you use your personal experience to respond to a text, you show how your experience relates in some way to the text, allowing it to make its point. For example, if you were responding to a poem, you might use your personal experience of an event similar to the one described in the poem as evidence for your strong emotional response to the poem.

≡ Using Evidence from the Text

Evidence from the text itself is of key importance when you are writing to respond. You cannot make any kind of claim about a text without supporting that claim with specific evidence from the text itself. For example, if you want to argue that an artist's use of color in a painting creates emotional tension, you have to identify the specific colors used in the painting and explain their emotional effect.

≡ Using Evidence from Other Sources

It is always a good idea to back up evidence you create or discover in a text with evidence from other sources. The fact that other people support your opinion gives your response credibility—especially if the other people are well-known in their field. For example, if you were writing in response to a film based on one of Dr. Seuss's books, you might take evidence from the review that appears later in this chapter.

CHOOSING STRATEGIES FOR RESPONDING

When you write to respond, you will find that argumentation, example, and definition are three very useful strategies.

≡ Argumentation

When you use argumentation as a writing strategy, you have a specific opinion you want to share. Your goal is to persuade your readers to accept your opinion. When you write to respond to a text, you can begin with an argumentative thesis:

> In the play, Trifles, Susan Glaspell uses the symbolism of the dead, caged canary to allude to the motive behind Mrs. Wright's murder of her husband.

> Why is it [*Mona Lisa*] so famous now, when for some 200 years— from the 17th to the 19th centuries—it was ignored?

> . . . watching the new, mega-budget Mike Myers vehicle *Dr. Seuss' The Cat in the Hat* (Universal) is like being run over by a garbage truck that backs up and dumps its load on top of you. It's a sloppy and vulgar burlesque, one of the most repulsive kiddie movies ever made.

Each of these thesis statements takes a stand about a particular text. In the first thesis, a student makes a claim about the writer's use of symbolism in relation to a motive for the murder at the play's center. In the second thesis statement, the writer questions the recent popularity of the *Mona Lisa*, pointing out that it had been ignored for centuries. In the third thesis, the writer bluntly characterizes the film *The Cat in the Hat* as a repulsive burlesque.

Once you identify the text to which you wish to respond, you must develop a thesis in which you clearly state the claim you have chosen to make about that text. Without such a thesis, your essay will lack focus.

☰ Example

Exemplification is the process of using specific examples to support a general statement. When you are responding to some aspect of a text—a particular meaning, a reccurring theme, a specific technique—you must begin by proving that that element does exist within the text. You do this by giving examples. Further, when you state an opinion about a text you must support this statement with specific examples from the text. In the review of *The Cat in the Hat*, the writer carefully includes examples to support his claim that the movie is vulgar burlesque:

> The movie is aggressively unpleasant: The music is grating and the colors garishly ugly--pea-soup green and egg-yolk yellow mixed with pink and lilac.

> Sean Hayes of *Will & Grace* gives not one but two disgraceful performances, as the twitty boss of the kids' pert blond mom (Kelly Preston) and the voice of a computer-generated killjoy goldfish. I can't make up my mind which is worse. Maybe the

goldfish: He actually has some verses of Seuss, which Hayes rushes through impatiently to get to the potty jokes.

The essay contains many other examples besides these, and it is these examples, taken directly from the film itself, that allow the writer to support the accuracy of the claim he made in his thesis statement.

In the next essay, a student responds to a poem, effectively explaining what he believes is the poem's primary message by using a number of examples from its text.

For the White Person Who Wants to Know

How to Be My Stereotypical Friend

Joel Adrian Villanueva

"For the white person who wants to know how to be my friend," is a poem written by Pat Parker, author of several books of poems and essays. Within the poem, Parker brings into play a sampling of the stereotypes placed on blacks by whites. Parker employs these stereotypes within the poem, along with sarcasm and humor, which soften but do not lessen the impact of her message, to demonstrate common interactions between black and white people and illustrate the difficulties of forming friendships that are based on stereotypes rather than an appreciation of all people's uniqueness. In "For the white person who wants to know how to be my friend," Pat Parker offers humorous examples of white people's stereotypical responses to black people in order to amplify the magnitude of stereotypes that are placed on African Americans.

Parker begins by offering a situation in which the stereotypical preference of music that black and white people listen to is highlighted. The basis for this specific situation is the idea that when a black person goes to a white person's house, the white person feels like he or she must play some "black music" in order to make the black person feel welcomed. With a clever play of words, Parker announces, from her own perspective as a black: "You should be able to dig Aretha / but don't play her every time I come over" (3-4). This request helps Parker to establish a present day stereotype of African Americans. Aretha Franklin, queen of the blues, is a popular African American vocal artist. Parker suggests with her request that white people instinctively reach for the nearest "black music" when a black person comes over. Parker maintains this idea by letting the white person know that black people even know about musicians like Beethoven. For as Parker explains: "They make us take music appreciation too" (6). Parker uses that line in order to reveal how African Americans are stereotyped into a genre of music and even more so, how their intelligence is insulted.

Furthermore, Parker tastefully discusses the stereotype of African American's taste in food. The poet brings up the association between "soul food" and African Americans in a few lines: "Eat soul food if you like it, but don't expect me / to locate your restaurants / or cook it for you" (7-9). In this example, Parker, with a pinch of wit, presents a stereotype of African Americans enjoying this type of food. This example suggests that all African Americans love the taste of soul food and always know where the nearest soul food restaurant is located. To continue, the addition of the line, "but don't expect me . . . / or cook it for you" (7, 9), reinforces the stereotype of the African American being expected to cook for the white person, cooking up delicious food that only an African American could master in the kitchen. This segment of the poem assists Parker in demonstrating that even after years since the ending of slavery, the demeaning stereotype that white people place on African

Americans in regard to African American's taste in food still exists.

Parker also explores the stereotypical beliefs of whites in regard to African Americans' and white people's response to crime within her poem. She illustrates several examples of how African Americans are stereotyped in these lines:

> And if some Black person insults you,
>
> Mugs you, rapes your sister, rapes you
>
> Rips your house or is just being an ass--
>
> Please do not apologize to me
>
> For wanting to do them bodily harm. (10-14)

Parker strongly believes that many times white people take on the task of balancing on a tightrope when talking about wanting justice to be served when an African American person commits a crime. The author suggests that white people often confuse the desire for justice with the concept of racism. In this instance, Parker highlights the stereotype that all African Americans are either criminals or potential criminals. Immediately after, Parker reaches into her bag of wit and humor to pull out the following line: "It makes me wonder if you're foolish" (15). Clearly, Parker questions the foolishness of feeling guilt over the desire to see a criminal brought to justice--regardless of his or her color.

Parker continues to assert her study of African American stereotypes by bringing up the conception by white people that illustrates African Americans as sexual dynamos. The poet uses another dynamic duo of humor and sarcasm when stating to white people: "And even if you really believe Blacks are better lovers than / whites--don't tell me" (16-17). Since the deplorable times of slavery, African Americans were thought of as better lovers than white people simply because they were mysterious people from a foreign land. That idea, when combined with the fact that slave owners knew very little about the people they owned, led to the misconception that African American slaves must have sexual prowess because they were naked savages-- little better than animals. Parker plays on this belief perfectly, when she says, sarcasm in hand: "I start thinking of charging stud fees" (17).

Parker concludes her poem with these lines: "In other words--if you really want to be my friend--don't / make a labor of it. I'm lazy. Remember" (18-19). By using the word "labor" in the line, Parker recalls the days of slavery, when African Americans were believed to be unfit for anything other than unskilled labor. She also smartly picks up on the stereotype of "lazy blacks." By correlating the social stereotypes of past and present, Parker helps to reveal the many stereotypes of African Americans that are still believed today.

Pat Parker amplifies throughout "For the white person who wants to know how to be my friend," the magnitude of the stereotypes that are placed on African Americans by offering overly extreme versions of how white people, who truly do not wish to be racist, become racist when they overcompensate and try too hard. In other words--if black and white people want to be friends--white people should throw out the stereotypes. Humans are all unique. Remember.

Consider this . . .

■ Is this writer's thesis argumentative?
■ Where in the essay does the writer use the technique of example?
■ Does the writer use definition?

☰ Definition

A definition tell us what something is by listing its parts, explaining how it works, telling us what it does, or comparing it to similar things. Frequently, when you write in response to a text, you have to define some aspect of the text or your argument in order to make your point. For example, if you want readers to understand what you mean by "Mona Lisa's aura," you need to define it:

> The painting entered the modern era's newly constructed publicity machinery without anyone intending to put it there, and has long since emerged as much more than a painting with a spectacular aura; "Mona Lisa" has become an aura that has left its physical canvas behind. It doesn't matter how little time you are given to look at it. It doesn't matter how dark the encrusted canvas is. Anyway, everyone knows exactly what it looks like. The point of "seeing" the Mona Lisa is not even to stand in its aura; the point is to have stood there.

The next essay, a review of the film *The Cat in the Hat*, claims that the movie falls short of the classic book on which it was based. This is an argumentative essay that uses logical organization of several kinds of evidence as well as definition and example.

THIS CAT'S A DOG

David Edelstein

If you've ever read a book by Dr. Seuss out loud, you know there's nothing like having those long, serpentine, nonsense words flying out of your mouth on their own current: Your voice seems to rise and fall on waves of anapestic tetrameter. On the other hand, watching the new, mega-budget Mike Myers vehicle *Dr. Seuss' The Cat in the Hat* (Universal) is like being run over by a garbage truck that backs up and dumps its load on top of you. It's a sloppy and vulgar burlesque, one of the most repulsive kiddie movies ever made.   1

"Vulgar" sounds prudish, so it's important to add that when Dr. Seuss (born Theodore Geisel) began writing his books for children more than half a century   2 ago, they were a frisky antidote to the Dick and Jane school of moral hygiene. In a universe in which parents compulsively reined in their kids (sometimes for their kids' own good, more often for the good of their furniture and upholstery), his Cat in the Hat gave permission for frenzied destruction—destruction that could even discomfit the kids themselves, who'd inevitably internalized some of their parents' edgy materialism. In their biography *Dr. Seuss and Mr. Geisel,* Judith and Neil Morgan quote Maurice Sendak: "[Geisel] wrote great big noisy books with noisy pictures and noisy language. . . . He was a bull in a china shop. . . . He appealed to the animalistic nature of children." Dr. Seuss never had his own kids, which I think kept him pure: Many of us zanies don't discover our Inner Repressive Parent until we're worn down by children screaming in our ears, spilling stuff on things we care about, and toddling toward staircases like little suicide machines.

3   Sendak might have framed his Seuss assessment like that because noisy, animalistic kids are at the heart of his own classic, *Where the Wild Things Are.* In the books of Dr. Seuss, there's actually something more than liberating anarchism: There's high elegance. The title character of *The Cat in the Hat* is a force of disorder, but he's disorder in a top hat, bow tie, and white gloves—the daintiest, most radiantly serene of tornados. The miracle of the Seussian universe is its balance between chaos and formality—that its whirligig cacophony arrives in all those gorgeously meticulous stanzas.

4   What Myers and director Bo Welch and a battery of screenwriters have done is turn *The Cat in the Hat* into *Austin Powers* with fur balls. It's now a low-camp universe, in which a vaguely 1950s conformity is undermined by scatological humor—belch and fart gags, plus sniggery allusions to four-letter words and cas-

Universal Studios/Zuma Press

tration. The movie is aggressively unpleasant: The music is grating and the colors garishly ugly—pea-soup green and egg-yolk yellow mixed with pink and lilac. Director Welch is a production designer who did playfully surreal work with Tim Burton on *Beetlejuice* (1988) and *Edward Scissorhands* (1990), but he doesn't want to move the camera, and he keeps the action in the center of the frame, where it congeals. The audience spends the first 15 minutes praying for the arrival of Myers, then the next hour praying for an anvil to fall on his head.

Myers doesn't have the lean silhouette of Dr. Seuss' cat. Physically, he's closer to Bert Lahr's Cowardly Lion, and his voice is Lahr's with a dash of Cawffee Tawk Long Island: The person he really sounds like is Joanne Worley from *Laugh-In*. He works like mad to bring *The Cat in the Hat* to life: He prances around those inert frames; he even throws in a *Saturday Night Live*–style mock infomercial that ends with his tail being inadvertently whacked off. You can see the logic behind this gross-out sketch-comedy approach, but it's alien to Dr. Seuss— and, more important, it's third-rate Myers. With his genius comic radar, Myers must have sensed the slant was wrong but couldn't turn back. Even under all that hair you can detect the expression of someone flapping his arms to keep a lead balloon aloft.

The movie comes with icky life lessons for the kids in the Cat's charge, Sally (Dakota Fanning) and Conrad (Spencer Breslin). The Cat has come to loosen up Sally and harness the creative energy of Conrad, who has run afoul of his single mom's suitor, a conniving sharpie named Quinn (Alec Baldwin). Quinn is the bad, repressive surrogate dad who wants to send Conrad to military school; the Cat is the good, liberating surrogate dad who wants him to care. But it's hard to

Universal Studios/Zuma Press

concentrate on the struggle when both dads are so revolting. The movie's grim sub-text is the wreck of Baldwin's career—how puffy he looks, and how he never manages to rise above his material.

7   Sean Hayes of *Will & Grace* gives not one but two disgraceful performances, as the twitty boss of the kids' pert blond mom (Kelly Preston) and the voice of a computer-generated killjoy goldfish. I can't make up my mind which is worse. Maybe the goldfish: He actually has some verses of Seuss, which Hayes rushes through impatiently to get to the potty jokes. The kids, especially Fanning, stay recognizably human, and there's some imagination in the scene in which the Cat and his antic Things, One and Two, finally clean the house up with their impossible clackety cleaning machines. But it might be that the scene is so enlivening because we know it means the movie is almost over.

8   Geisel swore off movies after a bad experience collaborating on *The 5,000 Fingers of Dr. T* (1953), but softened toward Hollywood after lively cartoons by Chuck Jones and an evocative treatment of *The Lorax*. But now, a dozen years after his death, after the bloated, pointless *How the Grinch Stole Christmas* (2000) and this latest desecration, it's clear that his heirs have sold out the good doctor's legacy. What could be next: Adam Sandler in *Horton Hears a Poo*?

Consider this . . .

- What point is this writer trying to make?
- What techniques does he use to make it?
- Is his argument persuasive?

CHOOSING AN ORGANIZATIONAL METHOD

The organizational methods used for responsive essays are conceptual, logical, and alternating order.

☰ Conceptual Order

When you use conceptual organization for an essay, you introduce points related to your topic and then develop and link them. In the essay "Doonesburied," the writer introduces the comic strip *Doonesbury* as his topic and then makes points related to that topic. The points support his argument that the quality of the strip has been damaged by the writer's increasing sense of his own relevance.

DOONESBURIED

Jesse Walker

A kid calls the FBI's terrorism tip line. "I am very serious," he says, "I know of several Americans who have helped train and finance Osama bin Laden." The feds ask him for the names. "Well, let's see. First one is Reagan. That's R-E-A-G . . . Hello? Hello?"

That was an October edition of *The Boondocks*, Aaron McGruder's comic strip about a precocious black radical. The cartoon caused a small furor, with several newspapers refusing to run it. The New York *Daily News* went further, dropping the strip for a month and a half, while other papers shuttled it to the opinion page.

If that sounds familiar, it's because McGruder is scarcely the first cartoonist to have run into such troubles. Walt Kelly's *Pogo*—a much better strip—paved the way in 1953, when it caricatured Joseph McCarthy as a wildcat named Simple J. Malarkey, prompting papers to move the strip to the opinion page, to threaten to drop it entirely, and, in one case, to alter Malarkey's face to tone down the senatorial resemblance. But the king of the controversial cartoonists was Garry Trudeau, whose *Doonesbury* first caused an uproar in 1972, a year before Kelly's death.

It was a Sunday strip. Zonker, Trudeau's permanently blissed-out hippie, was asked to entertain a boy at a day care center. He obliged with a tale of a "gentle freak named Douglas," whose kindness to rabbits was rewarded with a weekend in Nirvana. There, the gods gave him "his weight in fine, uncut hashish."

As soon as the episode appeared, complaints poured in. The editor of *The Abilene Reporter-News* wrote, "I have seldom experienced such an angry reaction on anything in my 20 years as chief editorial executive of this newspaper."

1   Organizational method—conceptual

2   Essay introduces points related to the topic and ties them together.

3

4

5

6   I found that quote on doonesbury.com, Trudeau's newly revamped Web site, which includes a self-congratulatory archive of "controversial strips." There is a pattern to these ire-inspiring cartoons. The early ones—the aforementioned tale of rabbits and hash, or the 1973 strip declaring that Watergate conspirator John Mitchell was "Guilty, guilty, guilty!!"—are famous, at least to those of us who follow the funny papers. These episodes made Trudeau's reputation and built his audience; for every editor who refused to run them, another two picked up the strip. Sometimes the figure being satirized even issued an angry public rebuttal. The original George Bush, in his vice presidential days, declared that "the American people are going to be speaking out, and we'll see whether they side with *Doonesbury* or the Reagan-Bush message."

7   The controversies kept coming, through the '70s and the early '80s: A law student reveals he's gay; a woman goes to bed with a man not her husband; a reporter takes a tour of Reagan's brain. When Frank Sinatra was awarded the Medal of Freedom, Trudeau ran a series on the singer's mob ties. In 1985 the Universal Press Syndicate, which distributes *Doonesbury*, implored Trudeau to withdraw a series mocking the anti-abortion film *Silent Scream*. He published it instead in *The New Republic*.

8   If there was brilliant satire here, there was also brilliant marketing: *Doonesbury* was now branded as a strip for smart people. Trudeau has already won the Pulitzer Prize for editorial cartooning, an award never before given to a comic strip (and rarely given to someone who is actually funny). Now he was being published in *The New Republic*, which in those days stood at the commanding heights of the Washington pundit class. When Trudeau won his Pulitzer in 1975, the Editorial Cartoonists' Society passed a resolution condemning the decision. No cabal of thinkocrats issued a similar dictate 10 years later.

9   With influence came power. While newspapers steadily reduced the size of the strips in their funny pages, Trudeau alone was able to insist that his cartoon stay unshrunk. Not that it always mattered what went on in the comics section: Like *Pogo* before it, *Doonesbury* was often printed on the opinion page, away from all the cartoon rabble. Papers originally shifted the strip to the op-ed page to ward off children's eyes and reader anger, but its new residence soon became a mark not just of danger, but of seriousness.

Point of essay—Trudeau destroyed his comic strip by taking himself too seriously.

10   But for a humorist, the wrong kind of seriousness can be fatal. Keep reading that archive of controversial strips, or examine the Web site's even more extensive timeline of *Doonesbury*'s history. Gradually, two things happen: The controversies become less familiar, and the strips become less funny. The two phenomenon were conjoined in 1990, when some papers refused to run a bland series mocking

Dan Quayle's notorious purchase of "Pedro, the anatomically explicit gag doll." When the *Pine Bluff Commercial* blocked the strips, its editor wrote, "Those of us in the newspaper business are obliged to cover the tasteless, but we see no reason to publish material on this page that is both tasteless and boring." The site quotes *Commercial*'s complaint. It fails to note that the paper had a point.

By 2001, while McGruder was stirring up trouble with *The Boondocks*, Trudeau was quietly withdrawing the cartoons originally slated to run the week after September 11. The strips had questioned the president's intelligence, you see, and now just wasn't the time for that sort of thing. A handful of papers accidentally printed the withdrawn strips, and Trudeau received some angry e-mails. One appears on the Doonesbury site: "How can you possibly be so insensitive and out of touch with the national sentiment? I am shocked and dismayed that your September 17 strip would attack the president in a time of national crisis." 11

The scathing reply: "In response to the 9-11 attacks Trudeau withdrew a week-long series of daily strips critical of Bush—already mailed to client newspapers—replacing them with 'Flashback' strips. Unfortunately a handful of papers, including the one you read, did not follow these instructions for the first few days of the week of 9-17." 12

Not that Trudeau gave up on satire. In a November strip—a good one, to give the cartoonist his due—Karl Rove informs the president that "it turned out that the missile defense program, and corporate tax cuts, and subsidies for the power industry, and oil drilling in Alaska . . . in fact, most of the items on our political agenda . . . are *all* justified by the war against terrorism!" 13

"Wow . . . what a coincidence . . . thanks, evildoers!" replies Bush. 14

Neither Rove nor Bush felt the need to respond to the cartoon, and no newspapers refused to run it—or if they did, doonesbury.com uncharacteristically fails to mention it. Instead, the site has printed a selection of e-mails attacking the strip. "Garry, the blood of Sept. 11 victims is on your hands," says one. Another asks, "What junior college did you drop out of?" 15

So Trudeau still has the power to piss people off. It says something, though, that he has to publish their complaints himself. 16

Controversy and quality are not the same thing, of course. But there is a direct link between *Doonesbury*'s declining relevance and *Doonesbury*'s declining merit, a common cause for both afflictions. Trudeau's career arc mirrors the evolution of baby-boom liberalism, from the anti-authoritarian skepticism of the 1970s to the smug paternalism of the Clinton years. In 1972 the strip was engaged with the world; in 2002 it is engaged with itself. 17

18   I mean that literally. In 1972 *Doonesbury* rewarded intelligence; in 2002 it rewards familiarity with its own mythology and conventions. In 1972 it trusted readers to know the politics and pop culture of the day; in 2002 it trusts us to understand a floating waffle represents Bill Clinton, a floating bomb represents Newt Gingrich, and a floating asterisk represents George W. Bush. The strip has grown so self-referential that it makes jokes about its own self-referentiality, with Sunday strips devoted to charting the relationships among the characters. And so *Doonesbury* folds in upon itself, and Trudeau ends up producing his own fan fiction.

19   This becomes even more obvious at the Web site—not just because it is filled with trivia games and the like, but because it now includes every single *Doonesbury* since the strip was launched in 1970 (plus the two years of Trudeau's college strip *Bull Tales*, featuring the same characters, that preceded that). The result is one giant hypertext novel, a nearly complete guide to the *Doonesbury* universe. Only a 1977 TV special, a 1983 Broadway musical, and some Web-only material produced during the 2000 election are missing.

20   One effect of this is to put the oldest and most recent strips on the same plane, to let one jump easily from the '70s and to today and back. The results do not flatter the modern cartoon. True, the drawing is better crafted now, though that's not necessarily an improvement: There's something to be said for the static poses of the strip's first decade and a half, at least when compared with the sometimes self-indulgent shifts in lighting and camera angles that prevail today. In its art as in its humor, the early *Doonesbury* combined understated irony with bursts of absurdity. The later strip never stops hitting you over the head.

21   A subtler change: how young people talk. Trudeau was in his 20s during the strip's early run and thus had no trouble imagining that college students—at that time, most of his major characters were in college—would be smart and engaged with the world. (Or, in the case of Zonker, smart and engaged with his own world.) They have the same self-awareness as the strip, and they speak like educated people. When the draft registration returned in 1980, for example, the cast discussed it like this:

22   Zonker: It's not fair! Why is it we 20-year-olds have to pay for the failures of U.S. foreign policy?

23   Mark: That's the way it's always been, man.

24   Mike: Well, it's not like we've been drafted. Carter's just trying to send the Kremlin a message.

Those characters, like their creator, are now middle-aged, and they still speak   25
the same way. Meanwhile, there's a new crop of college kids in the strip, and they
don't know much about the world. They speak the way an older man expects
teenagers to speak: They say "yo" a lot, and they ask questions like, "Can you teach
us how to get shaggy with the babes?" If Trudeau no longer captures the *Zeitgeist*,
it might be because he's started writing about it from the outside.

But the biggest change is political. There was a libertarian streak to '70s liber-   26
alism: Disillusioned by Watergate and Vietnam, invigorated by the rebellions of the
'60s, it was socially tolerant, supportive of civil liberties, suspicious of executive
power, ready to investigate and dismantle the national security state, and even open
to deregulation when it was presented in populist garb. (Few remember that it was
Ted Kennedy and Ralph Nader, not Ronald Reagan who pushed through airline
deregulation.) Needless to say, this current quickly disappeared—banished from
the Democratic mainstream by the '80s, its last gasp in that party was Jerry
Brown's presidential campaign of 1992. But it had an effect on popular culture, not
least with the pox-on-all-houses tone of the younger satirists and their outlets:
Trudeau, the *Rolling Stone* that published Hunter Thompson in his heyday, the
early *Saturday Night Live*. This obviously wasn't a strong strain, or else it wouldn't
have vanished so quickly in the '80s, either capitulating to the new political tone
or adopting the anybody-but-Reagan stance that flung liberals back into the arms
of Hubert Humphrey. (Walter Mondale, actually, but for practical purposes
they're the same thing.) Still, for nearly a decade, an anti-authoritarian style was
regnant within American liberalism.

Not, mind you, that Trudeau was a libertarian then, any more than he was a   27
Clintonite 20 years later. But there was an unmistakable shift in the strip's political tone, even when the strip's politics stayed the same; it moved from the clever
to the loud, from the smart ass to the ass. If there was a turning point, it was the
late-'80s introduction of Mr. Butts, the enormous talking cigarette who soon
came to embody the entire tobacco industry. ("Hey *teens*! . . . Getting hooked on
cigarettes is *fun*—and surprisingly easy! For just a few dollars a day, you'll have a
glamorous new habit for *life!*") Similar characters followed, notably Mr. Jay, Mr.
Brewski, and Mr. Dum-Dum, representing pot, alcohol, and firearms.

What did this mean for the strip? Consider one issue where Trudeau's opinion   28
hasn't changed but his tone has: gun control. First examine this 1981 exchange
between the strip's resident outlaw and a flunky from the National Rifle Association, set in a Washington bar:

29   Springfield: Duke . . . it's me, Springfield! From the N.R.A., remember?

30   Duke: Oh . . . Springfield, what's the idea of sneaking up on me like that? I coulda blown you away!

31   Springfield: I'm sorry. That would have been your right.

32   Now jump to 1993, as a giant cigarette and a giant bullet prepare to lobby Congress.

33   Mr. Butts: Still on a tear, Mr. Dum-Dum?

34   Mr. Dum-Dum: Hey! The N.R.A. never rests! The gun-control nuts keep trying to slip the Brady Bill past us! But it ain't gonna happen! No way! We've been shooting our way out of tight squeezes since 1871! And *look* at the *results!* Over 70 *million* happy gun owners ready and able to defend our way of life!

35   Mr. Butts: Wow . . . are we safe yet?

36   Mr. Dum-Dum: Not yet. Tragically, many children are *still* unarmed!

37   I disagree with Trudeau about gun control, but I still think the first strip is funny. The second one just hectors us. It isn't controversial so much as it's annoying.

38   Trudeau is not the only cartoonist to decline with age. Frank King's *Gasoline Alley* brought high art to the Sunday funnies in the 1920s and '30s, but it never matched those masterpieces in the decades that followed. Charles Schulz's *Peanuts* was in top form from the mid '50s through the mid '70s, then grew blander; by the end, it was not so much a comic as an outgrowth of the greeting card industry. Even *Pogo* peaked early, in the 1950s, though it stayed funny, relevant, and controversial until its creator's death in 1973.

39   If Trudeau's only sin were not living up to his early work, that would be understandable. But he's moving toward a far less pleasant future, toward a fate like that of *Li'l Abner* auteur Al Capp. Capp's strip, insightful and hilarious in its day, was little more than a permanent tantrum at the end; it felt like the product of a befuddled old man, desperately angry at the youth movements of the '60s but too far removed from them to lampoon them effectively. (There was sharper satire of the hippies in the underground comics of Robert Crumb, wiser cracks about the New Left—well, in the early years of *Doonesbury*.) There's an unpleasant parallel between *Li'l Abner* making dumb jokes about "Joanie Phoanie" Baez the millionaire folk singer and Doonesbury shooting witless potshots at Mr. Dum-Dum. And there's another parallel, no less ugly, between the decay of Capp's generation of liberals and the decay of the later left that shocked Capp in the '60s, reinvigorated liberalism in the '70s, then suffered its own sad decline.

If *Doonesbury* is still sometimes interesting, it is because its world is so vast, so　40
sprawling, that it cannot help intersecting with ours. After losing his way in the late
'80s, Trudeau recovered temporarily, with the Gulf War. His barbs weren't as
sharp as they were during Vietnam, but the universe he'd built allowed him to
examine the new war from multiple angles—one week in Iraq, the next in Washington, the next in Hollywood. Even Mr. Butts briefly became funny, putting
down his satiric sledgehammer to tend bar in Kuwait, where his fumes mixed with
those of the burning oil wells.

In that way, occasionally, *Doonesbury* returns to form: when the strip's Vietnam　41
veteran returns to Southeast Asia, when its title character starts a dot-com, and
even, yes, after September 11, when each of the comic's scattered characters
responded to the crisis in his or her own context. Garry Trudeau's fans surely
enjoyed such moments, and perhaps a crank or two even sent some angry e-mail
to the cartoonist.

It's not clear, though, that anyone else noticed. The strip still appears in　42
almost 1,400 newspapers, but it's lost its cultural cachet. Years ago, Henry
Kissinger remarked that the only thing worse than being in *Doonesbury* would be
not to be in *Doonesbury*. At some point since then, the strip simply stopped being
a fashionable place to be seen.

Consider this . . .

■ What is this writer's thesis?

■ What organizational method does he use?

■ What writing strategies does he use?

≡ Logical Order

A logically ordered essay can begin with a general statement followed by specific details that support it, or can begin with specific
details followed by a general statement. In the essay "This Cat's a
Dog," the writer begins by stating very generally that the movie is
"sloppy and vulgar burlesque, one of the most repulsive kiddie

movies ever made." He follows this general statement with specific details intended to support it. The writer of "This Magic Mona" uses basically the same organizational method. He first asks, "Why is it so famous now, when for some 200 years—from the 17th to the 19th centuries—it was ignored?" He then explores this question in detail and provides evidence to support his answer to it.

THIS MAGIC MONA

Charles Paul Freund

Organizational method—logical

Essay begins with specific details and concludes with a general statement.

1   When Mona Lisa came to Washington's National Gallery in 1963, the lines of people wanting to see her were so long that each art lover was allowed less than 30 seconds to commune in front of her. The event became notorious for its apparent absurdity; everyone had a good laugh at the spectacle. A decade later, Mona Lisa went to Japan, where viewing time was reduced to an estimated two seconds per visitor.

2   Why bother? Why, for that matter, do the Louvre's hordes snatch their floorplans and rush to the X that marks the painting's spot? Is "La Gioconda"'s smile any more mysterious than any other painted Renaissance smile? The 500-year-old canvas has become so grimy that the image is actually hard to see, yet no one dares clean the thing. Why is it so famous now, when for some 200 years—from the 17th to the 19th centuries—it was ignored?

3   "It's a snowball effect," Donald Sassoon recently told *The Washington Post.* Sassoon, for years a historian of the left, has now taken up the study of taste, and how elite opinion influences popular reception. He calls

The original Mona Lisa by Da Vinci

Gianni Dagli Orti/Corbis

Marcel Duchamp's Mona Lisa

his subject the "social canon," and his most recent project is *Becoming Mona Lisa: The Making of a Global Icon* (Harcourt Brace).

Sassoon focuses on the process of fame, especially how a little fame can lead to a lot more fame. "It's a very special painting," he told the *Post*, "so Raphael and other people copied it. And it was by Leonardo. And it was in Paris. And intellectuals wrote about it. And it got stolen [in 1912]. And [artist Marcel] Duchamp made fun of it. And it visited the United States. And each is due to the thing before. It gets stolen because it was pretty well known; then Duchamp puts a mustache on it, because he needs something that everybody knows; it gets sent to New York and Washington, because it is a popular painting; it is used in advertising because it was sent all over."

Sassoon's right, of course. The painting entered the modern era's newly constructed publicity machinery without anyone intending to put it there, and has long since emerged as much more than a painting with a spectacular aura; "Mona Lisa" has become an aura that has left its physical canvas behind. It doesn't matter how little time you are given to look at it. It doesn't matter how dark the encrusted canvas is. Anyway, everyone knows exactly what it looks like. The point of "seeing" the Mona Lisa is not even to stand in its aura; the point is to have stood there.

Mona is a woman of power, and that power emerges from "mystery"; Sassoon describes how French author Theophile Gautier established her as a modern *femme fatale*. Yet, for all the modernity of the painting's fame—constructed of endless press coverage, an infinity of cheap reproductions, the praise of the popularizing critical establishment (notably the "decadent" critic Walter Pater), the growth of art museums as uplifters of "mass" taste, etc.—the experience of the Mona Lisa isn't modern at all. In fact, the painting's popular reception is actually a link to the time before art.

7   For centuries prior to the Renaissance, there was neither art nor artist; there was only the image. Most imagery was religious; some of it was created to be didactic, some to exert spiritual power. So important were the functions of such images, especially those portraying or symbolizing spiritual glory that in the West their forms were often dictated down to the most minute detail. To deviate from an established form of an image was to risk debilitating its power and therefore its spiritual function. Creative artisans who experimented with these forms were accused of undermining faith and doing harm to the faithful; they could be punished as if they were criminals.

8   One rarely if ever looked at a "painting"; one was in the presence of an image. One didn't contemplate the meaning of imagery; rather, imagery had innate power. It's not at all unlike the experience of Louvre patrons and others hurrying past the Mona Lisa. It is not so much a painting that they are given the opportunity to see, but rather a powerful likeness in whose presence they are allowed to pause. Though they attend a palace of Enlightenment bourgeois uplift to see a Renaissance portrait, the experience they have is a medieval one. It comes from a time before art, and suggests a time after it.

Consider this . . .

- Did this writer make a clear analysis of the appeal of Mona Lisa? Why or why not?
- What techniques did the writer use to make his argument?
- Can you identify any other "landmarks" such as the Mona Lisa that have become icons?

≡ Alternating Order

When you choose comparison/contrast as a writing strategy for an essay, you may compare two things to show how they are similar or contrast them to show how they are different. You can organize such an essay in alternating order: by discussing first one topic and then the other or by using a point-by-point alternating pattern. In

"This Cat's a Dog," the writer compares the film version of *The Cat in the Hat* to the classic book.

WHEN WE WRITE to respond, we have the opportunity to analyze a text to which we have had a strong response. By sharing such responses, we are able to help others to make decisions regarding the texts with which they choose to engage. We live in a world full of information, and this is both a blessing and a curse. We are blessed to have access to so much information, but we are cursed in that we cannot possibly read, see, or hear every text that exists. By reading others' responses to various texts, we can gain further understanding of those texts and choose the ones we wish to explore further. ▪

COLLABORATIVE EXERCISES

Group Exercise One

- As a group, select a familiar cultural icon. For example, you might choose a celebrity, a television or cartoon character, or a well-known image.

- Spend some time talking within the group about the icon you selected. What does it mean to you? Do you like or dislike it? Why do you think it has become so famous?

- Write a few paragraphs in response to the icon, incorporating what you learned from your discussion.

Group Exercise Two

- Read the paragraphs about icons written by each of the other groups.

- Write a one-paragraph response to each one. Place each response on a separate sheet of paper, and give it to the appropriate group.

- As a group, read the one-paragraph responses you receive from other groups.

- Discuss whether the responses are fair and well supported. Why or why not?

Group Exercise Three

- As a group, compile a list of questions to ask when peer reviewing one another's response essays. (For example, you might ask whether the response is supported by evidence or experience or both.)

- As individuals, list the concerns you have regarding your response essays.

- Work in groups or as a whole class to ensure that everyone's personal concerns have been incorporated into the list of peer review questions.

WRITING PICKS

Option One

Textual analysis

Choose a written text—for example, a story, a poem, a song, or an essay—and offer a response to it based on one of three possible focuses:

- Analyze the effectiveness of the text
- Agree or disagree with the main idea of the text
- Interpret some aspect of the text

Whichever focus you choose, be sure to include evidence to support your response. Some of this evidence can come from your personal experience or other sources, but you must also include evidence from the text.

Option Two

A visual focus

Choose a visual text—such as a movie, an advertisement, a photo, or a painting—and offer a response to it based on one of three possible focuses:

- Analyze the effectiveness of the text
- Agree or disagree with the main idea of the text
- Interpret some aspect of the text

Whichever focus you choose, be sure to include evidence to support your response. Some of this evidence can come from your personal experience or other sources, but you must also include evidence from the text.

"Trailer Camp Children" by Ansel Adams, copyright 1986, Trustees of Ansel Adams Publishing Rights Trust

This photo of indigent children offers an opportunity to respond with analysis or interpretation.

Option Three

Picture this

We all have images that we have collected because they have meaning for us. You may have posters hanging on your walls or photos in your drawers that hold special meaning for you. You may have artwork that was given to you by a family member or a friend or a collection of album covers or even drawings that you've done yourself. Choose an image you own that has special meaning for you and analyze the source of that meaning. What about the image evokes a response in you? In an essay, analyze your response, and try to explain its significance to others.

Option Four

M-I-C-K-E-Y M-O-U-S-E

Mickey Mouse
© Disney Enterprises, Inc.

Decades after his creation, Mickey Mouse continues to be as popular as ever and is, in fact, an industry himself. What is it about this big-footed mouse with the squeaky voice that keeps generations of children and adults asking for more? And Mickey isn't just an American icon— Mickey has gone global. In an essay, explore the mystery of Mickey. What makes him a global icon of such enduring power?

APPLYING THE RHETORICAL SITUATION

As always, you must consider the rhetorical situation throughout the process of making choices when you write to respond. Use the questions here to guide your decision making.

Audience

- How familiar is your audience with the text, image, or object that you have chosen?

- What do you want to tell your audience about it?

- What information does your audience need in order to understand the significance of your response?

Purpose

- What point are your trying to make?

- What techniques can you use to make it?

- How can you structure your paper to emphasize that point?

- What do you want readers to understand after reading your analysis?

Occasion

- How can you make your analysis have pertinence for readers?

- How can you make them understand the significance of your topic without lecturing?

- Have you thoroughly analyzed the subject?

FOCUSING ON PROCESS

Prewriting

Once you choose your text, image, or object, read or study it carefully, and then answer these questions:

- Why did you choose it?
- How would you describe your response to it? Emotional? Logical?
- What specific aspect of it interests you most? Its message? The technique the writer or artist used? Do you agree or disagree with the main idea?

Drafting

- Begin by writing your thesis. Is it argumentative? Do you clearly identify the stance you will take in your essay?
- Identify three to five specific points you can use to support your thesis.
- Find at least one example from your text for each point.
- Write your draft.

Revising

- Identify the subject and the verb in each sentence of your draft.
- Ask yourself these questions:

  Is the subject doing the action of the sentence?
  Can the subject do the action of the sentence?
  Does the subject agree in number with the verb?
  Do the verbs have appropriate tenses?

- Make any necessary corrections.

Editing

- Review each of your previously graded essays. Which grammar or punctuation error do you make most often?

- Read your draft carefully. Have you made this error in the draft?

- Correct the error if you find it.

Grammar Choices

DANGLING MODIFIERS

Have you ever come across a sentence that made you either laugh or wonder because it didn't make sense? Look at these sentences:

After proofreading your papers, more corrections are often necessary.

Having started the assignment late, an extension was requested.

To be a good writer, hard work is needed.

These sentences do not make sense because each of them contains a dangling modifier. A modifier is a word or group of words that relates to another word in the sentence. A modifier dangles when the thing referred to is not clearly identified in the sentence.

Look at these revisions of the previous sentences:

After proofreading your papers, **you** might need to make more corrections.

Having started the assignment late, **she** requested an extension.

To be a good writer, **you** must work hard.

In each case, the sentence was corrected by the addition of the something the modifier of the original sentence was meant to modify.

Most sentences that contain dangling modifiers share these qualities:

■ The dangling modifier occurs at the beginning of the sentence.

■ The dangling modifer often has an *ing* form of a verb or a verb phrase containing the infinitive form of a verb (such as *to be*). This often results in a passive construction.

In the following sentences, the verbs are identified for you:

After freewriting, more research **is** often **required**.

Having finished the paper, a folder **was needed**.

To be a good writer, creativity **is to be desired**.

By simply eliminating the passive voice in the second half of the sentence by adding an actor, the writer can also correct the dangling modifier:

> After freewriting, **I** often decide I require more research.

> Having finished the paper, **I** needed a folder.

> To be a good writer, **a person** must have creativity.

Making It Work

- Underline each sentence in your draft or essay that contains a form of the verb to be.

- Locate the actor in each underlined sentence.

- Correct any sentence that has a dangling modifier by adding an actor and removing the passive voice.

Style Choices

USING QUALIFIERS

When we write, we often use *qualifiers*, or words that restrict or fine-tune the meaning of another word. Qualifiers—especially those of number, such as *all*, *some*, and *several*—can be very important.

Using Qualifiers Wisely

All students must attend the orientation.

Only dogs with complete vaccination records will be boarded.

This example suggests that **all** African Americans love the taste of soul food and always know where the nearest soul food restaurant is located.

The cartoon caused a small furor, with **several** newspapers refusing to run it.

In each of these cases, the qualifier allows the writer to specifically identify the class of things to which the information applies.

Dangers of Not Using Qualifiers

Sometimes, however, when writers choose not to use qualifiers, they make statements that might be considered questionable.

The movie is aggressively unpleasant.

Because the writer does not use a qualifier, the reader may assume that he literally means that every second of the film is unpleasant. However, later in his review, he identifies one redeeming moment in the film. Occasionally, a writer may choose not to use a qualifier in order to add weight or forcefulness to an opinion. You need to be careful when making this choice.

The original George Bush, in his vice presidential days, declared that "the American people are going to be speaking out, and we'll see whether they side with *Doonesbury* or the Reagan-Bush message."

We might assume from this quote that the vice president expected every American in the country to speak out on this issue. Clearly, this is not true. The addition of a qualifier would have made this statement more accurate.

> When Frank Sinatra was awarded the Medal of Freedom, Trudeau ran a series on the singer's mob ties.

Because the writer does not use a qualifier to soften this statement (for example, "singer's *alleged* mob ties"), the reader has to assume that the writer has proof that this allegation is true. Perhaps he does. However, when you are writing your papers, you should never make a claim that you cannot prove, and you should provide the proof in the paper.

Using Qualifiers Incorrectly

Inexperienced writers often use qualifiers inappropriately in an attempt to give their writing weight; however, such usage can alienate the readers. Consider this statement:

> Apparently **all** managers believe that short people are not strong enough or capable enough.

The writer of this essay needed to remember that some of her readers may disagree with her; in fact, some of her readers may be managers who do not believe that short people are less qualified.

> **All** humans view Mother Nature not as a benevolent mother who loves us unconditionally, but as a raging stepmother who apparently resents our existence.

Again, many of the readers of this essay may not believe the writer's statement, and they may resent being lumped together with others who do.

Qualifiers are very useful, but be sure to use them judiciously.

Making It Work

- ■ Underline every qualifier of number in your draft or essay.

- ■ Did you use these qualifiers correctly?

- ■ Look for sentences that need to be qualified.

- ■ Add or remove qualifiers wherever necessary.

PART THREE

Conducting Research

Web sites such as this one contain massive amounts of information that you will find useful when conducting research.

CHAPTER ELEVEN

WORKING IN THE LIBRARY AND ONLINE

Collecting Information

In this chapter, you will learn:

- How your purpose for writing affects the information you collect for a research paper

- How to use the library for research

- How to use the Internet for research

Spencer Grant/PhotoEdit

Research begins in the library.

You collect information every day. Looking at *TV Guide* to see when your favorite television program will be on, using the Internet to find out where your favorite band will be touring, perusing travel brochures to plan your ideal vacation, and comparing cars in *Consumer Reports* to decide what kind to buy are all forms of research. These types of research are not particularly difficult or at all intimidating because you are familiar with the tools and processes that you need to collect the information. The research you do for college papers is not fundamentally different from the research you do every day. You just have to make yourself as familiar with the tools and processes of college-level scholarly research as you are with those you use regularly.

Traditionally, scholarly research has been done in college or university libraries. Today, the World Wide Web has opened a whole new set of doors for collecting information. Whether you will be collecting information at your college or university library, at your public library, or on the Web, there are specialized tools and methods for collecting information. Understanding and knowing how to use these will make your search for information more efficient.

RESEARCH AND THE PURPOSE FOR WRITING

What reasons do you have for collecting information? In college, you collect information for your writing for any of three reasons:

- To learn something that you don't know
- To confirm the reliability of information for your readers
- To enter an academic conversation

You choose your reason based on your purpose for writing. Deciding what kind of information you need to collect is another one of the choices you make when writing.

Gathering information to learn something that you don't know can be as quick and casual as looking up a fact on the Internet or as formal as doing exhaustive library research. For example, if you needed to know the date of the Norman conquest of England, you could quickly find that information on the Internet or in an encyclopedia. You could also get plenty of in-depth information about this historical event at the library. Paula Mathis, the student whose research paper appears in Chapter Thirteen, chose the art of Matt Groening as her topic, and she needed both types of information from her research:

Quick fact: Name of each of the characters in *The Simpsons*

In-depth research: The use of satire in *The Simpsons*

You may already know quite a bit about your topic. However, you need to confirm the reliability of that information for your readers in order to add credibility to your writing. Even if you know very specific details or statistics that relate to your topic, your reader may question the reliability of the information if you don't support it with research. Although she knew that Groening had been drawing before he created *The Simpsons*, Paula Mathis couldn't simply say this in her paper. Her readers have no reason to accept her as an authority. She needed to support what she already knew with research:

> According to biographer Rachel Sprovtsoff-Mangus, Groening began drawing cartoons as a teenager, and his father Homer, a cartoonist as well, took great pride in young Matt's budding interest in the medium. Groening often drew cartoons as a part of his various school activities and in letters to friends and family, but not until 1980 did he achieve much commercial success as a cartoonist (Sprovtsoff-Mangus).

Collecting information to enter an academic conversation is the kind of research that separates college-level scholarly writing from the kind of writing you probably did in high school. When you enter an academic conversation, you learn what other scholars have to say about your topic. Then you use that research as a springboard for presenting your own ideas. Rather than simply using someone else's research to confirm facts, you enter into a dialogue of sorts with your sources by agreeing with, disagreeing with, and adding to the information that they provide. In the following passage, Mathis uses a quote from another source to support both her own opinion and her observations:

Ott goes on to say that "the Waltons of the 1970s and the Cosbys of the 1980s simply no longer possessed any fidelity, they no longer accurately reflected reality" (60). In episode 178, "The Secret War of Lisa Simpson," the Simpson children visited a military academy where the students ably demanded (quoting Keats, though harshly), "Truth is beauty, and beauty truth, Sir!" (<u>Simpsons Archive</u>). <u>The Simpsons'</u> truth, though often outlandishly presented, is what helps make it such a beautifully silly show.

WORKING IN THE LIBRARY

Working in a library is the traditional way to collect information. Despite the convenience of the World Wide Web, there are still many benefits to library research. When working in a library, you can ask a reference librarian to help you. The main job of these librarians is to help library patrons find information. Get to know the reference librarians at your college or university library (or even your public library). You'll be surprised at how willing they are to help you and how helpful they will be.

When you collect information in the library, especially a university library, you don't have to worry about the reliability of your sources as you do when you search on the World Wide Web. The information you find in the library has been subject to more quality control because it has been published by an established press or appears in a reputable journal or magazine. The process to select what is purchased for a library is highly controlled, while anyone can publish on the Internet. Another benefit of using a library is that some professors might be wary of—or simply not willing to accept—Internet research because they worry about the quality of the information available. Therefore, never assume that you can get through your college years relying solely on the Internet for research. You may encounter a professor who requires library research either exclusively or at least in addition to online research. So, learn to use your library's resources.

☰ Using the Library's Catalog

A library's catalog is a listing of all the books, magazines, periodicals, microfilm, microfiche, theses, and dissertations that the library has on site. The catalog may even include music, videos, and DVDs. Your library's catalog is always the first place you should start when seeking information. Databases will give you lists of sources that may or may not be owned by your library, but you will know that the sources listed in your library's catalog are easily accessible because they are right there.

You can search a card catalog by subject, author, or title. Generally, you will have more options for searching an online catalog. In addition to subject, author, and title, most online catalogs also

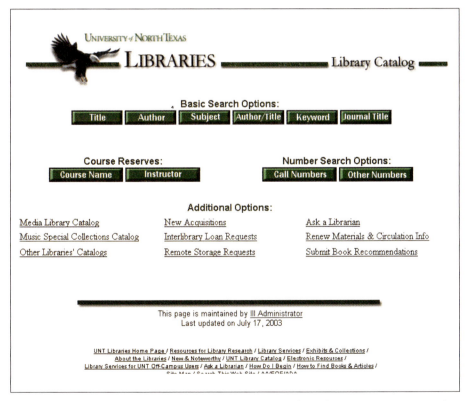

This is the online catalog for the libraries at the University of North Texas. As you can see, the search options are clearly labeled.

have a keyword search option. Some online catalogs even let you search by year of publication, which can be useful if you know the date of an article that you wish to find.

Whether you are using a card catalog or an online catalog, knowing how to search in it is the key to finding the information you need. Searching by title or author is relatively easy; however, searching by subject can be more difficult. If your library still uses a card catalog, you may need to ask a reference librarian to help you begin because the subject phrases in a card catalog are specific and limited in number. However, if your library has an online catalog, you should be able to sit down at the computer terminal and get started.

When you are searching by subject, make sure that you narrow your search. Narrowing your search will help you find information that is directly related to your topic and will prevent you from having to sift through countless sources. For example, rather than searching for "wives of Henry VIII," let your purpose determine how you narrow your search. You could search for a specific wife, such as "Anne Boleyn," or you could search for "beheaded wives of Henry VIII" or "divorced wives of Henry VIII." As another example, if you were doing research on the topic of medieval architecture, you could do a subject search under the broad topic of "historical architecture," but in order to ensure that you find as much information as possible, you would also need to narrow your topic and try other phrases, such as these:

Medieval architecture

Medieval architects

Medieval buildings

Medieval homes

Medieval structures

Architecture of the Middle Ages

Medieval builders

Medieval craftsmen

By describing your topic in as many ways as possible, you optimize your chances of finding useful information.

≡ Using Databases

Databases are large lists of sources organized so that you can find the information easily. Databases are not available on the Internet because they have to be purchased. A reference librarian will be able to tell you which databases your library owns and how you can access them.

You use the same strategies to search databases as you use to search a library catalog, but the sources you find in databases will not necessarily be owned by your library. After you find works through a database, you need to check your library's catalog to see if the library owns the source you need.

You might find the following databases useful:

- **InfoTrac College Edition** provides access to ten million full-text articles from nearly five thousand academic and popular journals. Because this database provides the full text of articles from a wide range of journals on many topics, it is highly useful for any type of research project.

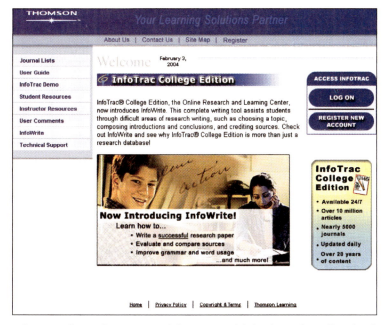

InfoTrac College Edition is one of the most useful databases for college-level research.

Articles from thousands of scholarly journals can be accessed through Academic Search Premier.

▪ **Academic Search Premier** provides full-text coverage of over three thousand scholarly journals. This is a useful database because a wealth of information is right there for you; you can simply print out the material you need. Academic Search Premier also provides abstracts (brief summaries) and indexing for more than four thousand other scholarly journals.

Periodical Abstracts Research indexes academic journals and popular magazines.

▪ **Periodical Abstracts Research** contains abstracts and full-text articles from academic journals, popular magazines, and key business publications. You can search Periodical Abstracts Research by publication, keyword, or topic. This is a great database to turn to if a professor requires you to have sources from journals or magazines.

■ **Literature Resource Center** contains biographies, literary criticism, work overviews, bibliographies, timelines, and many additional resources, including directories of reliable Web sites for more than 120,000 authors from every period and literary discipline. This database is the place to start when you need to learn about a specific author.

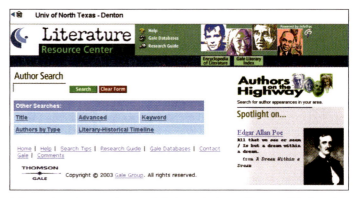

Information about authors and their works is readily accessible by using Literature Resource Center.

■ **The MLA International Bibliography** contains the bibliographic records of sources relating to literature, language, linguistics, and folklore. This database covers sources from 1963 to the present and is the best place to search for information about literature and the English language.

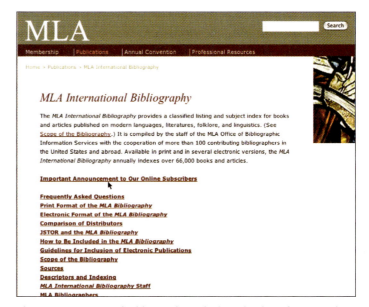

The MLA International Bibliography is the best database for researching papers about literature.

Educational materials can be searched for efficiently using GEM.

■ **GEM (The Gateway to Educational Materials)** provides access to educational materials, including lesson plans, activities, and projects. You can browse by subject or keyword, or search by subject, keyword, title, or grade level. You can limit search results to free resources.

PubMed is useful for research in the life sciences.

■ **PubMed** allows you to search more than twelve million references to articles published in 4,500 biomedical and life science journals. Coverage extends from the mid-1960s to the present.

■ **Business Source Premier** is a database containing articles from scholarly and trade business journals. This database is useful if you are researching companies, industries, products, management, marketing, accounting, real estate, finance, insurance, business law, and technology.

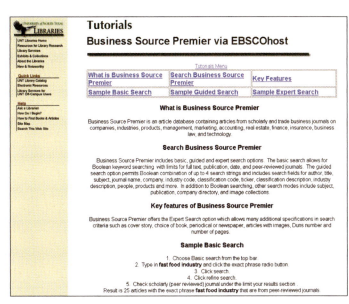

For a research paper on any business-related topic, Business Source Premier is a useful resource.

■ **PsycINFO** allows you to search for articles and information in the field of behavioral sciences.

PsycINFO accesses articles and other sources dealing with psychology and other behavioral sciences.

Sources in the biological sciences can be accessed through Biological
Abstracts.

■ **Biological Abstracts** allows you to search for abstracts of published articles in the field of biological sciences.

≡ Using Interlibrary Loan

If you come across a source that you need on a database and you can't find it in your library's catalog, what should you do? Many libraries offer interlibrary loan: You can request that your library borrow a source from a library that does own it. Ask the reference librarian whether your library participates in interlibrary loan and what the procedure is for using it.

WORKING ON THE WEB

Working online is the truly modern way to conduct research. You can access the Web wherever you have a hook-up—your house, your dorm room, or your favorite coffee shop. You don't have to worry about library hours, so you can search at your convenience. And sometimes you can even access the sources themselves directly from your computer. So why not just collect information from cyberspace and boycott the library altogether? There are several reasons: The Internet still does not contain the amount of information that libraries do. Also, when you are collecting information from the Internet in your home at 3:00 a.m., you don't have access to a librarian who can help you. The last reason you don't want to rely solely on the Internet is because you have to be very discriminating about your research sources.

Here, then, is a checklist of how to begin your research:

1. Search your library's catalog to locate books.

2. Choose the electronic databases that are appropriate to your topic, and search for articles.

3. Use a search engine such as Google or Yahoo! and conduct a search for information available on the Web.

4. After you make a list of every book, article, and Web site that you wish to read, begin collecting your materials and determining which you will use.

Google is one of the most popular search engines for finding text or graphics by topic: a word, name, or phrase.

≡ Using Boolean Operators

Boolean operators are terms you can use to refine a search when working with any search engine. For example, if you were researching iguanas and you did a search using "iguana" as a key word, the computer would search for all records with that word in them, and you would get a complete list of every source that included it. This simple search did not use Boolean operators. If you wanted to expand or narrow this search, you could use Boolean operators. For example, if you wanted to find all sources that had the term "iguana" or the term "iguanadon" or both, you would use the Boolean operator OR: "iguana OR iguanadon." If you wanted sources with the term "iguana" but not the term "iguanadon," you would use the Boolean term NOT: "iguana NOT iguanadon." If you wanted to find sources that included both "iguana" and "iguanadon," you would use the Boolean operator AND: "iguana AND iguanadon."

To summarize, the three Boolean operators refine a search as follows:

> **OR** can be used to broaden your search to sources that include either of two works, phrases, or concepts.
>
> **NOT** can be used to exclude a specific word, phrase, or concept when you search.
>
> **AND** can be used to narrow your search to sources that include two words, phrases, or concepts.

Using these operators can help you optimize your efforts and get the search results you want.

≡ Using Directories

So, how do you discriminate between reliable and unreliable Web sources? You'll learn some specific strategies for evaluating information on the Internet in Chapter Twelve. The first step is to learn that there are directories out there that do it for you. The following examples will get you started.

▪ **Best Information on the Net (BIOTN)**, at **http://library.sau.edu/bestinfo/**, lists resources by discipline and topic with links to relevant sites. This directory is maintained by St. Ambrose University's O'Keefe Library.

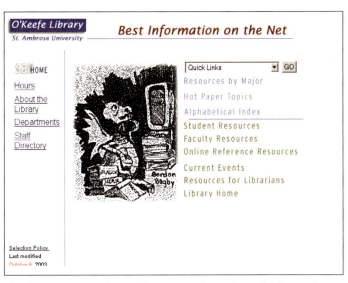

The directory BIOTN lists Web resources for students, faculty, and librarians.

▪ **BUBL Link**, at **http://bubl.ac.uk/link/**, is a directory of selected Internet resources that covers all major academic subject areas. Links are classified according to the Dewey decimal system and are updated monthly.

BUBL Link covers all major academic subject areas.

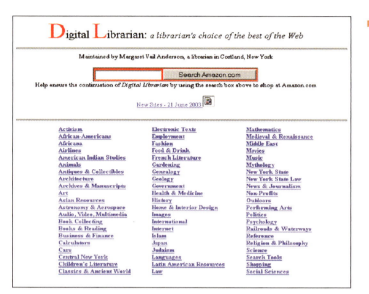

Digital Librarian offers an extensive list of subject areas.

■ **Digital Librarian**, at **http://www.digital-librarian.com/**, a directory that lists Internet sites by subject, is updated only periodically.

■ **Education Index**, at **http://www.educationindex.com/**, is an annotated guide to education-related Web sites sorted by subject and by age level.

Education-related Web sites are sorted by subject and age level on Education Index.

■ **INFOMINE**, at **http://infomine.ucr.edu/**, is a virtual library of resources such as databases, electronic journals, electronic books, and articles. It is maintained by the University of California, Riverside.

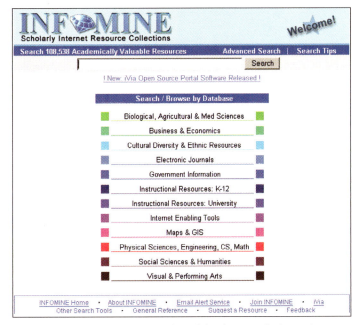

INFOMINE offers access to a number of databases and other online resources for scholarly research.

■ **Librarians' Index to the Internet**, at **http://lii.org/**, is an annotated directory of Internet sites sorted by category and subject.

The slogan of Librarians' Index to the Internet is "Information You Can Trust."

Web resources in the humanities can be accessed through Voice of the Shuttle.

▪ **Voice of the Shuttle**, at **http://vos.ucsb.edu/**, is a comprehensive and highly reliable Web directory and database for academic research. Strongest in the humanities, but also covering some other disciplines, it is maintained by the English Department at the University of California, Santa Barbara.

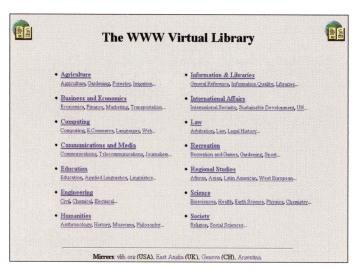

Links to a range of sites for a variety of subjects are provided by the WWW Virtual Library.

▪ **The WWW Virtual Library**, at **http://vlib.org/**, is a high-quality catalog that provides links to Web sites for a variety of subjects.

ALTHOUGH EXPRESSIVE WRITING based on personal experience can be highly useful for expressing your feelings and honing your writing skills, the majority of the writing you will do, especially in the work world, will be based on information of a nonpersonal nature. Sometimes you will be provided with the information on which to base a piece of writing, but more often you will be expected to find it. Consequently, you need to have strong research skills. There is a wide world of information out there, but if you can't find it, you can't use it. ▪

COLLABORATIVE EXERCISES

Group Exercise One

- As a group, choose one of the Research-Based Writing Picks.

- For that topic, find at least one possible source using each of the search engines listed in this chapter.

- Identify one search engine not listed here.

- Share your material with the class.

Group Exercise Two

- Use search engines to find at least five graphics to use with the topic you chose in Group Exercise One.

- Learn how to save the graphics so that you can download them.

- Which search engine worked most effectively for graphics?

- Did you find any new search engines?

- Share your information with the class.

RESEARCH-BASED WRITING PICKS

In this chapter, you will pick a topic for a research paper from the options on the following pages. Your paper should meet these criteria:

- It must contain an arguable thesis.
- You must use MLA or APA style.
- You must document all sources.
- You must use both direct quotes and paraphrases.
- You must use a minimum of five secondary sources.
- Your paper must be six to eight pages long.
- Your paper must include a Works Cited or References list.

In the next two chapters, you will be introduced to the skills you need in order to satisfy these criteria.

Option One

Art critic at large

Select an artist whose work you admire, and make his or her work the focus of a research paper. Remember, you can choose a graphic artist, a musician, a cartoonist, a writer, a photographer, or any other type of artist. Focus your research not just on the artist—his or her education, influences, medium, and so on—but also on the significance of his or her work. What makes it noteworthy? What do the critics have to say? Can you offer a close analysis of a specific work? Remember, in addition to a verbal analysis of the artist's work, you also need to include examples of that work.

The work of Andy Warhol redefined popular culture.

Houdini was a master magician and escape artist. Many of his tricks have never been reproduced.

Option Two

People who have shaped our world

Research the accomplishments of someone, living or dead, whom you admire for some significant reason. For example, you might admire Mother Theresa for her humanitarian work or Albert Einstein for his genius in developing the theory of relativity. You might admire Buddy Holly for writing music that paved the way for rock and roll. Be sure the person you choose has contributed in a truly significant way. For example, if you wanted to write about an athlete, you might choose Lance Armstrong, who won the Tour de France six times. However, more importantly, he is a cancer survivor who has devoted time and money to finding a cure for a terrible disease. So don't just write about your favorite singer or your favorite actor—unless that person has contributed to the world in a significant way.

Mahatma Gandhi was born in India and is known for his work as a peace activist.

Lance Armstrong, who rides for Team USPS, is the founder of Cycle of Hope, an organization seeking to find a cure for cancer.

Born in Poland in 1867, Marie Curie discovered two radioactive elements: radium and polonium.

Option Three

Surviving the information explosion

We are living in an information explosion. Because of the World Wide Web and satellite communications, we have twenty-four-hour access to news from around the world. Consequently, we have access to a larger amount of information about a broader range of topics than ever before. However, we have to learn to filter this information. For this research topic, choose a current event or issue about which you would like to know more, and use it as the focus of your research. Be careful not to choose a topic that is too broad for the scope of this paper. For example, you might effectively research recent scientific advancements in the separation of conjoined twins, but not the history of conjoined twins.

The popular CNN.com Web site allows uninterrupted access to worldwide news events.

Grammar Choices

FAULTY PREDICATION

You have already learned that every simple sentence has two parts: a subject (a noun or pronoun) and a predicate (a verb plus object, complement, and/or modifier). Because the subject of the sentence carries out any action stated by the verb, the **subject** and the **verb** have to match. In other words, you can't combine a verb with a subject that is not capable of doing the action the verb describes. Doing so results in **faulty predication**, as in these examples:

> The **dog begged** me to take it home.

You might argue that dogs do beg, but, strictly speaking, *to beg* implies the ability to talk, which dogs do not have.

> The **book said** it is difficult to become a published writer.

A book cannot *say* anything. The author of the book *said* something.

When to Avoid Faulty Predication

Faulty predication may seem like a technical detail, but it can cause your readers to misunderstand you. Look at the following sentences:

> Even the **notes** he had taken so carefully **could not recall** the name of the woman he met in Paris.

People use notes to recall information, but the notes themselves cannot do any recalling.

> Her **faded prom dress**, which she had saved so carefully, **captured** a moment of her youth and preserved it for all time.

A photograph of someone in a prom dress can be said to capture a moment, but the dress itself cannot capture anything.

In order to avoid faulty predication, remember to be sure that the subjects of your sentences can do what the verbs logically require. Writers of poetry or song lyrics sometimes use faulty predication intentionally, but it is not usually appropriate when writing essays.

When to Use Faulty Predication

As you've learned, there are usually exceptions to rules, and you may occasionally use faulty predication for stylistic effect—but only when you understand it well enough to choose it intentionally. In each of the following sentences, the writer used faulty predication for stylistic effect:

The **chocolate cake was screaming** her name.

At night in his dreams, his overdrawn **bank account wept** in shame.

Though it is no longer the tallest building in New York City, many visitors still answer when the **Empire State Building sings** its siren song of glamor and mystery.

As you can tell, these intentional uses of faulty predication allow the writers to emphasize their feelings about the inanimate objects they are describing. Faulty predication can be a useful technique, but use it carefully.

Making It Work

■ Identify the subject of every independent clause in your draft or paper.

■ Is each subject capable of performing the action expressed by its verb?

■ Correct any instances of faulty predication that you find.

Style Choices

NEGATIVE OR POSITIVE LANGUAGE

When we communicate, we often have the opportunity to choose between negative or positive language.

Negative Language

Do not use the computer behind the desk.

Never wait until the night before a paper is due to begin writing.

Never make a major purchase without reading *Consumer Reports* first.

Positive Language

Use the computers in the student lounge.

Begin writing your paper several days before it is due.

Read *Consumer Reports* before you make a major purchase.

Though the difference between the first set of sentences and the second may seem relatively superficial, the difference can have a psychological impact on a reader's response. Most people resist being told that they cannot do something; however, they tend to respond more favorably to positive suggestions. Consequently, it is always more effective to use positive language when possible.

In the following passage, positive language is in color:

Having concluded that the appeal to color blindness **is** a dangerous distraction from the lingering effects of prejudice, Loury **calls** for major structural remedies to **speed up progress** toward racial equality. Most prominently, he **adamantly and impatiently defends** the affirmative action programs **widely used** in American higher education. He **sees affirmative action as a means of propelling** blacks into positions of influence, thereby **changing social attitudes** ingrained by many years of private and institutionalized bigotry. "What is required," he says, "**is a commitment** on the part of the public, the political elite, the opinion-shaping media, and so on **to take responsibility** for such situations as the contemporary plight of the urban black poor, and **to understand** them in a general way as a consequence of an ethically indefensible past." While **there is some merit** to Loury's observations about the inadequacy of color blindness, his explanation of racial inequality is only partly successful, and his critique of liberal individualism misses the mark.

Focusing on what Loury has said and has proposed, the writer emphasizes the positive aspects of his work.

Making It Work

- Underline any negative words in your draft or essay.

- Are any of your uses of negative language justified?

- Rewrite any passages with unnecessary negative language and present the information in positive language instead.

CHAPTER TWELVE

PRINT AND ELECTRONIC MEDIA

Evaluating Sources

In this chapter, you will learn:

- How to evaluate print sources in terms of currency, reputability, reliability, and level of detail

- How to evaluate Internet sources in terms of accuracy, credibility, objectivity, currency, and thoroughness

- How to use sources effectively and responsibly by recording bibliographic and other information accurately and by acknowledging your sources

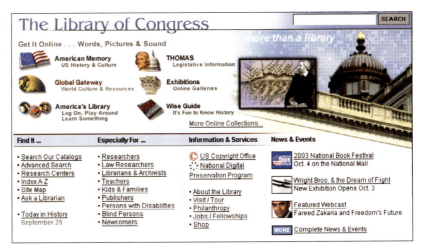

The Internet can be a wonderful research tool—but you must be sure that the sites you use are accurate and credible.

The information explosion brought about by the World Wide Web has both advantages and disadvantages for you as a writer. On the plus side, you have information at your fingertips. You can access both print sources from libraries and Internet sources from the Web without ever leaving your computer. On the negative side, because so many sources of information are available to you, you must be selective about the sources you choose and vigilant in determining which sources are reputable. Before the Internet, the fact that all research material came from the library ensured that it was likely to be reputable. However, now anyone can publish on the Web, and it is often hard to distinguish a good source from a bad source. We can divide the types of research sources you will use into two groups:

- Print sources
- Internet sources

PRINT SOURCES

Print sources include any information that was published in the form of a book or a periodical (journal, magazine, newsletter, or newspaper). You will do most of your research for print sources at the library, but you might occasionally find very recent material at a bookstore.

Books

The databases that were discussed in Chapter Eleven will help you identify the titles of books about your topic. Once you have a list of the books you wish to read, you can consult your library's catalog to find their locations within the library. If your library does not have a book you need, you may have to order it through interlibrary loan.

A database will help you find books on your research topic.

☰ Periodicals

Periodicals are of three basic types: scholarly journals, popular magazines, and newspapers.

Scholarly journals

Scholarly journals are typically published by professional organizations or university presses, and they contain articles about topics in a particular field. For example, if you were doing research on a method of teaching writing, you might find an article in *College English*, which is published by the National Council of Teachers of English. In addition to being categorized by their subject matter, scholarly journals can also be classified as regional, national, or international publications:

Regional publications have a relatively small circulation in one geographical area. For example, *MLA* is a national publication, and *Rocky Mountain MLA* is a regional publication. Regional publications often contain good material, but they have less prestige than national or international publications.

National publications have a larger circulation and subscribers across the country. National publications are prestigious.

International publications have subscribers from around the world. Because their articles are read by people in many countries, they are also prestigious.

Popular magazines

Popular magazines are published by private organizations for non-academic audiences. For example, *People*, *Newsweek*, and *Harper's*, are considered popular magazines. Popular magazines have their own editorial policies that determine how submissions are selected. The larger the circulation of the publication, the more strenuous the review process tends to be.

Popular magazines may provide information for certain research topics.

Some popular magazines are more reliable than others in terms of the accuracy of the information that is presented. For your research, give more credibility to magazines that focus on objective presentations of the news rather than on movie stars, millionaires, or other aspects of popular culture. For example, if you are looking for information on global warming, a magazine like *Time*, *Discover*, or *Scientific American* is more likely to provide solid information than *People* or *Look*.

Newspapers

Newspapers can also be excellent sources of information, especially if you are writing about a current event or topical issue. Most libraries have back issues of the major newspapers. You can also find newspaper archives online. Again, remember that some newspapers have better reputations than others. Newspapers like the *New York Times*, *Washington Post*, and *Wall Street Journal* are known for their accurate reporting. The *Enquirer* and the *Star* are known for their fantastic stories.

Many newspapers also publish online versions.

☰ Reference Materials

Reference materials are stored in a separate area of the library, and they cannot be checked out. Examples of reference materials are encyclopedias, bibliographies, atlases, and dictionaries. You can use reference materials for many types of research topics. For example, if you are looking for information about a specific writer, you can consult the *Dictionary of Literary Figures*. You can also consult any number of encyclopedias to gather information about specific people, events, or things. Other useful reference materials are bibliographies, or lists of works on a specific topic, as well as the *Oxford English Dictionary* (*OED*), where you can find historical information about every word in the English language. Some highly useful and reputable reference works, such as the *OED*, are now available online as well as in bound volumes.

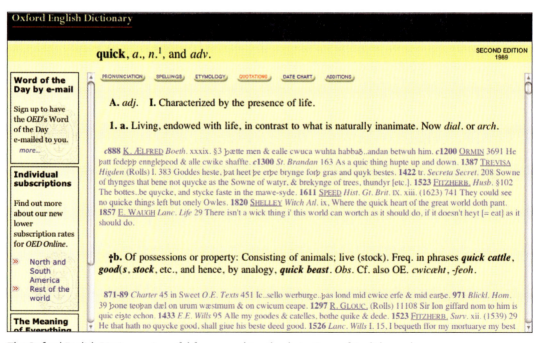

The Oxford English Dictionary *is useful for researching the derivations of English words.*

EVALUATING PRINT SOURCES

Searching in various databases and reference works is likely to yield a number of written sources about your topic—probably more than you can use. You have to evaluate these sources to determine whether you should use the information they contain. When you evaluate a print source, ask these questions:

- Is the source current?
- Is the source reputable?
- Is the source reliable?
- Is the source thorough?

Is the Source Current?

All printed sources have a publication date, and to what extent that date will affect the usefulness of a source depends on your topic. For example, if you are writing about cloning, any articles that were written more than a year ago may contain information that is no longer accurate. However, if you are writing about a historical event, such as the development of the first nuclear bomb, you might need to read articles that were written in the 1940s. For most nonhistorical topics, however, you should use the most current material possible. Facts change as new information is discovered, and opinions change as a result of new discoveries. Unless you are using the most recent material available, you can't depend on the accuracy of the information.

Is the Source Reputable?

In general, scholarly sources are considered more reputable than popular sources. Articles published in scholarly journals are often based on primary research and are written by experts in a field for other experts in the field. Popular magazines, on the other hand,

As sources for research papers, magazines written for general audiences, such as Smithsonian, *are generally not considered as reputable as scholarly journals covering similar subject matter.*

are written for general audiences who have no special expertise. Consequently, they do not have the same level of complexity and may contain less information. Among popular magazines, some are more reputable than others, however. For example, which would you consider more reputable—*National Enquirer* or *Time*?

Is the Source Reliable?

When you are dealing with a reputable printed source, you normally assume that the information within it is correct and reliable. However, you should select articles that are thoroughly documented and, if necessary, cross-check pertinent facts with other sources. This way you can be sure that the information you use is accurate. Also, be sure to look at enough sources to determine whether there are differing opinions about your topic.

☰ Is the Source Thorough?

You are likely to find more sources than you can either read or use. When that is the case, you need to have a method of selecting the best options. One important criterion to consider is how thoroughly a source covers your topic. Obviously, the more detail about your topic the source contains, the more useful it is likely to be. In addition, remember that the bibliography at the end of a book or article might be a useful tool. Bibliographies can steer you toward other sources that you might not have found.

INTERNET SOURCES

As you have probably noticed, Web sites have one of several endings. Each of these means that the site has a particular type of affiliation:

.com—the site has a commercial sponsor, such as eBay or Google.

.net—the site also has a commercial sponsor, but it serves as an umbrella site, managing a number of related .com sites.

.org—the site is sponsored by a nonprofit organization, such as the Sierra Club or National Public Radio.

.edu—the site is sponsored by an educational organization, such as a school or university.

.gov—the site is sponsored by a government organization, such as the IRS.

EVALUATING INTERNET SOURCES

Clearly, you have to question the reliability of commercial Web sites. Anyone can publish on a .com or .net site if he or she is willing to pay for the space. Also, many of these commercial sites have one primary purpose—to make money. The other types of sites are more stringently controlled by the organizations that create and manage them.

There is much useful information on the Web, but it is necessary to evaluate it carefully. You must evaluate all Web sites based on these criteria:

- Is the site accurate?

- Is the site credible?

- Is the site objective?

- Is the site current?

- Is the site thorough?

Is the Site Accurate?

When a Web site is accurate, it is free of errors: grammatical errors, factual errors, any kind of error. Furthermore, both the author of the Web site and his or her credentials and sources should be available. This information allows you to evaluate the author's qualifications and to cross-check the information if necessary. Does the creator of the site include links to other sources? Can you verify the sources of the information if necessary? Be highly suspicious of any Web site that does not meet these criteria.

Consider, for example, the Film Noir site. It contains a great deal of information, and the information seems factual. However, although the author is identified at the bottom of the screen, he never gives his qualifications as a scholar of film noir, and he does not include the sources from which he gathered his information. Thus, you should be wary of using this site as a research source.

FILM NOIR

Film Noir (literally 'black film or cinema') was coined by French film critics who noticed the trend of how dark and black the looks and themes were of many American crime and detective films released in France following the war. It is a style of American films that first evolved in the 1940s, became prominent in the post-war era, and lasted in a classic period until about 1960.

Film noir is a distinct branch, sub-genre or offshoot of the *crime/gangster* sagas from the 1930s (i.e., Little Caesar (1930), Public Enemy (1931) and Scarface (1932)), but different in tone and characterization. The criminal, violence or greed elements in film noir are a metaphoric symptom of society's evils, with a strong undercurrent of moral conflict. Strictly speaking, however, film noir is <u>not</u> a genre, but rather the mood, style or tone of a film.

The themes of noir, derived from sources in Europe, were imported to Hollywood by emigre film-makers. (Noirs were rooted in German Expressionism of the 1920s and 1930s, such as in **The Cabinet of Dr. Caligari (1919)** or Fritz Lang's **M (1931)**, and in the French sound films of the 30s.) Classic *film noir* developed during and after World War II, taking advantage of the post-war ambience of anxiety, pessimism, and suspicion. So-called *post-noirs* (modern, tech-noirs or neo-noirs) appeared after the classic period with a revival of the themes of classic noir.

Primary Characteristics and Conventions of Film Noir:

- In Lewis Milestone's **The Strange Love of Martha Ivers (1946)**, Barbara Stanwyck's murderous past may be revealed by her alcoholic, unrespected husband Kirk Douglas
- Rita Hayworth's gave a sultry performance as the black glove-stripping Gilda (1946) in Charles Vidor's classic - portraying the sexy wife of a casino owner (George Macready) who becomes involved with her husband's abusive croupier (Glenn Ford)
- Robert Siodmak's adaptation of Ernest Hemingway's tale of a twisting double-cross, The Killers (1946), with Burt Lancaster (as the doomed "Swede") and the stunning Ava Gardner as the manipulative vixen Kitty Collins
- in director John Cromwell's **Dead Reckoning (1947)**, an on-the-run WWII veteran's alluring Southern girlfriend (Lizabeth Scott) threatens military buddy Humphrey Bogart
- director Jacques Tourneur's quintessential film noir ★ Out of the Past (1947) featured Robert Mitchum playing the doomed, double-crossed private eye who falls for the icy femme fatale (Jane Greer) he is trailing for gangster Kirk Douglas [remade as **Against All Odds (1984)**]
- Nicholas Ray's doomed lover film **They Live By Night (1949)** with Farley Granger and Cathy O'Donnell as fugitive, misfit criminals on the run [remade as **Thieves Like Us (1974)**]
- Joseph H. Lewis' tabloid romantic/crime B movie melodrama Gun Crazy (1949) - another *amour fou* 'Bonnie and Clyde' tale with two disturbed and doomed, gun-loving, sharpshooting lovers (John Dall and Peggy Cummins)
- Otto Preminger's **Angel Face (1953)** with Jean Simmons as a psychotic 'angel of death' who talks chauffeur Robert Mitchum into a murder scheme

◄ Previous   Next ►

The Greatest Films

This site offers a lot of information about film noir, but it may not be accurate.

≡ Is the Site Credible?

Credibility arises from the credentials of the person or organization that created a Web site. Generally speaking, the sites of well-known organizations such as the American Film Institute or a major university are highly credible.

For example, the sponsoring organization of the second film noir site is clearly identified as Media Resources Center, Moffit Library, UC Berkeley. Because the site is associated with a major university library, you can assume that the information is credible. The credibility of the site is further established by information given on the last page, which identifies the individuals responsible for the content and for updating. Again, when evaluating Web sites, steer clear of those that lack credibility. If you don't know who created a site or if you have only a name and no credentials, be suspicious of the information the site contains.

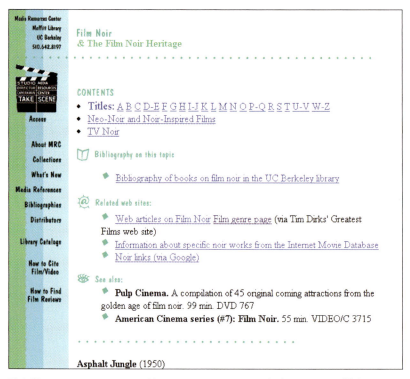

This film noir site is sponsored by a major university, which gives it credibility.

≡ Is the Site Objective?

To be objective, a Web site must have a low level of bias. All sites contain some bias; however, sites that sell a product are much more likely to be biased than sites that merely provide information. The organization that sponsors a site is also an indicator of potential bias. For example, the Web site devoted to beef clearly offers a specific viewpoint: Beef is good for you; eat more beef. This site lacks objectivity; however, even though it makes no attempt to hide its bias, you might find it useful if you were researching how the beef industry promotes the sale of beef. If you were looking for unbiased statistics regarding the consumption of beef in the United States, you might want to look elsewhere for confirmation.

This site is devoted to the marketing and consumption of beef, and thus is not very objective.

Look at the Web site for the U.S. Air Force on the next page. Is this site objective, or does it have an agenda? The purpose of this site is to persuade viewers to enlist in the Air Force. If someone is looking at this site to get information about enlisting, he or she

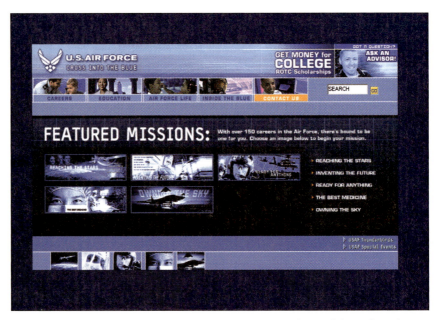

The U.S. Air Force site is devoted to convincing viewers to enlist, and thus is biased toward positive aspects of military service.

may already be prepared to like the site. For the undecided, the site emphasizes the positive aspects of joining the Air Force by showing "Featured Missions" in a James Bond sort of format. What about the site makes you believe that it is less than objective? Nowhere do you see any of the realities of military life. There are no statistics about death rates or references to boot camp. Is this a problem? It could be if a reader is trying to make a decision and he or she hasn't been given access to the full story.

≡ Is the Site Current?

If a Web site is not updated regularly, you should not use it as a source. A key benefit of the Web is the speed with which information can be updated. Without regular updating, the information may be inaccurate or even obsolete. Every site should contain a notification of when it was last updated. On a site that is updated daily, the information is as current as possible.

The eBay site is updated every day, and the date and time of the updating are shown near the bottom of the page. In contrast, the site on women, race, and culture in Disney's movies hasn't been updated since June 19, 1999.

☰ Is the Site Thorough?

If you are not convinced that a Web site offers thorough coverage of the topic you are researching, you probably need to keep looking. For example, if you were looking for information regarding John Steinbeck or one of his novels, you would find many sites, including the one sponsored by San José State University. It offers comprehensive coverage of the author and his works, the Center for Steinbeck Studies, and related works. The other Steinbeck site does not offer good coverage. In fact, the only information it contains is one student's research paper.

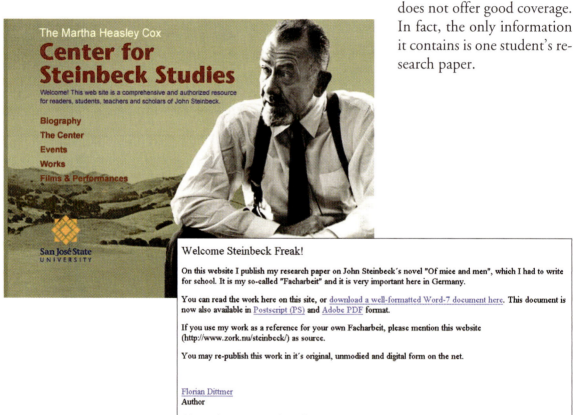

The site sponsored by San José State University offers more thorough coverage of John Steinbeck and his works than does the site authored by an individual German student.

USING INFORMATION RESPONSIBLY

Once you have identified the sources you want to use, you have to be sure that you use the information within them responsibly. In order to use sources responsibly and avoid unintentional plagiarism, you have to have a system for taking notes and keeping track of your sources. Developing such a system will increase your efficiency and ensure that you keep track of what information came from what source.

≡ Recording Bibliographical Information

A bibliographic entry contains all of the information that you need in order to document information you use in your paper. For example, if you are creating a bibliographic entry for a book, you include the author, title, publishing information, and date of publication:

> Hoffman, Frederick J. The Twenties. New York: Free Press, 1962.

Notice that the writer put this information in the correct MLA format. This allows the information to simply be transferred into the bibliography if the source is used in the paper. You may write your bibliographic information on note cards by hand or enter it into a file on your computer. But be sure to make records of all sources. You may think you will remember every source you use, but it is very frustrating to discover that you forgot a key piece of information at midnight when you are trying to finish your paper.

≡ Taking Notes

You will not use all of every source that you find. In fact, in some cases, you may use only a single idea or a phrase or sentence. As you read through the sources you have selected, you need to keep notes on the material you intend to use. For example, if you find a direct quote you want to use, make a note card of it, including the source and topic:

Hoffman, <u>The Twenties</u>. Intellectual climate

"The 1920s were a time least likely to produce substantial support among intellectuals for any sound, rational, and logical program. Prewar stability and convention were condemned because all evidences of stability seemed illusory and artificial" (32).

At the top of this entry, the writer noted the author and title of the book from which the question came, and a brief heading identifying the topic to which the information on the card relates. Below that she placed the material in quotation marks so that she won't unintentionally assume that it was a paraphrase. She also included the page number where the quote can be found.

You can also use notes for paraphrasing ideas:

Hoffman, <u>The Twenties</u> Cultural immaturity

Many Americans believed that it was necessary to go to Europe to develop cultural "finish." They believed that Europe and Europeans had a culture that the United States lacked; when they went abroad, Americans apologized for their own country's lack of culture and blamed it on a lack of time in which to develop it (23).

In this case, the writer did not put the material in quotes because it is not a direct quotation—she paraphrased information that she found on page 23 of the book by Hoffman.

By taking careful notes, you can keep track of the useful information that you find. You can also use the notes as a way of organizing your thoughts. Notetaking may seem time-consuming, but you will find later that it was time well spent.

≡ Avoiding Plagiarism

You all know what plagiarism is and that you shouldn't turn in material that you did not write without giving credit to the author of the work. However, if you don't organize your work and keep careful records of the sources you are using, you may find that you have plagiarized unintentionally.

"Really? Someone told me it's not plagiarism if they're dead."

Distinguishing someone else's ideas from your own

When you use secondary sources in a paper, it is important to distinguish your ideas from those of the other writers whose material you are using. Look at this passage:

> Most students read both the <u>Iliad</u> and the <u>Odyssey</u> of Homer at some point in their education. Like many readers, you may think the <u>Iliad</u> and the <u>Odyssey</u> are just good stories full of action and adventure. You may even know that they are normally identified as epic poems. What you may not know is that, though many ancient and modern scholars disagree, both poems have much to teach us about the history and development of rhetoric.

Because the writer doesn't cite any secondary sources, readers might assume that all of these ideas were her own. However, one of her notes reveals that she is using an idea from one of her sources:

> Enos, <u>Greek Rhetoric</u> Why Homer wasn't studied as rhetoric in classical times

> Enos believes that the writings of Homer have not been studied as examples of rhetoric because many ancient rhetoricians believed that because it predated the development of rhetoric in the fourth century BCE, it could not be rhetoric but was the product of Homer's poetic genius instead. Quintilian did admire Homer, but he was the exception (2). Many modern scholars feel the same way and disregard the poem's contribution to the history of rhetoric.

In order to avoid plagiarizing, the writer needs to distinguish her own ideas from Enos's ideas:

> Most students read both the Iliad and the Odyssey of Homer at some point in their education. Like many readers, you may think the Iliad and the Odyssey are just good stories full of action and adventure. You may even know that they are normally identified as epic poems. What you may not know is what scholar Richard Enos has suggested: although many ancient and modern scholars disagree, both poems have much to teach us about the history and development of rhetoric (2).

In this revised passage, the writer clearly credits an idea to one of her sources by introducing the paraphrase with "Richard Enos has suggested" and by giving the page number where the information can be found. This is an example of how to use secondary sources responsibly.

It is even more important to identify the source of any direct quote:

> According to Enos: "To say that Homer's Iliad and Odyssey are paradigms in the history of literature is to utter a commonplace, but their contribution to the history and development of writing and rhetorical theory have received far less attention" (1). In this paper, I analyze both poems for their contribution to the study of the history of rhetoric.

Here again, the writer separated her own ideas from those of Enos, and she carefully identified the direct quote that she integrated into her paper.

Documenting your sources

The only certain way to avoid plagiarizing is to document every source you use. This means not only written texts, but also interviews, Web sites, and graphics. In Chapter Thirteen, you will be introduced to the basics of documenting sources.

You may sometimes wonder whether information you know must be documented. This can be a complex issue. Some widely known information—for example, that Plato was a philosopher or that rhetoric is persuasive speech—can be considered common knowledge. You don't have to cite any source for this information. However, any ideas that you did not have before finding them in other sources—books, articles, Web sites, interviews—must be documented, even if you put the ideas in your own words. The words may be yours, but the ideas are not. When in doubt, document.

Integrating Direct Quotes

When you use information from a secondary source, you must integrate it smoothly into your text; otherwise, your writing will be choppy. Furthermore, the words you use to integrate direct quotes can help your readers understand their significance.

> When we study the works of great writers, we very rarely study the setting in which the writing took place. This can result in an incomplete understanding of writers' works because in many cases writers' houses "provided the context in which the occupants spent the most fertile years of their creative lives" (Premoli-Droulers and Lennard 7). In fact, as Premoli-Droulers and Lennard further suggest, "Houses play an all-important role in the lives of writers, bringing order to their memories, calming their fears, stimulating their ideas" (7).

The writer of this passage begins with an idea of his own and follows with a direct quotation of part of a sentence that completes his own. He next integrates a complete quoted sentence, introducing it with the phrase *In fact*, which allows the reader to see the relationship between his original idea and the information in the quote.

☰ Paraphrasing

A direct quote is useful when a writer has used a particular phrase or sentence in a way that is important to your thesis. However, if you use too many direct quotes, the paper ceases to be yours. Another way of including information from secondary sources without using direct quotes is to paraphrase the information. You paraphrase when you put someone else's ideas into your own words. Unlike a summary, which is more general, a paraphrase is an intentional attempt to reword. Thus, a paraphrase is often as long as the original. A paraphrase does not include the writer's opinions. Look at this quote and paraphrase:

Direct quote

"Every episode of <u>The Simpsons</u> is multifaceted, allowing it to have different interpretations. There is the superficial layer, which is sprinkled with physical humor and elementary jokes that any audience member can understand. Then there is the more profound level that is replete with allusions to historical occurrences, current events, and popular culture, the mass media, and literature" (Basner 2).

Paraphrase

Each episode of <u>The Simpsons</u> has two layers: the shallow layer and the deep layer. The shallow layer contains the body humor and childish jokes that anyone can understand. The deep layer contains the more difficult references to topics such as history and culture (Banser 2).

Notice that the paraphrase does not change the meaning of the original or add any new information. The writer simply put the idea into her own words.

☰ Summarizing

Like a paraphrase, a summary is a rewording of the original source. However, unlike a paraphrase, which is detailed and may be as long as the original material, a summary is a more concise, generalized restatement. Consider the following passage from a source and its summary:

Original source

"Each person who watches The Simpsons is sure to be made fun of, causing all sorts of disorder. The writers of the show know Poirier's concept that, as artists, each time they air an episode, they risk offending their audience. The makers of the show toy with this idea and are sure to use at least one joke in each episode that pokes at their audience's religion, occupation, status, or character. This allows the audience to lie back a little from their hectic lives, take a step back, and laugh at themselves. Every episode of The Simpsons has some aspect in it that causes the members of the audience to analyze what is going on around them or within them. The allusions ridicule society and the characters are hyperboles of some undesired traits, causing tension and disorder in the viewers, only to be released as laughter." (Basner 2)

Summary

Matt Groening's ability to poke fun at some aspect of each person watching The Simpsons allows viewers to take themselves a little less seriously and enjoy laughing at their own flaws--even as they are forced to consider the often serious underlying issues being ridiculed (Basner 2).

Here, the writer summarizes a passage from a secondary source in order to concisely highlight the points that are important to her argument; however, even though she has put the information in her own words, she still gives credit to the author who owns the ideas.

BECAUSE RESEARCH PAPERS are based on research, they are only as good as the information you gather. Consequently, if you do not carefully evaluate the quality of the sources you use, your final paper will not be as effective as it could be. It is easy to get caught up in the race against a deadline and settle for the sources you find first. This is a bad choice. Give yourself the time to evaluate your research thoroughly, and you will see positive effects on the quality of your papers. ■

RESEARCH-BASED WRITING BRIEFS

You chose your research topic in Chapter Eleven. As the next part of your research assignment, you must complete a research portfolio. Your research portfolio will contain the following items:

Abstract—a short summary of your research paper that clearly presents your thesis and highlights your argument

Outline—a detailed outline of your paper, including both primary and secondary development of the points you will cover

Annotated bibliography—a list of your sources with a brief annotation—critical comments or explanatory notes—for each source you include

Use the information that follows to write your abstract, outline and annotated bibliography.

Your Abstract

An *abstract* is a short summary of a scholarly paper. In this case, you are writing an abstract of the research paper that you will be writing. Because you are summarizing a paper you have not yet written, your abstract may ultimately differ slightly from your final paper. Just be sure that your abstract contains your thesis statement and clearly highlights the main points of your argument. Look at the example on the next page.

The writer begins by providing some background information about her topic—*The Simpsons*. Next, she presents her thesis. This thesis makes an arguable claim and specifically identifies three aspects of the show that she will discuss in the essay. When you read the completed essay in Chapter Thirteen, you will see that she slightly altered her thesis, but the basic premise of the paper remained the same. Writing an abstract such as this will help you focus your thesis and organize the content of your paper.

Abstract

In 1987 Matt Groening created <u>The Simpsons</u>, and in 1989 it became a prime-time television show. <u>The Simpsons</u>' honesty, its intelligent use of humor and satire, and its characters' genuine affection for one another have all helped this cartoon surpass being merely cartoon and become, truly, the best television show ever. This paper gives a brief history of Groening's work. Next, using several critics' perspectives and examples from the show itself, it shows how the inventiveness, humor, intellect, use of satire, and love the characters show one another all move the show beyond typical television sitcoms into a socially conscious satire of American family life.

Your Outline

Your outline is a road map of your research paper. While an abstract presents your paper's thesis and highlights its arguments, an outline gives a more detailed presentation of the content of the paper, section by section.

Again, when you compare the outline on the following pages with the actual paper in Chapter Thirteen, you will find some differences. This is not unusual. However, you will find that writing your outline before you begin writing your paper will help you to produce an organized and coherent paper with less effort.

Outline

I. Thesis: <u>The Simpsons</u>' honesty, its intelligent use of humor and satire, and its characters' genuine affection for one another have all helped this cartoon surpass being merely art and become, truly, the best television show ever.

II. Biography of Matt Groenig

   A. Development of cartoon

   B. Father's interest in cartooning

   C. First work as cartoonist--<u>Life in Hell</u>, 1980

   D. The Simpson's first airing on <u>The Tracey Ullman Show</u>

III. The inventiveness of the show

   A. Cartoon-within-a-cartoon: Itchy and Scratchy Show

   B. Treehouse of Horrors Halloween Specials

   C. Musical numbers and shows

IV. <u>The Simpsons</u> as an honest and realistic show

   A. Characters doing everyday things such as going to the bathroom

   B. Even the fantastic seems realistic

   C. Displaced the false reality of shows like <u>The Cosby Show</u>.

V. <u>The Simpsons</u> as intelligent and thought-provoking

   A. Titles of shows as a reference to other literary works

   B. <u>The Simpsons</u> satire compared to Twain's

VI. The characters' love for one another

   A. Strongest episodes showing the family's loyalty

   B. Example of an episode that shows the family's bonds

VII. Conclusion: The show admired and loved.

Your Annotated Bibliography

An *annotated bibliography* is a list of sources in which each source is followed by a critical comment or explanatory note. To create an annotated bibliography, follow these steps:

- Prepare your bibliography using the MLA format outlined in Chapter Thirteen.

- Directly following each source, provide a brief description of the work (two to four sentences that will remind you of the main points) that relates to how you will use it as you construct your argument.

An example of an annotated bibliography for the paper outlined above is presented on the following pages.

Annotated Bibliography

Cantor, Paul A. "The Greatest TV Show Ever." <u>American Enterprise</u>
Sept./Oct. 1997: 34–37. Cantor, a Shakespeare scholar, says <u>The
Simpsons</u> may be the greatest television show ever. Cantor discusses the use of a cartoon within a cartoon, <u>Itchy and Scratchy</u>,
and compares it to Shakespeare's play within a play. He also discusses the history of <u>Itchy and Scratchy</u> and examines its significance as part of <u>The Simpsons</u>' genius.

Corliss, Richard. "Simpsons Forever!" <u>Time</u> 2 May 1994: 73. On the
show's 100th episode celebration, Corliss discusses ten reasons why
<u>The Simpsons</u> are America's ideal family. He says humor and intelli-
gence in the show, the bond among Simpson family members, and
the societal impact of the show make <u>The Simpsons</u> the most satis-
fying show on television.

Kantor, Ken, Nancy Lerner Kantor, Josh Kantor, Mary Eaton, and Ben-
jamin Kantor. " 'I Will Not Expose the Ignorance of the Faculty':
<u>The Simpsons</u> as School Satire." <u>Images of Schoolteachers in Amer-
ica</u>. Ed. Pamela Bolotin Joseph and Gail E. Burnaford. New Jersey:
Erlbaum, 2001. 185–200. The authors discuss <u>The Simpsons</u>' use of
satire in its representation of students, teachers, administrators,
and parents. The authors contend that the show uses a balance of

cynicism and sentiment to portray the various characters and uses

multiple stereotypes to highlight problems with America's schools.

Ott, Brian L. " 'I'm Bart Simpson, Who the Hell Are You?' A Study in

Postmodern Identity (Re)Construction." <u>Journal of Popular Culture</u>

37 (2003): 56–81. Ott examines postmodern identity in the context

of <u>The Simpsons</u> television show. He discusses the history of the

show and its cultural relevance and investigates the identity mod-

els portrayed in characters Bart, Lisa, and Homer. He contends that

viewers find identity models within the show that they incorporate

into their own identities.

<u>Simpsons Archive</u>. Ed. Jouni Paakkinen. (18 Oct. 2003) <http://

www.snpp.com>. This unofficial Web site lists every episode of the

television cartoon. This site also contains a plot summary of each

show, memorable quotes, entire scripts of many episodes, guest

stars for each episode, and commentary by fans.

Sprovtsoff-Mangus, Rachel. "Matt Groening Biography." (18 Oct. 2003)

<http://www.allmovie.com/cg/avg.dll>. Sprovtsoff-Mangus reviews

the career of Matt Groening, creator of the television cartoon <u>The

Simpsons</u> and the comic strip <u>Life in Hell</u>. She discusses the influ-

ences on Groening as a cartoonist and how he developed the long-

running show.

Grammar Choices

PRONOUN CASES

One of the choices inexperienced writers often struggle with involves whether to use *I* or *me*, or *we* or *us*, or *who* or *whom*. These choices are based on the case of the pronoun. Pronouns can have one of three cases:

Subjective case—when a pronoun is the subject of a sentence, it is in the subjective case.

Objective case—when a pronoun acts as the object of a verb or preposition, it is in the objective case.

Possessive case—when a pronoun is used to show possession, it is in the possessive case.

Subjective	Objective	Possessive
I	me	my, mine
we	us	our, ours
you	you	your, yours
he	him	his
she	her	her, hers
it	it	its
they	them	their, theirs
who	whom	whose

He helped **her** move into **her** new apartment.

She is **my** best friend.

[*You* is understood to be the subject here.] Ask not for **whom** the bell tolls. It tolls for **you**.

Who was at the door?

The manager asked **you** and **me** to close the store tonight.

Tom and **I** are going to the movies later.

His knowledge of algebra is greater than mine.

Major corporations are required to give 5 percent of their annual profits to nonprofit organizations.

Making It Work

- Identify each pronoun in your draft or essay.

- Determine if it is in the subjective, objective, or possessive case.

- Check the list of pronoun cases, and be sure you have used the correct form for each pronoun.

- Make any necessary changes.

Style Choices

USING TRANSITIONS

Transitional words or phrases show relationships between ideas. These are only a few of the transitional words or phrases from which you can choose:

For example—introduces an example

In other words—introduces an explanation

However—introduces a contrast or comparison

On the other hand—introduces a contrast

Next—indicates a time sequence

When—indicates a time sequence

Transitions are important because they create coherence, increase the clarity of communication, and help readers to understand the relationships between ideas. Writers use transitions for three common purposes:

- To show time shifts
- To show relationships between ideas
- To introduce quotes

Consider this passage, written by a student, Dan Kidd:

The first time my youngest child, a boy four years old, visited Scarborough Faire brings back a flood of memories, of which one has bearing on our deliberation. Mama had escaped our attention, and both he and I were browsing through one of the many booths. I felt an urgent tugging at my shirt. "Dad, Dad, come see. We got to get one of these." He repeated his plea a few times. I relented and followed him to one side of the display. Deeply serious, carefully, gently, with awe and respect, he picked out an item, handing it to me for my inspection. "D-d-dad, we really need one of these!" He was right. I did need one of those. You do, too. He handed me a magic wand. No, I had not eaten the mushroom the witch tried to sell me. I was not in my cups, as they would say. Like my son, I too am deeply serious. We all need more magic in our lives. If distributing one of these magic wands is what it takes, so be it. Let it be done.

Although this passage is fairly well-written, it lacks transitions. Consequently, the sentences do not flow. It is also difficult to understand the relationships between ideas. Look at this revised version of the passage:

The first time my youngest child, a boy four years old, visited Scarborough Faire brings back a flood of memories. His mother had escaped our attention, and both he and I were browsing through one of the many booths when I felt an urgent tugging at my shirt. "Dad, Dad," my son exclaimed, "Come see. We got to get one of these." Only after he repeated his plea a few times, did I relent and follow him to one side of the display. Deeply serious, carefully, gently, with awe and respect, he picked out an item, handing it to me for my inspection. He stuttered in his eagerness, "D-d-dad, we really need one of these!" He was right. I did need one of those, and you do, too. He handed me a magic wand. No, I had not eaten the mushroom the witch tried to sell me. I was not in my cups, as they would say. However, like my son, I too am deeply serious. After all, we all need more magic in our lives, and if distributing one of these magic wands is what it takes, so be it. Let it be done.

In this version, the writer makes his message stronger by using transitions to create coherence and to show relationships between ideas. Not only is this passage clearer, it is more pleasurable to read.

Making It Work

- Look over your draft or essay. Are you using transitions successfully?

- Check to see if you have used transitions to show time shifts, to show relationships between ideas, or to introduce quotes.

- Incorporate transitions whenever possible, but especially when you are using direct quotes.

MLA AND APA STYLES

Documenting Sources

In this chapter, you will learn:

- How to document sources using MLA style guidelines

- How to document sources using APA style guidelines

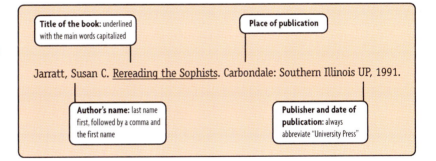

> **Title of the book:** underlined with the main words capitalized
>
> **Place of publication**
>
> Jarratt, Susan C. Rereading the Sophists. Carbondale: Southern Illinois UP, 1991.
>
> **Author's name:** last name first, followed by a comma and the first name
>
> **Publisher and date of publication:** always abbreviate "University Press"

MLA-style bibliographic entry for a book

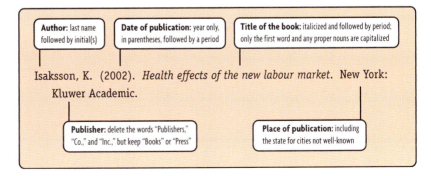

> **Author:** last name followed by initial(s)
>
> **Date of publication:** year only, in parentheses, followed by a period
>
> **Title of the book:** italicized and followed by period; only the first word and any proper nouns are capitalized
>
> Isaksson, K. (2002). *Health effects of the new labour market.* New York: Kluwer Academic.
>
> **Publisher:** delete the words "Publishers," "Co.," and "Inc.," but keep "Books" or "Press"
>
> **Place of publication:** including the state for cities not well-known

APA-style bibliographic entry for a book

CHOOSING A METHOD OF DOCUMENTATION

There are several different methods you can use to document your sources when writing a research paper: MLA (Modern Language Association), APA (American Psychological Association), Chicago, and CSE (Council of Science Editors). The documentation method you use depends on the discipline for which you are writing. For example, if you are writing an English or history paper, you will probably be expected to use MLA style. If you are writing a paper for journalism or psychology, you will use APA. If you are writing in the sciences, you will use CSE. The only way to be sure you are using the correct method is to verify your choice with your instructor. Because you will primarily use MLA and APA style, this book concentrates on those methods. If you need more information than is provided here, you can refer to the *MLA Handbook for Writers of Research Papers* or the *Publication Manual of the American Psychological Association*—both of which are available at any bookstore or library.

USING MLA STYLE

If you are majoring in the humanities, you are most likely to be asked to use MLA format, so it is important to be familiar with it.

≡ Parenthetical References in the Text

When you use MLA style, you cite the source of quotes and paraphrases within the text of your paper. You do this by mentioning the name(s) of the author(s) and the page number(s) you are using. This information is linked to a list at the end of the paper that gives complete bibliographic information for each source you cite parenthetically. This Works Cited list is discussed later in this section.

There are two ways you can introduce quotes, and they determine the information you include in the citation. First, when you mention the author's name in the text, the parenthetical citation contains only the page number:

> As Paul Cantor states, "No other show can match the way <u>The Simpsons</u> has combined consistency of quality with an inventiveness and willingness to take chances over the years" (34).

Alternatively, when you use a quote from a source but do not mention the author's name in the text, the citation includes both the author's name and the page number:

> In order to set off <u>Itchy and Scratchy</u> from the main cartoon of <u>The Simpsons</u>, Groening and his writers have "stripped away" the excess material--dialogue, plot lines, character development--and left <u>Itchy and Scratchy</u> with "the meaningless and gratuitous violence that is the quintessence of cartoon" (Cantor 36).

How you punctuate when you include parenthetical citations in the text of your research paper depends on the type of information. There are three options:

Paraphrases. You do not use quotation marks, and the citation is placed before the sentence's end punctuation.

> Further, among the topics listed by D'Angelo are definition, cause and effect, and iteration and negation (44).

Quotes within the text. The citation is placed after the closing quotation mark but before the end punctuation.

> The use of preconceptual theories is a natural progression in the development of any theory, as humans' growing awareness of a precognitive process leads them to conceptualize an innate ability in an attempt to understand and more fully utilize the patterns by which they think because "All arts including the arts of discourse, employ techniques to accomplish their purposes" (Kennedy 8).

Quotes set off from the text (those more than four lines long). The citation is placed after the end punctuation.

Kennedy corroborates this view saying:

> In the middle of the second century before Christ, the rhetorician Hermagoras reorganized the theory of topics in a form more adapted to lawcourts and more easily memorized by students in rhetorical schools. As such, it is known as the stasis theory. (83)

Even though you have basically only two options regarding where you put the author's name when citing sources, there are many forms of parenthetical citations with which you must be familiar.

≡ Forms of Parenthetical Citations

Listed below are the thirteen primary forms of parenthetical citations. If you have a situation that this list does not cover, refer to the *MLA Handbook*.

Work by a single author

Marlow describes Kurtz's last moments "as though a veil had been rent" (Conrad 239).

Work by two or three authors

This law was to prevent freed slaves from going north for religious training as they had in 1815 (Johnson and Roark 105).

Work by more than three authors

Those who upheld the king's belief would prosper, while those who did not would suffer the consequences (Ramey et al. 174).

Distinguishing sources by the same author

"As shows like The Simpsons and Malcolm in the Middle have proven, you can be as satirical as you want about the family on American TV as long as you remember to show that, when all the shouting is over, mom and dad and the kids really love each other" (Cantor, "Ozz Fest," 5).

Work in multiple volumes

For people who suffer from alcohol addiction, attending twelve-step meetings is often not the only step to recovery, but is an important one nonetheless (Scott 2: 35-36).

Work without a listed author

The fact that three-week-old chickens often die of cardiac arrest during transport to the slaughter house is a testament to the horrific conditions under which they live ("Poultry").

An indirect source

Roberts wanted no part of the "impending onslaught of criticism" that she felt surely awaited her upon her return to the United States (qtd. in Sturgeon 79).

More than one work in the same parenthetical citation

Nixon knew his presidency was doomed, yet he refused to back down to his detractors until he simply had no other choice (Lane 90; Ararat 126).

A literary work

A story

In The Lifted Veil, George Eliot uses aphorisms reminiscent of those used by Oscar Wilde (39).

An epic poem

In Beowulf, the poet makes reference to Cain and Abel, perhaps to cast Christian overtones over an otherwise pagan work (19: 1261).

A poem

Robert Frost, in "The Road Not Taken," says, "Two roads diverged in a wood and I / I took the one less traveled by / And that has made all the difference" (lines 18-20).

An entire work

Phillip Roth's <u>The Human Stain</u> examines the notion of "passing," and its lifelong repercussions for protagonist Coleman Silk.

Two or more authors with the same last name

The number of Vietnam veterans receiving psychiatric treatment has gone down as the men move closer to their retirement years (F. Fisher 301). However, many of these vets will likely remain on psychotropic medication for the rest of their lives (J. Fisher 36).

An electronic source

African Americans indeed have a high rate of kidney disease, frequently due to "complications from diabetes and hypertension" (Bjorklie, par. 1).

A government document with a corporate author

The Centers for Disease Control has stated that children, the elderly, and people with compromised immune systems are most at risk for contracting the West Nile virus (12).

≡ Creating the Works Cited List

When using MLA style, in addition to placing parenthetical citations within the text of your paper, you also have to include bibliographic information for each of your sources in a Works Cited list at the end of your paper. The purpose of this list is to allow readers who want more information than you have provided to find the works you used when writing your paper. When you create your Works Cited list, you need to remember:

- Include the first and last name(s) and middle initial(s), if available, for the author(s) for each entry.

- Capitalize every important word in the titles of books, articles, and journals.

- Underline the titles of books, journals, magazines, and newspapers.

- Indent the second and subsequent line of every entry.

The following subsections cover the most common types of sources you will include in your Works Cited List.

Books

Here is an example of an MLA bibliographic entry for a book with a single author, with its major components labeled:

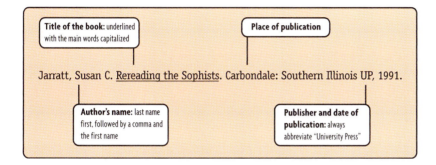

Book by one author

Greene, Bob. <u>Duty: A Father, His Son, and the Man Who Won the War</u>. New York: Morrow, 2000.

Book by two or three authors

Dragga, Sam, and Gwendolyn Gong. <u>Editing: The Design of Rhetoric</u>. Amityville, NY: Baywood, 1989.

Book by more than three authors

Belenky, Mary Field, et al. <u>Women's Ways of Knowing</u>. New York: Basic, 1986.

Two or more books by the same author

Burke, Kenneth. <u>A Grammar of Motives</u>. Berkeley: U of California P, 1969.

---. <u>A Rhetoric of Motives</u>. Berkeley: U of California P, 1969.

Edited book

Bizzell, Patricia, ed. <u>The Rhetorical Tradition</u>. Boston: St. Martin's, 1990.

Book by a corporate author

Rand McNally. <u>The Road Atlas: United States, Canada & Mexico</u>.
    Chicago: Rand 2001.

Selection in an anthology

Collier, Michael, "The Truant Pen." <u>Touchstones: American Poets on
    a Favorite Poem</u>. Ed. Robert Pack and Jay Parini. Hanover: UP
    of New England, 1996. 37-39.

More than one selection from the same anthology

Gombrich, Ernst. "Style." Preziosi 150-63.

Kant, Immanuel. "The Critique of Judgement." Preziosi 76-96.

Preziosi, Donald, ed. <u>The Art of Art History</u>. New York: Oxford UP,
    1998.

Multivolume work

Davis, Paul, et al. <u>The Bedford Anthology of World Literature</u>. Vol.
    4. Boston: Bedford/St. Martin's, 2003.

Book in a series

Hill, Randal Myron. <u>Silicone Surfactants</u>. Surfactant Science Ser.
    86. New York: Dekker, 1999.

Foreword, preface, or afterword of a book

Frommer, Arthur. Foreword. <u>The Complete Idiot's Guide to
    Geography</u>. By Thomas E. Sherer. New York: Alpha, 1997. xxii.

Short story, play, or poem in an anthology

Jen, Gish. "Birthmates." <u>The Best American Short Stories of the
    Century</u>. Ed. John Updike and Katrina Kenison. Boston:
    Houghton, 1999. 720-34.

Short story, play, or poem in a collection of an author's work

Dickinson, Emily. "I." <u>Collected Poems</u>. Philadelphia: Running, 1991. 17.

Book with a title within its title

Herz, Sarah K., and Donald R. Gallo. <u>From Hinton to</u> Hamlet<u>: Building Bridges Between Young Adult Literature and the Classics</u>. Westport: Greenwood, 1996.

Wiener, Hon. <u>"Come Together": John Lennon in His Time</u>. New York: Random, 1984.

Translation of a book

Tolstoy, Leo. <u>Anna Karenina</u>. Trans. Louise Maude and Aylmer Maude. Oxford: Oxford UP, 1998.

Republished book

Lawrence, D. H. <u>The Rainbow</u>. 1915. New York: Viking, 1968.

Dissertation

Unpublished

Jackson, E. P. "Meta-analysis of School-based Consultation Outcome Research." Diss. U of Pittsburgh, 1986.

Published

Pak, Dorothy Kim. <u>Paleocene and Eocene Deep-Water Circulation, Climate, and Sea Level (Foraminafera)</u>. Diss. Columbia U, 1995. Ann Arbor: UMI, 1996. ATT 9611167.

Pamphlet

<u>Women's Studies: Beyond the Stereotype</u>. Denton: U of North Texas, 2003.

Government publication

United States. Food and Drug Administration. <u>FDA Consumer</u>.
 Washington: GPO, Sept-Oct 2003.

Articles

Here is an example of an MLA bibliographic entry for an article
with a single author, with its major components labeled:

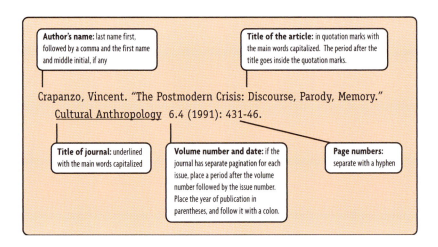

Author's name: last name first, followed by a comma and the first name and middle initial, if any

Title of the article: in quotation marks with the main words capitalized. The period after the title goes inside the quotation marks.

Crapanzo, Vincent. "The Postmodern Crisis: Discourse, Parody, Memory."
 <u>Cultural Anthropology</u> 6.4 (1991): 431-46.

Title of journal: underlined with the main words capitalized

Volume number and date: if the journal has separate pagination for each issue, place a period after the volume number followed by the issue number. Place the year of publication in parentheses, and follow it with a colon.

Page numbers: separate with a hyphen

Article in a scholarly journal with continuous pagination

Hairston, Maxine. "Diversity, Ideology, and Teaching Writing."
 <u>College Composition and Communication</u> 43 (1992): 179-93.

Article in a scholarly journal with separate pagination in each issue

Pritchett, Lant. "Divergence, Big Time." <u>Journal of Economic
 Perspectives</u> 11.3 (1997): 3-17.

Article in a weekly magazine

Gilman, John J. "Strength of Spider Silk." <u>Science</u> 5 Apr. 1996: 17.

Article in a monthly magazine

Koblitz, Neal. "Problems That Teach the Obvious But Difficult."
    American Mathematical Monthly Mar. 1998: 254-57.

Article in newspaper (signed)

Johnson, David, and Eric Lichtblau. "A Critical Study, Minus
    Criticism." New York Times 31 Oct. 2003, late ed.: A1-A2.

Article that does not appear on consecutive pages

Wilonsky, Robert. "Nobody's Fool." Dallas Observer 30 Oct. 2003:
    31+.

Editorial (untitled)

Dunsby, Jonathan. Editorial. Musical Analysis 12 Jul. 1982: 119-24.

Letter to the editor

Cook, Jacki. Letter. Time 27 Oct. 2003: 10.

Book review

Freeman, John. "A Common Story Told with Uncommon Skill." Rev.
    of The Namesake, by Jhumpa Lahiri. Dallas Morning News 24
    Oct. 2003: C15.

Article with a title within its title

Graver, Bruce Edward. "Alison Hickey's Impure Conceits: A Review."
    Poetics Today 21 (2000): 443-47.
Lachman, Lilach. "Keats's 'Hyperion': Time, Space, and the Long
    Poem." Poetics Today 22 (2001): 89-127.

Article in a reference book

Signed

Berman, Tressa L. "Man Dan." Encyclopedia of North American
    Indians. Ed. Frederick E. Hoxie. New York: Houghton, 1996.

Unsigned

"Kierkegaard." <u>The Blackwell Encyclopedia of Modern Christian
   Thought</u>. Ed. Alister E. McGrath. Oxford: Blackwell, 1993.

Other sources

Lecture

Parberry, Ian. "Dynamic Programming." Algorithm Analysis and
   Complexity Theory Lecture Series. Dept. of Computer Sciences,
   U of North Texas. 16 Oct. 1995.

Personal interview

Green, Pat. Telephone interview. 22 Jan. 2003.

Published interview

Lesesne, Teri. "Interview with John Ritter." <u>Teacher Librarian
   Magazine</u> Mar. 2001: 25.

Personal letter

Mathis, Audrey. Letter to the author. 11 May 2003.

Letter published in a collection

Nancy, Ted L. "Letter to Nordstrom Department Stores." 4 Aug.
   1995. <u>Letters from a Nut</u>. By Ted L. Nancy. New York: Avon,
   1999.

Letter in a library's archives

Dryer, Sidney. Letter to Charles S. Nutter. 10 Oct. 1885. School of
   Theology Lib. Boston U, Boston.

Film

<u>The Shawshank Redemption</u>. Dir. Frank Darabont. Perf. Tim
   Robbins, Morgan Freeman. Castle Rock, 1999.

Videotape, DVD, or laser disc

Kesey, Ken, interview. <u>One Flew Over the Cuckoo's Nest</u>. Dir. Milos
Forman. DVD. Warner Home Video, 2002.

Radio or television program

"Reality Bites." Writ. Peter Overton. <u>60 Minutes</u>. CBS. KTVT, Dallas.
26 Oct. 2003.

Recording

Winston, George. "Variations on the Kanon." Comp. Johann
Pachelbel. <u>December</u>. Windham Hill Records, 1982.

Cartoon or comic strip

Cannon, Max. "Red Meat." Comic strip. <u>Dallas Observer</u> 30 Oct.
2003: 9.

Advertisement

Cookie Bouquet. Advertisement. <u>Denton Connection</u> Nov. 2003: 32.

Electronic sources

Here is an example of an MLA bibliographic entry for an online
source, with its major components labeled:

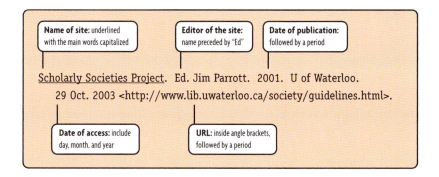

Scholarly project or information database on the Internet

<u>Margaret Atwood Society</u>. 28 June 1998. Metropolitan State College
    of Denver. 2 June 2002 <http://www.mscd.edu/~atwoodso/
    index.htm>.

Document within a scholarly project or information database on the Internet

"The Negro National Anthem." <u>African American Studies Scholarly</u>
    <u>Resources</u>. 2003. Columbia U. 29 Oct. 2003 <http://
    www.columbia.edu/cu/lweb/eguides/afam/resource.html>.

Home page for a course or a personal home page on the Internet

Brow, James. Cultural Anthropology. Course home page. Spring
    2003. Dept. of Anthropology, U of Texas. 7 May 2003
    <http://www.utexas.edu/cola/depts/anthropology/
    courses/03Spring/ant302/>.
Lyman family. Home page. 30 Mar. 2001 <http://
    www.lymanfamily.org/>.

≡ Sample Research Paper

The following research paper was written in response to Option
One of the Research-Based Writing Picks at the end of Chapter
Eleven: "Art Critic at Large." Notice the number of textual cita-
tions the writer uses.

The Art of Bart

Paula Mathis

Professor Thompson

English 1302

20 November 2004

The word "art" can evoke a wide variety of images for different people. One person might picture museums with beautiful
paintings and sculptures, while someone else imagines a sym-
phony hall with the music of Beethoven or Bach floating in the
air. However, people rarely consider television shows art, and
even less frequently do cartoons make it to that exalted status.
But with his television cartoon The Simpsons, Matt Groening has
in fact given the world a true work of art--thirty minutes at a
time, once a week, for fourteen years running. As Paul Cantor
states, "No other show can match the way The Simpsons has
combined consistency of quality with an inventiveness and will-
ingness to take chances over the years" (34). Indeed, the inventiveness Cantor mentions, along with The Simpsons' honesty, its
intelligent use of humor and satire, and its characters' genuine
affection for one another have all helped this cartoon surpass

being merely art and become, truly, the best television show ever.

Matt Groening has a long history with cartoons. According to biographer Rachel Sprovtsoff-Mangus, Groening began drawing cartoons as a teenager, and his father Homer, a cartoonist as well, took great pride in young Matt's budding interest in the medium. Groening often drew cartoons as a part of his various school activities and in letters to friends and family, but not until 1980 did he achieve much commercial success as a cartoonist (Sprovtsoff-Mangus). At that time, Groening, then twenty-six years old, began publishing his comic strip <u>Life in Hell</u> in the <u>Los Angeles Reader</u>. Now printed in 250 newspapers, <u>Life in Hell</u> was born of Groening's experiences performing such mind-numbing jobs as chauffeur and sewage treatment plant worker to earn his living while perfecting his craft. Then in 1987, the Fox network began airing brief snippets of Groening's cartoon <u>The Simpsons</u> during <u>The Tracy Ullman Show</u> (perhaps Ms. Ullman's greatest claim to fame), and the yellow-toned, dysfunctional family from Springfield, USA soon attracted quite a following. Finally, after spending two years as an animated short, the Simpsons were granted their own half-hour animated television show in December of 1989 (Sprovtsoff-Mangus). Matt Groening, along with his Simpson clan--parents Homer and Marge, and kids Bart, Lisa, and baby Maggie--quickly became household names, and with good reason.

The Simpsons has proven itself to be a truly inventive show, not just among cartoons, but also among television shows in general. Cantor discusses one aspect of the show that is truly unique, its cartoon-within-a-cartoon, Itchy and Scratchy. Groening's use of this cartoon can be compared to Shakespeare's instances of a play-within-a-play. Cantor notes that in his play Hamlet, Shakespeare "elevate[s] the diction and start[s] using rhyme when he wants the drama his hero calls the 'Mousetrap' to stand out from the surrounding blank verse" (35). In order to set off Itchy and Scratchy from the main cartoon of The Simpsons, Groening and his writers have "stripped away" the excess material--dialogue, plot lines, character development--and left Itchy and Scratchy with "the meaningless and gratuitous violence that is the quintessence of cartoon" (Cantor 36).

In addition to his cartoon-within-a-cartoon, Groening has provided his viewers with other unique episodes of The

<u>Simpsons</u>, including elaborate musical numbers, and he has even created entire episodes in the form of a musical production. Since its second season, <u>The Simpsons</u> has also presented an annual "Treehouse of Horror" Halloween episode. These Halloween episodes are unique in that, in many of the episodes, several characters are killed off in some horrific way, only to return the next week good as new. In these episodes, Groening takes advantage of the fact that his characters are not real, and does not allow himself to be confined to story lines that only result in the return of his characters, intact, to their pre-Halloween well-being. While these extraordinary features of <u>The Simpsons</u> are a significant part of what makes the show so brilliant, the show has much more to offer than mere distinctiveness.

In the fourteen years that <u>The Simpsons</u> has been on the air, viewers in general and critics in particular have hailed the show as being both more honest and more realistic than many shows with live actors. The Simpsons do all the things that make up most people's daily routines, but that most sit-com characters almost never do--they go to the bathroom and to church, they mow the yard, and they even watch television.

Additionally, the Simpsons, both as a family and as individuals within their community of Springfield, have problems in
their lives that aren't always easily resolved at the end of a thirty-minute program. Of course, they work on their problems and
go to the bathroom as cartoon characters, and therefore many of
their actions are much more absurd than anything that would
happen in real life. Regarding the fantastic nature of the show,
however, Groening "manages to capture a sense of reality, even
in far-fetched scenarios" (Kantor et al. 185). Hence, the arrival
in 1989 of The Simpsons on the airwaves marked a departure
from what Brian Ott calls "TV's idealistic families of early
decades, its nostalgic throwbacks of the 1980s, and its convenient, simplistic resolution of narrative conflicts" (59). Ott discusses how the Simpson family helped displace the Cosbys as
America's ideal family, stating that the Simpsons instead were
soon "being touted as the typical American family." Ott goes on
to say that "the Waltons of the 1970s and the Cosbys of the
1980s simply no longer possessed any fidelity, they no longer
accurately reflected reality" (60). In episode 178, "The Secret
War of Lisa Simpson," the Simpson children visited a military

academy where the students ably demanded (quoting Keats, though harshly), "Truth is beauty, and beauty truth, Sir!" (<u>Simpsons Archive</u>). <u>The Simpsons</u>' truth, though often outlandishly presented, is what helps make it such a beautifully silly show.

In addition to giving his viewers a cartoon that is closer to reality than many live-action shows, Matt Groening has also given us a show that is truly thought-provoking and insightful. While nearly everyone can enjoy watching <u>The Simpsons</u>, most episodes contain at least some bits that are clearly aimed at people with a little higher education under their belts. One need only look at the titles of various <u>Simpsons</u> episodes to know that Groening and his staff like to exhibit their knowledge to those who can appreciate it: "A Milhouse Divided," "The Canine Mutiny," "The Old Man and the 'C' Student," and, of course, "Homer's Odyssey" (<u>Simpsons Archive</u>). Groening also regularly employs social satire to both entertain and enlighten his audience. Kantor et al praise the show's use of satire, stating that "the show deserves a place alongside the works of Twain," who is said to have called satire both "the deriding of shams" and "the laughing of stupid superstitions out of existence" (qtd. in Kantor et al. 198). Thus when <u>Simpsons</u> announcer Troy McClure asks satirically, "Who knows what adventures [the Simpsons] will have between now and the time the show becomes unprofitable?" we know that Groening and his staff make no pretense, to themselves or to <u>Simpsons'</u> fans, about the true reason for the show's longevity (<u>Simpsons Archive</u>). Groening respects his audience's intelligence enough to provide viewers with not only sharp wit but also insightful commentary on the nature of his business.

"As shows like <u>The Simpsons</u> and <u>Malcolm in the Middle</u> have proven, you can be as satirical as you want about the family on American TV as long as you remember to show that, when all the shouting is over, mom and dad and the kids really love each other" (Cantor, "Ozz Fest"). Groening and his writers ensure that the Simpsons show their love for one another on a regular basis, which humanizes the sometimes over-the-top characters. Even though Homer has the tendency to try to choke the life out of Bart, he truly loves the boy and the rest of his family as well. The Simpsons have survived being ostracized by their town, having their home taken over by squatters, and dozens of other situations that might have torn other families apart but only served to draw the Simpsons closer together. As Richard Corliss states, "the strongest episodes are those that reveal the bedrock fondness, desperation and loyalty that bond this or any other frazzled clan" (73). For example, in one episode, Bart is caught shoplifting a video game, and when his mother Marge discovers his crime, she expresses both her disappointment in Bart and her weariness at always trying to discipline him, and thus declines to discipline him at all. Bart soon feels the emotional isolation that comes from Marge's disappointment, and though he works to win his mother's trust back, Bart's sadness at his mother's loss of faith in him is actually quite moving. He realizes that he will always need his mother, no matter how old he is. Of course, when Marge discovers that Bart can be a very good boy when he wants to be, she showers him with kisses just as any mother would do (<u>Simpsons Archive</u>). Without this love that the Simpson family shows each other, despite the frequent disruptions of blissful family life that various members (especially Homer and Bart) cause, the show would not be as touching as it has often proven itself to be, and perhaps would not have lasted as long as it has.

Matt Groening's cartoon <u>The Simpsons</u> has all the basic elements of a true work of art. Although this particular work of art
is found on television rather than in a museum, it still deserves
its place among other masterpieces. People watch <u>The Simpsons</u>
for entertainment, certainly, but they are also moved to tears by
Groening's work--through laughter or otherwise. By combining
ingenuity with humor, intellect, and a true passion for his work,
Groening has assembled one yellow-toned, dysfunctional family
that people around the world truly love and admire.

Works Cited

Basner, David M. "'The Simpsons' as Fart, D'oh!, Art." <u>Simpsons</u>
    <u>Archive</u>. 9 Feb. 2004 <http://www.snpp.com.other/papers/
    db.paper.html>.

Cantor, Paul A. "The Greatest TV Show Ever." <u>American Enterprise</u>
    Sept./Oct. 1997: 34-37.

---. "Ozz Fest." <u>reasononline</u> 24 May 2002 <http://reason.com/
    hod/pc052402.shtml>.

Corliss, Richard. "Simpsons Forever!" <u>Time</u> 2 May 1994: 73.

Kantor, Ken, Nancy Lerner Kantor, Josh Kantor, Mary Eaton, and
    Benjamin Kantor. " 'I Will Not Expose the Ignorance of the

Faculty': The Simpsons as School Satire." Images of School-

teachers in America. Ed. Pamela Bolotin Joseph and Gail E.

Burnaford. New Jersey: Erlbaum, 2001. 185-200.

Ott, Brian L. " 'I'm Bart Simpson, Who the Hell Are You?' A Study in

Postmodern Identity (Re)Construction." Journal of Popular

Culture 37 (2003): 56-81.

Sprovtsoff-Mangus, Rachel. "Matt Groening Biography." 18 Oct. 2003

<http://entertainment.msn.com>.

Simpsons Archive. Ed. Jouni Paakkinen. 18 Oct 2003

<http://www.snpp.com>.

"The Secret War of Lisa Simpson." The Simpsons. Writ. Richard

Appel. Dir. Mike B. Anderson. Fox. KTTV, Los Angeles. 18 May

1997.

Consider this . . .

- Did the writer use sufficient sources to support her argument?
- Did she integrate her quotes successfully?
- Did she use a broad range of sources for her research?

USING APA STYLE

The second most commonly used form of documentation for college papers is APA style. APA style accomplishes the same goal as MLA style, but it follows a different format.

≡ Parenthetical References in the Text

As you do when using MLA style, when you use APA style, you cite the source of quotes and paraphrases within the text of your paper. Again, the author's name appears either in the sentence itself or in the parenthetical citation. The citation also includes the year the source was published, and if you are quoting directly, the page number(s) on which the quote appears. The parenthetical information is linked to a reference list at the end of the paper, which gives complete bibliographic information for each source.

The method you use to introduce a direct quote determines the information you include in the parenthetical citation. If the author's name is mentioned in the text, it is followed by the date in parentheses; the page number, in parentheses, follows the closing quote marks:

> As Paul Cantor (1997) states, "No other show can match the way *The Simpsons* has combined consistency of quality with an inventiveness and willingness to take chances over the years" (p. 34).

Alternatively, if the author's name is not mentioned in the text, the citation follows the quotation and includes the author's name, the date, and the page number(s):

> In order to set off *Itchy and Scratchy* from the main cartoon of *The Simpsons*, Groening and his writers have "stripped away" the excess material—dialogue, plot lines, character development—and left *Itchy and Scratchy* with "the meaningless and gratuitous violence that is the quintessence of cartoon" (Cantor, 1997, p. 36).

☰ Forms of In-text Citations

As with MLA style, APA style has many forms of parenthetical citations with which you must be familiar.

Work by a single author

The occurrence of developmental disabilities has increased sharply with the rise in births to older mothers (Harrison, 2001).

Work by two authors

The fact that more and more doctors are prescribing mood-altering drugs to school-aged children has many parents and teachers concerned (O'Flaherty & Connor, 2003).

Work by three to five authors

First reference

(Jackson, Bolger, & Ashley, 2000)

Later references

(Jackson et al., 2000)

Work by six or more authors

(Scott et al., 1999)

Works by authors with the same last name

F. Fisher (2002) and J. Fisher (2002) have each stated that . . . .

Work authored by a group

First reference

(American Psychiatric Association [APA], 1998)

Later references

(APA, 1998)

Work without an author

("Poultry," 1997)

Personal communication

(L. Simpson, personal communication, November 4, 2003)

Note that personal communications are cited in the text but not listed in the reference list.

Indirect source

Roberts has stated that she disagrees with the majority of experts when discussing the causes of this disease (as cited in Sturgeon, 2001).

Specific part of a source

Until recently, scientists have focused almost exclusively on men when researching the recidivism rate among parolees (Silvan, 2002, chap. 4).

Electronic source

African Americans indeed have a high rate of kidney disease, frequently due to "complications from diabetes and hypertension" (Bjorklie, 2003, ¶ 1).

Two or more works within the same parenthetical citation

Different authors

Several studies have shown this theory to be valid (Canton, 2000; Mables & White, 1994; Williamson, 1998).

Same author, different years

Several studies have shown this theory to be valid (Morriss & Logan, 1995, 1999, 2003).

Same author, same year

Several studies have shown this theory to be valid (Sophia, 2001a, 2001b).

☰ Creating the Reference List

In addition to citing the material you use within the text of your paper, when using APA style, you also have to include bibliographic information for each of your sources in a reference list at the end of your paper. Just like a Works Cited list, this list allows readers who want more information than you have provided to find the works you used when writing your paper.

The following subsections are the most common types of sources you will include in your reference list.

Books

Here is an example of an APA-style bibliographic entry for a book with a single author, with its major components labeled:

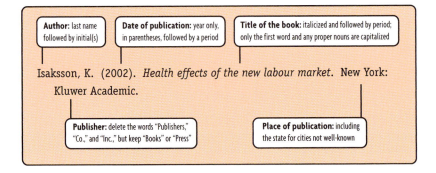

Book with one author

Damasio, A. R. (1994). *Descartes' error: Emotion, reason, and the human brain*. New York: Lyons Press.

Book with more than one but less than six authors

Bradshaw, J., Stimson, C., Skinner, C., & Williams, J. (2002). *Absent fathers?* New York: Routledge.

Edited book

Jacobi, J. (Ed.). (1953). *Psychological reflections: An anthology of the writings of C. G. Jung*. New York: Harper & Row.

Book with no author or editor

Research and service programs in the PHS: Challenges in organization. (1991). Washington DC: National Academy Press.

Work in several volumes

Cicchetti, D. (1999). *Developmental approaches to prevention and intervention* (Vol. 9). Rochester, NY: University of Rochester Press.

Work with a corporate author

American Civil Liberties Union. (1996). *American Civil Liberties Union handbook.* Carbondale: Southern Illinois University Press.

Government report

Alcohol, Drug Abuse, and Mental Health Administration. (1981). *ADAMHA research programs* (DHHS Publication No. ADM 81-942). Rockville, MD: U.S. Government Printing Office.

One selection from an anthology

Adams, A. (1997). Molding women's bodies: The surgeon as sculptor. In D. S. Wilson (Ed.), *Bodily discursions: Genders, representations, technologies* (pp. 56–81). Albany: State University of New York Press.

Article in a reference book

Magill, F. N. (Ed.). (1993). Gender identity formation. In *Psychology basics* (pp. 254–259). Pasadena, CA: Salem Press.

Foreword, preface, or afterword of a book

Essed, P. (1996). Preface. In *Diversity: Gender, color, and culture* (pp. vii–viii). Amherst: University of Massachusetts Press.

Articles

Here is an example of an APA-style bibliographic entry for an article with a single author, with its major components labeled:

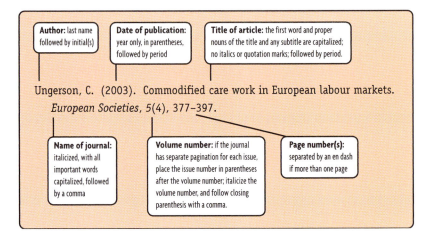

Here is an example of an APA-syle bibliographic entry for a newspaper article with a single author, with its major components labeled:

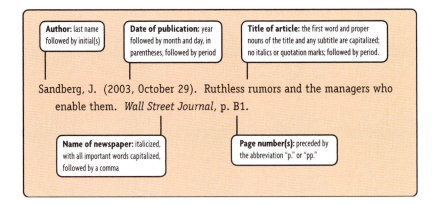

Article in a scholarly journal with continuous pagination through an annual volume

Macassa, G., Ghilagaber, G., Bernhardt, E., Diderichsen, F., & Burstrom, B. (2003). Inequalities in child mortality in Mozambique: Differentials by parental socio-economic position. *Social Science & Medicine, 57*, 2255–2265.

Magazine article

Brown, R. (1994). Pragmatics vs. semantics. *Times Higher Education Supplement, 1125*, 30.

Newspaper article

Johnson, J., & Lichtblau, E. (2003, October 31). A critical study, minus criticism, *New York Times*, p. A1.

Letter to the editor

Daly, W. (2003, October 27). When the illness is real [Letter to the editor]. *Time*, p. 11.

Electronic sources

Here is an example of an APA-style bibliographic entry for an article from a searchable database, with its major components labeled:

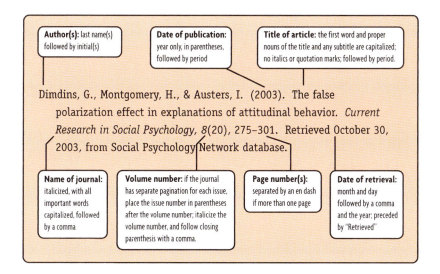

Internet article based on a print source

Scott, E., & Panksepp, J. (2003). Rough-and-tumble play in human children [Electronic version]. *Aggressive Behavior, 29*, 539–551.

Article in an Internet-only journal

Imam, A. A. (2003). Assessing transfer of response speed and
    nodality via conditional discriminations. *Experimental Analysis
    of Human Behavior Bulletin, 21*, 1–7. Retrieved November 6,
    2003, from http://www.eahb.org/NewSitePages/
    CitationIndex.htm

Article in an online daily newspaper

Millman, J. (2002, October 24). Americans head to Mexico to buy
    cut-rate drugs. *Wall Street Journal*. Retrieved November 6,
    2003, from http://online.wsj.com/public/us

Document from a university Web site

Hoyenski, E. (2003). *It came from the vault: Unusual items from the
    rare book & Texana collections*. Retrieved October 28, 2003,
    from University of North Texas Library Web site: http://
    www.library.unt.edu/rarebooks/newsletter/2003Fall/
    rarebks.htm

Abstract from a university Web site

Beach, E. A. (1990). *Schelling's contributions to the development of
    religious psychology* (University of Wisconsin–Eau Claire,
    Department of Philosophy and Religious Studies). Abstract
    retrieved October 21, 2003, from http://www.uwec.edu/
    philrel/faculty/beach/ publications/relpsych.html

Web document (no author, no date)

*Finding freedom: A review of the death row writings of Jarvis
    Masters*. (n.d.). Retrieved November 8, 2003, from
    http://www.prisonwall.org/ffreedom.htm

Message posted to a newsgroup

Mazis, G. (2003, April 9). Dark poetic magic [Msg 5]. Message
    posted to http://humanityquest.com/themes/inspiration/
    Newsletter/2003-04-9/index.asp#8

Journal article retrieved from a database

Dimdins, G., Montgomery, H., & Austers, I. (2003). The false polarization effect in explanations of attitudinal behavior. *Current Research in Social Psychology, 8*(20), 275–301. Retrieved October 30, 2003, from Social Psychology Network database.

Computer software

Froming, K. B., Levy, C. M., & Ekman, P. (2003). Comprehensive Affect Testing Systems (CATS) [Computer software]. Gainesville, FL: Psychology Software.

Nonprint sources

Television show

Jones, S. (Executive producer). (2003, October 23). *ABC world news tonight* [Television broadcast]. New York: American Broadcasting Company.

Television series

Ball, A., & Kaplan, B. E. (Executive producers). (2003). *Six feet under* [Television series]. New York: Home Box Office.

Motion picture

Darabont, F. (Director). (1994). *The Shawshank redemption* [Motion picture]. United States: Castle Rock.

CD recording

Winston, G. (1982). Variations on the Kanon. On *December* [CD]. San Francisco: Windham Hill Records.

Audio recording on cassette

Libath, T. O. (Speaker). (1982). *History of the Pagan-Fletcher restoration* [Cassette recording]. Valley Stream, NY: Valley Stream Historical Society Oral History Recordings.

CAREFULLY DOCUMENTING your work can be tedious, but it is incredibly important. Because of computer technology, we have the ability to spread information at an alarming rate; consequently, it is increasingly important to remember to give credit to the people who created the information you are using in your papers. You certainly wouldn't want someone to borrow one of your possessions without your permission. Imagine how outraged you would feel if a stranger borrowed your car without asking you first. Writers own their words just as you own your car or any of your other possessions. Don't use someone else's work without giving him or her credit.   ■

RESEARCH-BASED WRITING BRIEFS

Your Works Cited List

In order to complete your research portfolio, you must prepare the following item: Works Cited list. Follow the steps below to create this list:

- Collect all of the bibliographic notes that you made while researching your paper. Make sure that you have included every source you use in your paper.

- Make sure each bibliographic entry is in MLA format. Check the examples in this chapter or consult the *MLA Handbook* if you have questions.

- Put the entries in alphabetical order.

- Carefully proofread each entry.

Paraphrasing and Summarizing

Any research paper requires the writer to use paraphrases and summaries. The following will allow you to practice that skill.

- Read the two passages below.

- When you are done, summarize each passage.

- Next, paraphrase each passage.

- How is the summary different from the paraphrase?

Passage One

There's really no way to explain the TV taste of Americans, and when you get right down to it, the viewing public likes a show because its characters are likable. For all their foul language and vulgar behaviour, Ozzy and his clan are just plain likable.

In fact, they fit the tried-and-true formula for a television family, epitomized most recently by Fox's *Malcolm in the Middle*. There is a weak but lovable father (Ozzy), the strong-willed but caring mother (Sharon) and the obnoxious but witty children (Jack and Kelly). If you take away the curse words (and MTV tries mightily), the Osbournes are like any other TV family, regularly tearing apart and knitting back together in convenient chunks of 30 minutes at a time.

Passage Two

But MTV wasn't wasting its time all those years doing shows like *Real World* and *Road Rules*. Their producers have learned how to take raw candid footage and shape it up through skillful editing. What *The Osbournes* does so cleverly is to mold the daily life of this real family into the standard plot lines of traditional sitcoms. Thus we end up with the best of both worlds. When viewed today, a 1950's-era sitcom inevitably seems old-fashioned and even sappy. With *The Osbournes*, we can feel we're viewing something on the cutting edge and yet still see the nuclear family as an institution that is not outdated.

Integrating Quotations

Another necessary skill for writing research papers is integrating quotations from sources. Practice this skill now.

- Read the following article.
- Choose three sentences to use as quotes in a paragraph summarizing the main point of the essay.
- Write the paragraph, and integrate each of the three quotes differently.
- Share your work with the class.

GROUNDBREAKER

Dan Buettner

Deep in the rainforest of northeast Guatemala's Petén state, within earshot of El   1
Mirador—one of the largest of the ancient Mayan ruins—UCLA archaeologist
Richard Hansen believes he's found the perfect spot for a tourist attraction. "I envi-
sion a high-end eco-lodge," says Hansen, an internationally respected scientist
who since 1978 has excavated sites in the Petén's sprawling Maya Biosphere
Reserve. "There would be hot showers, clean sheets on the beds, and ice for your
drink."

Hansen isn't kidding, and his plans are notable both for their grandiosity and   2
his professed motives, which are to protect El Mirador and other sites from looters,
who cart off an estimated $50 million in Mayan artifacts from Guatemala
every year, and to safeguard one of the biggest remaining tracts of intact forest in
the country. After decades of watching the plunder, Hansen is convinced that the
only long-term hope for preservation is to make El Mirador a paying concern and
secure its borders with armed Guatemalan park guards trained by the U.S. Park
Service.

The development would be the centerpiece of a proposed Mirador Basin   3
National Monument, an 820-square-mile plot of jungle that Hansen hopes to
model on Tikal National Park, another Mayan site and Guatemala's top tourist
attraction since the 1950s. He pictures a lavish wilderness lodge complete with
gourmet dining and an airstrip—enough infrastructure to accommodate 80,000
visitors a year. Though it all sounds far-fetched, in the past 16 months Hansen has
nailed down the support of Guatemala's president, Alfonso Portillo, and other key
government officials, rounded up close to a million dollars to dig major ruins out
from under tons of dirt and get them ready for tourists, and kicked off a campaign
to court international investment. It's far from a done deal, but he's made surprising inroads, and he's not letting up.

"This is the pivotal year," says Hansen, a bullish 50-year-old who made his   4
name by proving that the Mirador Basin yielded Central American's earliest soci-
eties. "If I fail, the forest is gone and the sites will be destroyed."

Hansen's plans put him at odds with local loggers and powerful green groups,   5
who have their own ideas about preserving the region. For the past 12 years, the
Petén has been the setting for a sustainable-forestry program launched with

investment dollars from the United States Agency for International Development, a federal office that funds economic growth in developing nations. The goal was to give rural communities a stake in long-term forest health by granting them logging concessions. A number of U.S. environmental groups pitched in, among them the Nature Conservancy, and the World Wildlife Fund (WWF), spending some $40 million to teach locals about responsible forestry and promote their certified green timber on the global market.

6   But Hansen argues that the program has only hastened the destruction of the Petén and that new roads have made it easier for looters to transport Mayan treasures to market. "The grave robbers used to bushwhack in and cart out the artifacts on their backs," Hansen says. "Thanks to logging roads, they've switched to pickups."

7   In April 2002, after years of getting nowhere with his own idea, Hansen invited Portillo to the Mirador Basin and convinced him to nullify logging concessions that approach the archaeological sites—a critical step toward gaining national-monument status. This spring, he drummed up $880,000 from donors like the Global Heritage Foundation, a California-based preservation group, to restore four buildings in the 2,500-year-old city of Nakbé. As of June, the Inter-American Development Bank (IDB), Latin America's largest lender, was considering Hansen's proposal to help finance a 13-year, $35 million investment plan to refurbish and guard the rest of the Mirador Basin sites. If the IDB commits, Hansen will be positioned to convince developers to invest in a lodge.

8   Not surprisingly, the plan has fierce detractors who, while conceding that the forestry program may facilitate looting, counter that Hansen's scheme would destroy years of successful collaboration between Petén communities and international nonprofits. "It reeks of neocolonialism," says Darron A. Collins, 33, the Latin American and Caribbean forest coordinator for the WWF. "The gringo comes down, wraps up large chunks of forest, and builds a fence around it without considering the lives of the local people."

9   "Ninety-five percent of the people here are against him," adds Israel Giron, the 46-year-old vice-president of Gibor SA, a logging company that lost 40 percent of its concession to Portillo's decree.

10   As inflamed Guatemalans see it, foreign investors will fatten up on tourist dollars while locals will be stuck cleaning hotel rooms. Hansen, who says he'll take no part in the financial operation of the development, insists they're wrong, claiming that tourism would contribute up to $20 million to the economy by 2020. But his macroeconomic arguments fall flat in the lawless Petén, where locals may be

ready to take control of their future by whatever means necessary. After learning of an alleged plot to assassinate him, Hansen doesn't set foot in the jungle without four heavily armed Kaibiles—the Guatemalan version of the Green Berets—provided by Portillo.

Whatever happens next, the melee sounds painfully familiar to Arthur   11
Demarest, director of Vanderbilt University's Institute of Mesoamerican Archaeology. In the late 1990s, he supported an IDB-funded tourist development at Mayan sites in Guatemala's Petexbatún region, and says the whole thing was a disaster. Roads were built and sites were restored, but locals were left out of the loop. Disillusioned, many returned to logging.

"People want the wood too bad," says Demarest. "You'd have to put a wall   12
around the entire Mirador Basin, and that's not going to happen."

Grammar Choices

RESTRICTIVE AND NONRESTRICTIVE CLAUSES

By now you are familiar with the difference between independent and dependent clauses, but you also have to know the difference between two other types of clauses:

A **restrictive clause** restricts the meaning of the noun it modifies.

A **nonrestrictive clause** does not restrict the meaning of the noun it modifies.

Restrictive Clauses

A restrictive clause restricts, or limits, the meaning of the noun it modifies. Restrictive clauses begin with *that* unless you are referring to a person; in this case, you use *who*.

In the following sentences, the use of restrictive clauses allows the writer to develop his argument more specifically.

> In order to set off <u>Itchy and Scratchy</u> from the main cartoon of <u>The Simpsons</u>, Groening and his writers have "stripped away" the excess material--dialogue, plot lines, character development--and left <u>Itchy and Scratchy</u> with "the meaningless and gratuitous violence **that is the quintessence of cartoon**" (Cantor 36).

In this sentence, the restrictive clause modifies the noun violence.

> In addition to giving his viewers a cartoon **that is closer to reality than many live-action shows**, Matt Groening has also given us a show **that is truly thought-provoking and insightful**.

In this sentence, the first restrictive clause modifies *cartoon*, and the second restrictive clause modifies *show*.

> With the Osbournes we can feel we're viewing something on the cutting edge, and yet still see the nuclear family as an institution **that is not outdated**.

In this sentence, the restrictive clause modifies the noun *institution*.

Nonrestrictive Clauses

A nonrestrictive clause does not restrict the meaning of the noun it modifies—it is parenthetical information that the reader does not require. Because they are, in a sense, parenthetical, nonrestrictive clauses are set off by commas. A restrictive clause begins with *which* unless it refers to a person. When the clause refers to a person, it begins with *who*.

Hansen isn't kidding, and his plans are notable both for their grandiosity and his professed motives, **which are to protect El Mirador and other sites from looters**, who cart off an estimated $50 million in Mayan artifacts from Guatemala every year, **and to safeguard one of the biggest remaining tracts of intact forest in the country**.

Hansen's plans put him at odds with local loggers and powerful green groups, **who have their own ideas about preserving the region**.

Making It Work

- Identify each restrictive clause in your draft or essay. Does each one begin with that or who? Is it set off by a comma or commas?

- Identify each nonrestrictive clause in your draft or essay. Does each one begin with which or who? Is it set off by a comma or commas?

- Correct any errors you find.

Style Choices

USING TOPIC SENTENCES

A topic sentence identifies the main idea within a paragraph. It is often the first sentence in the paragraph. Topic sentences are very useful because they help readers keep their place in an essay—they provide a road map that the reader can follow. How many times have you read an essay that seemed to skip from one topic to another without any real direction? You may not have been able to identify the essay's problem at the time, but if you go back to it now and look for topic sentences, you may find that it has none. Not only do topic sentences help readers, they also help writers. Using topic sentences will help you keep your own place as you write and will improve the coherence of your essays.

A topic sentence normally meets these criteria:

- The **subject of the sentence** is the topic of the paragraph.

- The **information that follows the subject** provides a brief description of what the writer will say about the topic.

In many ways, a topic sentence is a thesis statement on a paragraph level. Look at these examples:

Matt Groening has a long history with cartoons.

The Simpsons has proven itself to be a truly inventive show, not just among cartoons, but also among television shows in general.

In the fourteen years that <u>The Simpsons</u> has been on the air, **viewers in general and critics in particular have hailed the show as being both more honest and more realistic than many shows with live actors**.

Additionally, **the Simpsons, both as a family and as individuals within their community of Springfield, have problems in their lives that aren't always easily resolved at the end of a thirty-minute program**.

In addition to giving his viewers a cartoon that is closer to reality than many live-action shows, **Matt Groening has also given us a show that is truly thought-provoking and insightful**.

"**As shows like The Simpsons and Malcolm in the Middle have proven**, you can be as satirical as you want about the family on American TV as long as you remember to show that, when all the shouting is over, mom and dad and the kids really love each other" (Cantor "Ozz Fest," 5).

Each of these topic sentences clearly identifies a subject and then tells the reader what the writer will say about that subject.

Making It Work

- Does each paragraph in your draft or essay begin with a topic sentence?

- Does each topic sentence accurately describe the information presented in the paragraph?

- Add or change topic sentences where necessary.

Credits

p. 362: Shark cartoon by Gary Brookins, from *Richmond Times-Dispatch.* Reprinted by permission of Gary Brookins.

p. 391: "This Cat's a Dog" by David Edelstein, *Slate* Magazine, November 20, 2003. SLATE ARTICLE reprinted by permission of Newspaper Enterprise Association, Inc.

p. 395: "Doonesburied" by Jesse Walker. Reprinted, with permission, from *Reason* magazine. Copyright © 2002 by Reason Foundation, 2415 S. Sepulveda Blvd., Suite 400, Los Angeles, CA 90034. www.reason.com

p. 402: "This Magic Mona" by Charles Paul Freund. Reprinted, with permission, from *Reason* magazine. Copyright © 2002 by Reason Foundation, 2415 S. Sepulveda Blvd., Suite 400, Los Angeles, CA 90034. www.reason.com

p. 408: Mickey Mouse © Disney Enterprises, Inc. Reprinted with permission.

p. 454: Mars scene on *Smithsonian Magazine* site, Pat Rawlings/SAIC/NASA.

p. 465: Cartoon © Marc Tyler Nobleman/ www.mtncartoons.com. Reprinted with permission.

p. 517: "Groundbreaker" by Dan Buettner, *Outside Magazine*, August 2003. Reprinted by permission of the author.

Photos

p. 1: (from left) Roger Ressmeyer/Corbis; AP Photo/Eric Risberg; Ben Martin/Time-Life Pictures/Getty Images.

p. 3: Warner Bros/Zuma Press.

p. 9: © Reuters/Corbis.

p. 11: © Reuters/Corbis.

p. 19: Photodisc/Getty RF.

p. 20: Photograph by Dina Bangdel, Courtesy of the Huntington Archive.

p. 43: Corbis/Sygma.

p. 44: (top) AP/Wide World Photos; (bottom) Landov Agency.

p. 51: (from top left) Roger Ressmeyer/Corbis; AP Photo/Eric Risberg; Ben Martin/Time-Life Pictures/Getty Images.

p. 59: Owali-Kulla/Corbis.

p. 60: Guildhall Library, Corporation of London, UK/Bridgeman Art Library.

p. 68: Corbis.

p. 80: (top) Mark Wilson/Getty Images; (bottom right) The Advertising Archive/The Picture Desk, Inc.

p. 81: Corbis.

p. 90: Courtesy Timex Corporation.

p. 93 "Free Trade" by J. Otto Seibold. Originally published in *The New Yorker.*

p. 94: (left) "Memories Second Phase/Stopped in Time" © 2002 Alice Aycock. Theoretical proposal for the World Trade Center site. Originally published in *The New Yorker.* (right) "Mirror of Memory/WTC" © 2002 Elyn Zimmerman. Originally published in *The New Yorker.*

p. 95: (left) © Komar and Melamid. Originally published in *The New Yorker.* (right) Photograph by David Fein. (left poem) © 1993 Estate of James Schuyler, Courtesy F.S.G., LLC. (right text) Translation, Stanislaw Baranczak and Clare Cavanagh © 1995 Harcourt, Inc. © 1975 Czytelnik. Originally published in *The New Yorker.*

p. 112: (left) © 2004 The M. C. Esher Company, Baarn, Holland. All rights reserved.

p. 115: ROB & SAS/Corbis.

p. 116: Corbis.

p. 123: Stelios Varias/Reuters/Landov.

p. 125: Roy Morsch/Corbis.

p. 129: Peter Byron/PhotoEdit.

p. 130: Jeff Greenberg/PhotoEdit.

p. 133: Corbis.

p. 135: CBS-TV/The Kobal Collection/The Picture Desk.

p. 141: Erich Lessing/Art Resource, NY.

p. 153: AP/Wide World Photo.

p. 156: The Huntington Library, Art Collections, and Botanical Gardens, San Marino, California/Superstock.

p. 157: Photofest.

p. 158: Abbas/Magnum Photos.

p. 167: Francis G. Mayer/Corbis.

p. 172: Photodisc/Getty RF.

p. 182: The AdvertisingArchive/The Picture Desk, Inc.

pp. 187, 188, 190, and 192: Robertstock/Retrofile.com.

p. 194: Dave Hahn/Mallory & Irvine/Getty Images.

p. 204: (top) Private Collection/Bridgeman Art Library, London/Superstock; (bottom) The Advertising Archive/The Picture Desk, Inc.

p. 205: The Advertising Archive/The Picture Desk, Inc.

p. 206: © Photodisc/Getty.

Index

529